AN ARMY DOCTOR'S WIFE ON THE FRONTIER

Mrs. Elizabeth F. Hiestand, called Bessie by her mother in these letters, with her grandson, Richard Michael Stark.

AN ARMY DOCTOR'S WIFE ON THE FRONTIER

THE LETTERS OF EMILY MCCORKLE FITZGERALD
FROM ALASKA AND THE FAR WEST, 1874–1878

By Emily McCorkle FitzGerald

Edited by
Abe Laufe

Foreword by Joan I. Biddle

University of Nebraska Press
Lincoln and London

Manufactured in the United States of America

First Bison Book printing: 1986
Most recent printing indicated by the first digit below:
1 2 3 4 5 6 7 8 9 10

Library of Congress Cataloging-in-Publication Data
FitzGerald, Emily McCorkle, 1850–1912.
An army doctor's wife on the frontier.
"Bison."
Reprint. Originally published: Pittsburgh,
Pennsylvania: University of Pittsburgh Press, 1962.
1. FitzGerald, Emily McCorkle, 1850–1912—
Correspondence. 2. Frontier and pioneer life—West
(U.S.) 3. Frontier and pioneer life—Alaska—Sitka.
4. West (U.S.)—History—1848–1950. 5. Sitka (Alaska)
—History. 6. United States. Army—Military life.
7. Officers' wives—West (U.S.)—Correspondence.
8. Officers' wives—Alaska—Sitka—Correspondence.
I. Laufe, Abe. II. Title.
F594.F56 1986 973.8'2'0924 [B] 85-29040
ISBN 0-8032-6859-9 (pbk.)

Reprinted by arrangement with the University of Pittsburgh Press

CONTENTS

LIST OF ILLUSTRATIONS

Foreword

By Joan I. Biddle

When I read Emily FitzGerald's letters for the first time a few years ago, I couldn't help being struck by how contemporary they seemed. Since then, after having reread the collection several times, I am still amazed that despite the passing of more than a century, Emily's experiences, feelings, and concerns are remarkably similar to those of many modern women who accompany their military husbands to remote, isolated, or overseas locations.

In recent years there has been a revival of interest in the written works of women, including those by army officers' wives who lived on the American frontier. Although a number of these accounts were written intentionally as books and published during the lifetime of their authors, *An Army Doctor's Wife on the Frontier* was first published only in 1962.

During the late 1950s, a collection of letters written by Emily L. FitzGerald was given to Dr. Abe Laufe at the University of Pittsburgh by Emily's daughter, Mrs. Elizabeth Hiestand, for editing. According to Miss Hannah Bechtel, who assisted Dr. Laufe, when the letters were received, they were found placed between the pages of a bound collection of magazines. Miss Bechtel recalled that many of the letters were repetitious and that a few were deleted from the published collection, but, she emphasized, every letter in the book is in Emily's own words. Nothing was changed.[1]

A particular value of Emily's letters is that they are impressions of events described *as they were happening*. Because the details were immediately fresh in her mind, it is possible to gain insights into life at frontier posts that may be clearer or more accurate than views from memoirs, which may have been written through a nostalgic haze. The repetitive nature of some of her letters allows us to observe the sometimes subtle shifts in the way Emily viewed the events and people around her as well as her changes of mood and mind. It is likely that many of Emily's thoughts and feelings mirrored those of the people around her.

Beyond their descriptions of historical events and day-to-day affairs, Emily's accounts of frontier life are valuable in demonstrating that women took an active part in events in the American West just as did the men whose names are predominant in history books. In a time in which letters were an essential form of communication between family and friends, Emily wrote consistently, sometimes every day. Because she did, many of the fine details of frontier life, and in particular the life of women at military posts in the 1870s, have been salvaged. Through Emily's eyes we learn about the life of a frontier army officer's wife, household management, and life behind the scenes at a military post during the Indian campaigns. The content of her letters varies from descriptions of clothes and household furnishings to feelings of anger at the government for its Indian policy. Emily's letters also reveal her feelings about the events and people surrounding her, as well as a little about her preferences, fears, and biases.

Although not much is known about the FitzGeralds after they left Idaho, it is known that during his subsequent leave in Columbia, Pennsylvania, Jenkins FitzGerald became ill and was diagnosed as having pneumonia. He consequently applied for sick leave. His condition continued to worsen, and on August 11, 1879, he died of "consumption resulting from pneumonia."[2]

On June 23, 1880, Emily filed for a widow's pension based on her husband's military service. Her claim was rejected on November 30, 1881, on the grounds that Dr. FitzGerald had been on leave at the time of his death and that his disease had not been contracted in the line of duty.[3]

During the years after her husband's death, Emily owned two homes, one in Marietta, the other in Columbia, Pennsylvania. She lived in the Marietta home in order to be near her daughter and grandchildren.[4] Emily employed a lawyer and continued to pursue her claim for a widow's pension on the grounds that Jenkins's disease had in reality been contracted while on active campaign duty. Her case lasted through several appeals over a number of years during which Emily and her lawyers continued to gather statements to back their claim. One such statement was given by

Nathan W. FitzGerald, Emily's brother-in-law and second lawyer, who stated Jenkins had told him "that he had had a hard siege of service, and took the worst cold of his life, on the campaign and he feared one lung was seriously affected."[5] Emily finally did receive her pension, in the amount of twenty dollars a month. She died on February 14, 1912, the eve of her fortieth wedding anniversary.

NOTES

1. Conversation with Hannah Bechtel, June 4, 1985.
2. War Department AG note, widow's pension file of Emily L. FitzGerald, National Archives and Records Service, Washington, D.C.
3. Widow's pension file of Emily L. FitzGerald, National Archives and Records Service, Washington, D.C. A slip of paper entitled "Incidental Matter" found in the pension file notes that the claim was "Rejected, on the ground of want of title. The evidence in the claim shows that the soldier was 'on leave' when his fatal disease was contracted. Under the provisions of Sec. 4694 R.S., the soldier being 'in service,' and not being 'actually in the field,' or 'on the march,' or 'at some post, fort or garrison,' or 'en-route by direction of competent authority to some post, fort or garrison' when his fatal disease was contracted, no title to pension exists under the general law. Other points not considered."
4. Mrs. Richard J. Stark to Joan Biddle, July 31, 1985.
5. Statement of Nathan W. FitzGerald, December 20, 1889, widow's pension file of Emily L. FitzGerald, National Archives and Records Service, Washington, D.C.

PREFACE

Written by Emily's daughter, Mrs. Elizabeth F. Hiestand, called Bessie by her mother in these letters.

There seems to be very little written or known of the early days in the far Northwest, our western frontiers of Idaho and Montana, the Indian outbreaks of that time, the Army Posts with their small garrisons, the daily contacts with the friendly Indians, and the fears and terrors in times when the Indians were hostile.

My parents happened to be in Idaho, then a territory, through two of the worst Indian outbreaks this country has ever known, the Nez Percé and Bannock Indian Wars. Recently, while going over the letters of my father "in the field" and my mother's letters to her mother and sister, I felt they were interesting enough to give to others.

Perhaps a few words about their lives previous to the time when they wrote the letters would be helpful. My father, born in Indiana of New England parents who had emigrated to Indiana early in 1800, was at Jefferson Medical College, Philadelphia, at the outbreak of the Civil War. He left college and enlisted in an Indiana regiment, under General Benjamin Harrison, to look after a very young brother who had run off from school to enlist. He served throughout the war and was in Sherman's March to the Sea. He had enlisted as a private, but he came home as surgeon of his regiment. His interest in surgery and his education along these lines brought him into quick prominence.

In 1898, General Harrison (the ex-president of the United States) wrote to my mother:

> I knew Surgeon FitzGerald well and admired him greatly. He was one of the bravest men I ever knew. I recall at the time of the Civil War, during a skirmish, coming upon him in a sheltered hollow, working over some wounded men. I shouted to him as I galloped by, "Get your wounded out of here quickly, Doctor. In a few min-

utes the bullets will be raining like Hell." He looked up and said, "I cannot move these wounded now, General, and my place is with them," and went quietly on with his work.

After the war, my father went back to Jefferson College, graduated, offered his services to the government, and was enrolled as Surgeon in the United States Army. He was sent first to Indian Territory, and on a trip to Fort Leavenworth, Kansas, met my mother, who was visiting there.

Mother was born in Columbia, Pennsylvania, of an old English Quaker family who lived on the land they bought from William Penn. When father met her, she had just graduated from school, was pretty, bright, and entertaining, and was at once attracted to the big, quiet, gentlemanly surgeon. After a short courtship, they were married, were ordered to West Point (where I was born), and after only a year and a half, were ordered to Sitka, Alaska, the "Jumping Off Place" in those days.

Mother's letters tell of the then most unusual trip by water down the Atlantic Coast from New York, across the Isthmus of Panama by rail, the long thirty-or-forty-day trip up the Pacific Coast to Portland, and finally through the narrow inside passage to Sitka, Alaska. For two years we lived at this new, little Post. We had only had it a short time from the Russians. (It was abandoned later as a post and is now one of our famous Indian schools.) Mother was one of the first American women up there. My brother was born in Sitka. Three little boys were born in as many months to three American families there.

The letters of that time would make a book in themselves. Everything was so new and strange. A mail steamer came only once a month. The Indians and half-Russians provided new experiences. Yet the families at the Army Post were happy and managed to have many good times together.

From Sitka we were ordered to Fort Lapwai in Idaho Territory, and there, almost at once, the Indian troubles began. As usual, it was about the land. The Nez Percé Indians, who objected to the increasing oncoming of the White Settlers in Wallowa Valley, would not stay on their reservations. Chief Joseph was a fine Indian and a friend to the Whites. Yet, as many a fine man before him, he had to "go with his people," and it was he who finally led his people to war. I often saw him. He came to our home and to the homes of other officers in the most friendly way.

It was at Lapwai that Miss McBeth, an early Presbyterian missionary, established her school for the Nez Percé Indians and did her wonderful work among them, but all that seemed forgotten by the Indians. The young braves wanted war, and war they had, all that first summer in 1877.

I remember the general unrest. I remember the big Pow-Wow or conference of the Indians and General Howard, who was then in command of the Army of the Northwest, in a huge tent upon our parade ground, trying to bring the Indians to a peaceful settlement; his failure to do so; the galloping into the Post of a rider with a sweated horse bringing news of the first Indian massacre; the marching out at sunset of almost the whole of our little garrison; the tension everywhere; the nervous waiting for news; the report that the Indians would attack the Post with its pitifully few defenders because there were "Heap plenty guns — heap plenty blankets," etc.; and finally I remember hours spent in the darkness of a cellar with frightened mothers and weeping children.

All these are vivid recollections of my childhood, but I want the letters to tell their own story. I hope the bitterness so often expressed in my mother's letters will be excused by those who live today in our safe and peaceful land, and that they will realize what those times must have meant to the young wives and mothers who have "gone before."

Elizabeth FitzGerald Hiestand

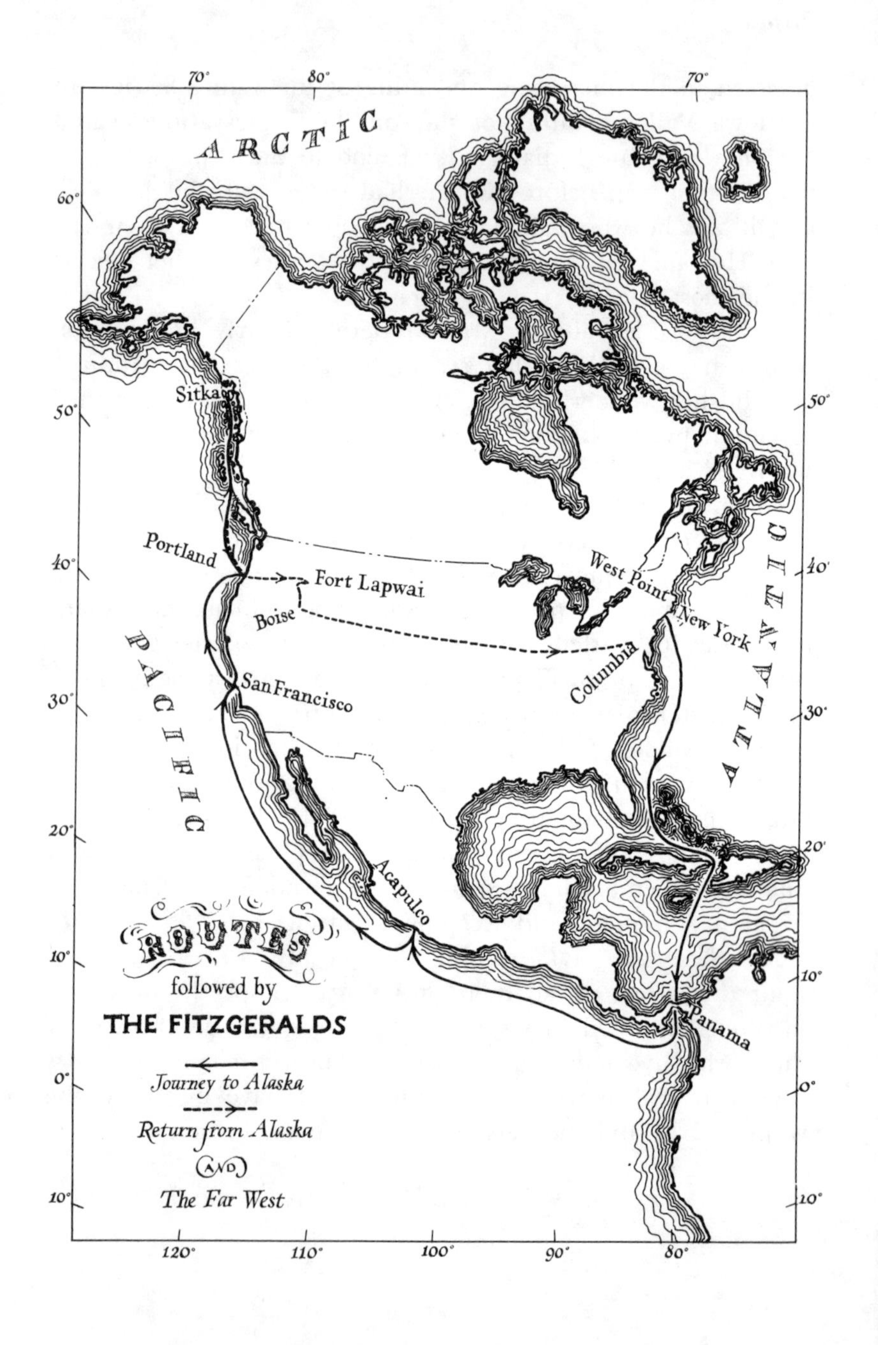
ARCTIC
PACIFIC
ATLANTIC
Sitka
Portland
Fort Lapwai
Boise
San Francisco
Acapulco
Panama
Columbia
West Point
New York
ROUTES
followed by
THE FITZGERALDS
Journey to Alaska
Return from Alaska
AND
The Far West
70°
80°
70°
60°
50°
40°
30°
20°
10°
0°
10°
120°
110°
100°
90°
80°

AN ARMY DOCTOR'S WIFE
ON THE FRONTIER

PART I

THE JOURNEY

From New York to Sitka, Alaska — 1874

In the latter part of 1870, Emily McCorkle left her home in Columbia, Pennsylvania, to visit her Aunt Patience Caldwell in Leavenworth, Kansas. Aunt "Pace" Caldwell was the youngest sister of Emily's mother, and Uncle "Alex" Caldwell was a wealthy businessman of Leavenworth and, subsequently, a United States Senator from Kansas.

Emily was a daughter of an old Pennsylvania family. She had attended Miss Dickson's School for Girls in Harrisburg, Pennsylvania, and had increased her social graces by many visits with her cousins in Philadelphia. She was short and slight, with dark brown hair with tints of gold, a slender face with fair skin, and a generous mouth around which dimples played.

At the Caldwell home in Leavenworth, she met Dr. Jenkins (John) A. FitzGerald, Post Surgeon at Camp Supply, Indian Territory, when he came to eastern Kansas on leave. He was tall, broad shouldered and muscular, had a dark complexion, dark hair and moustache, and gray eyes that suggested firmness.

When they met, Emily was twenty and John was thirty-one. He was at once attracted to her, but, despite his age and experience, was shy in her presence. Emily originally had planned to make her visit a short one. Her growing affection for Doctor FitzGerald, however, prompted her to stay longer.

According to Mrs. Elizabeth FitzGerald Hiestand, the nickname John originated one day while Dr. FitzGerald and Emily were out for a drive. In order to find out how Emily felt about him, Dr. FitzGerald began praising one of her other suitors. Emily turned to him and said, "Why don't you speak for yourself, John?"

When Dr. FitzGerald received orders to report for duty at West Point, he wrote to Emily's mother and begged for permission to be married at once, for he could get a delay in reporting for duty; he also said it would be very difficult for him to get a leave of absence in the immediate future after he took on his duties at the new post.

Dr. FitzGerald left Leavenworth on January 31, 1872. On February 15, 1872, he and Emily were married at Columbia, Pennsylvania, by Dr. Roger Owen, a Presbyterian minister from Chestnut Hill. In her letters, Emily referred to Dr. Owen as Uncle Owen.

From February 1872 until May 1874 the FitzGeralds lived at West Point where Doctor FitzGerald served as Assistant Surgeon at the United States Military Academy. Their first child, Elizabeth, or Bess as she was called in the letters, was born February 17, 1873.

In May 1874, Doctor FitzGerald received orders to report to the Military Department of the Columbia with headquarters at Fort Vancouver, six miles from Portland. This extensive Department included the State of Oregon, the Territory of Washington, parts of Idaho, and recently purchased Alaska. Doctor FitzGerald and Emily, their 15-month-old daughter Bess, and Mary, a negro nurse-maid aged 15, left New York aboard the Acapulco, *bound for Panama. They were to cross the Isthmus of Panama by rail and then sail up the Pacific Coast aboard the* Montana.

Emily began writing letters to her mother on May 25, 1874. At this time, she was in the fourth month of her second pregnancy.)

Emily McCorkle FitzGerald, who wrote most of these letters.

Dr. Jenkins (John) A. FitzGerald, Emily's husband, Army Surgeon.

Aboard the Acapulco
May 25, 1874

Dear Mamma,

This is Tuesday morning and we are about as far south as Florida, though, of course, out of sight of the coast. Bess is asleep and Mary is sitting outside of our stateroom door listening for her to awake. Doctor and I are on deck, and this is actually the first time I have been able to try to write since we came aboard, but now I do really feel better, though awfully shaky, and have not yet felt that I will lose my breakfast. If I don't, it will be the first meal I have kept down. Doctor was quite sick yesterday afternoon for the first time, and Mary has been real sick, too. Bess is the only well one of the party, and she seems to enjoy it. If we only can get to feeling comfortable, we will enjoy the trip, I know.

There are a great many pleasant people on board and Captain Dow is very kind. Doctor brought him a letter from General Morgan, who is an old friend, and we have seats at the table next to the Captain which, you know, is quite an honor, though an honor I have not once had the pleasure of enjoying. We expect to reach Jamaica Friday morning, and there I will mail this letter.

Right beside me is sitting a Mrs. Brown whose husband is in the Navy. She has not seen him for two years and is going to join him in San Francisco where his ship will put in for repairs. We have a young Naval Surgeon who is going to join his ship at Panama. He is awfully sick; poor prospect for a life on the water, isn't it?

Afternoon

Still improving. Took a little lunch and kept it down. The weather is growing much warmer. The first two days we could scarcely keep ourselves warm, but today it is as warm as July and fast growing warmer. Captain Dow says tomorrow we will begin to suffer with the heat, and from that time it will grow hotter. I managed, though I am terribly shaky, to give Bess a bath and clean clothes an hour ago. I changed her flannel and will change my own in the morning.

I have just heard we will pass a steamer homeward bound in a few hours, and a boat will go out from this one with mail, so I will have an opportunity of sending my letter sooner than I expected. Doctor joins me in love to all. I will write every chance.

Your daughter,
Emily FitzGerald

The *Acapulco*
Tuesday Afternoon
May 25, 1874

Dear Mamma,

Doctor just went down to the purser to have our letters sent off with other mail to the steamer going to New York. I will begin this and write a little every now and then and have this ready for the next chance. The sea is lovely this afternoon. I believe it is the first time I have thought so. All day we have passed seaweed, several varieties. Indeed, ever since Sunday afternoon when we crossed the Gulf Stream, we have seen quantities of it. I wish you were with us. Then, after I get over seasickness, we would enjoy it.

Wednesday Afternoon
May 26, 1874

Have had a horrible sick morning but no vomiting. The sea has been rough and we have some sails up which, though they make us go faster, give the ship an extra rocking which is awful. It has been the hardest day for seasick people, but as I am better than yesterday, I feel comforted.

I am up on deck again. About half an hour ago we sighted land. Everybody has rushed to this side of the deck and they are all using their glasses. You don't know what a comfort the sight of land is. Why I feel better already. But it is land I never expected to see — the San Salvador of Columbus. I believe the one we are passing now they call Watling Island. So you see we are pretty far south, 2 or 3 hundred miles southeast of Florida. Tomorrow morning we pass so near Cuba that we will see the houses on shore. We pass within a mile and a half of the coast and the next morning, Friday, we put in at Jamaica. We hear there is smallpox there, and the Captain will stay but a few hours.

Mary is getting along very well. Bess let her feed her today for the first time. Mary is a queer child. She came to me yesterday and said, "Oh Miss Emmie, isn't it awful? Did you see those girls? They are playing cards. Why I wouldn't for a hundred dollars."

Thursday Morning
May 27, 1874

We are all better this morning and everything is lovely. We are near Cuba. This morning while waiting on the guards for breakfast, we saw a dozen coconuts floating in the water and more beautiful varieties of seaweed. Some one fished some seaweed up yesterday and it was lovely. I wish I could have sent some for you to see. It looked like beautiful grapevines, full of grapes, clear and white.

Noon

A long range of mountains, which they tell us is Cuba, has just come in sight. We will pass it this afternoon and see both it and San Domingo. Bess had a bath in seawater this morning.

Later

We passed Cuba quite close. Saw the lighthouse distinctly and palm trees and coconut trees in abundance. San Domingo we saw way off in the distance. We only pass the end of the Island of Cuba and are more than a hundred miles east of Havana. The weather is and has been lovely. Today it is just charming. We all expected to be suffering with heat, but as yet we have had no real warm weather.

Quite a number of pleasant people are at our table. There is Mrs. Brown I spoke of, two Miss Messers from Boston going to San Francisco to visit a brother, and a Presbyterian minister,

Mr. Cameron, and his wife. He is very entertaining and always telling Scottish stories. Then there is a Mr. Brown who is always laughing, a young looking fellow, looks like a rowdy, who astonished me yesterday by telling me he has four children and then astonished everybody by turning out to be a Baptist minister!

We have on board a bride and groom who are awfully devoted. Mr. Cameron calls her the hanging bride, I suppose, because she is always hanging on his arms.

Saturday, May 29, 1874

A rough sea and another seasick day. I had to rush from the dinner table yesterday and have not been down there since. But I must tell you about Jamaica. Before we were up yesterday, Mary came in and said that we were near land. We got up and dressed and found we were sailing around the Island at a distance of about a mile. We could see villages, sugar plantations, palm trees, etc. Kingston, where we were to land, is in the southern part, so we skirted the whole eastern shore of the Island. About noon we got into the harbor and then were stopped in quarantine until the health officer came on board and saw our papers. I wish you could have ridden up that bay with us — such wonderful sights for northern people. Just at the entrance to the bay or harbor we passed right over a buried city, Port Royal. Only a few years ago an earthquake buried it in the sea. Captain Dow told us that sometimes, when the water is clear, you can see down the chimneys of the homes as you pass over. Up the bay on both sides we could see houses, people, and coconuts in quantities growing on the trees. The coconut foliage looks prettier at a distance. It looks like huge fern leaves and the trees are tall and straight with everything in a bunch at the top, the nuts growing close in with the leaves to the stem of the tree.

As we came up to the wharf at Kingston, about 20 naked negroes leaped into the water from it and from ships and boats around and swam towards our ship and called out to throw them "a silver or a copper, Sir." They would dive and catch it before it reached the bottom. Lots were thrown to them and they did dive every time and get them. At last they cried out, "Too much copper." They carried what they got in their mouths as if they had been pockets. And oh, the wharf! I wish you could have seen the negroes and the dressing of the ladies, etc.

After the health officer's visit to the ship, a notice was put up in the salon telling the passengers they could not go ashore at Jamaica owing to the smallpox. So the natives came down to the wharf with their wares to sell, principally fruit, but also other little matters that I should like to have carried you all from Jamaica, if we were only going home. The noise and jabber of various voices talking in half a dozen different languages was awful. They would hold up what they had to sell and call at the top of their voices, "This, lady (or gentleman) for a quarter." Their smallest charge was a quarter. Doctor went out on to the guards to get some oranges but came back without any, as they refuse to take anything but silver — greenbacks are below par with them. I sacrificed my new quarter and Doctor got a lovely little basket with a tight fitting lid and about eight or ten oranges in it. Then after a while Doctor got some silver from someone on the ship and made two or three little purchases — a Panama hat for himself for a dollar, not the very finest but very nice, such a one as you would have to give six or eight dollars for in New York. Then he got me a little light fan for a quarter and Bess four good, long, pretty strands of red coral for 50 cents. One more basket of fruit, I believe, concluded our purchases, but the noise and commotion kept up all afternoon. We left about four o'clock and were accompanied half way down the harbor by the swimming men and boys diving for "Silver or copper, Sir."

After we got out to sea we found it rough — awfully rough — and almost everybody was seasick this afternoon. I am better and do hope to keep so. By tomorrow night we expect to be at the Isthmus but will not land and cross until Monday morning. How I wish it was all over, I mean the rest of our journey. I am tired and want to be settled in a home of our own with some home comforts around us. We will be nearly three weeks more getting to San Francisco. We take the *Montana,* the ship that takes us to San Francisco, at Panama.

One other item about Jamaica. It has over four hundred thousand inhabitants and only 40 or 50 thousand whites. We saw lots of enormous birds flying around in all directions — a sort of buzzard — and we were told they act as scavengers all over the island, actually cleaning the streets. A fine is put upon anyone that injures or interferes with them.

Bess is well and happy. She wears her little wrappers and looks cute in them. She is known all over the ship and everybody makes a fuss over her. She is actually kissed to death. Last night Doctor said, "Em, can't you keep these people from pulling this poor baby to pieces?" People say to me, "Does she ever cry?" "What a sunny little baby," etc. She is cute and sweet but I wish I had her safely through the rest of the journey and comfortable and quiet at our own home.

We have quite a number of books and reading matter with us, but with Bess and seasickness, I have not been able to read a thing. Doctor joins me in love to all at home. I will have another letter ready and send it when we arrive at San Francisco. I will send this one from Panama.

Sunday, May 30, 1874

We are about 50 miles from Aspinwall and will sleep tonight in the harbor there, if nothing happens. [*Aspinwall, former name for Colon, which at present is the seaport on the Atlantic side of the Panama Canal.*]

How I wish I could see you. We are all well. Bess particularly so, though the poor child is bedbug bitten this morning. Breakfast tomorrow is the last meal we take in this ship.

I don't believe we would hear from you at San Francisco, so write to Portland in care of Medical Director, Department of the Columbia. Lots of love from us all.

Your daughter,
Emily FitzGerald

On the *Montana,*
at Panama Bay
June 5, 1874
. . . Roasting!

Dear Mamma,

Just after I finished your letter, we came in sight of Aspinwall and got in there about six o'clock That was Sunday night. We stayed on the *Acapulco* until Monday about noon, then came over here where we are roasting and have to wait until some freight is put aboard. Doctor went out and took a look at Aspinwall. I saw very little of it, but it was the dirtiest, hottest place that ever was! Goats, parrots, pigs, and naked people all live together. The little children, indeed quite big ones, are entirely in their "natural condition," and the women think a chemise is quite covering enough. The streets are smelling and filthy. The only pretty or refreshing things were the flowers and they were lovely — roses, great bunches of them, and other flowers that I don't know but that were so lovely and fresh looking.

Our ride across the Isthmus to Panama was interesting but hot, and we were glad to have it over. It took about three hours to cross. I don't think we saw as much as we expected to, but, of course, all was so different from any sight we could have up North that it was interesting. The trees don't look nearly as high and handsome as our own, but everything is a mass of vines. All the trees and bushes are covered. Then there are quantities of banana trees and very much larger coconut trees than any we had seen, two or three more varieties of palms, great large, coarse palm fern, and other things of the kind. Then we saw oranges, limes, mangoes, and other fruits growing, whole orchards of them. And such lovely flowers! We passed some nice looking little houses. I guess they belonged to whites; the natives live like pigs in little thatched houses, and oh, so dirty! Some places, there were four and five little naked black children standing in a row looking at the train.

The train cars are open, have cane seats, and no glass in the windows.

We arrived at Panama about five in the evening and came straight through a big, rough-looking crowd to a little steamboat that brought us off to the *Montana.* The big vessels can't come within three miles of the shore here because the tides are so unusual and rise and fall so suddenly. Just in this bay where we are now, the tide rises nearly thirty feet and falls very rapidly. This ship is not like the other one. In some respects it is more comfortable, but not so much in some others. We are on the deck; at least the deck is on the same story we are. In front of our stateroom, there are great white guards with a railing running all around. We are suffering with the heat but hope to feel better when we start. The Captain says we will, perhaps, start tonight. We are fortunate again in getting to the Captain's own table and we sit there with nearly the same party we had at Captain Dow's table.

Doctor went over to Panama last evening with a party to see the sights. I did not go because I did not like to leave Bess alone on the ship with Mary. Mary does very well, though she is not inclined to be at all submissive. She is very angry this morning because the steward has changed her place at the table where she takes her meals with all the other children. I don't know, but I think, perhaps, there was some trouble from a foolish mother whose children sit near Mary. Anyway, her seat was changed this morning to another, much to her indignation, and she looks like a thunder cloud. She doesn't care about the seat so much, but she is cross that she had to give it up to some child she did not like. I believe the child called her Spanish the other day. You know, all those negroes down here talk Spanish and look just like Mary, so it wasn't such an awful mistake, but Mary is very indignant. I talked to her and tried to explain, but I don't know whether she feels very much better about it.

Doctor is over in the town again this morning. He went with the captain to see about some of his baggage. I hear Panama is a very old town. There are some churches and a convent there of some interest. The fruits we get here, particularly the pineapples, are very fine. The Jamaica oranges were horrible, not nearly as nice as the little thin-skinned ones we get up North. They are better here but have the same fault — so much thick skin and pulpy skin inside the orange, it makes them coarse and ugly to eat.

We don't know when we will get to San Francisco and we are all tired and dirty. I have so many dirty clothes, particularly Bess' little things, I don't know what to do with them.

Friday, June 5, 1874

Yesterday at eleven o'clock we left Panama, much to our delight. Now we have a voyage of sixteen or eighteen days before us which I wish was over. I am a little seasick this morning, and so are most of my neighbors.

Did I tell you that boat loads of fruits—limes, oranges, coconuts, pineapples, etc. — were lying by the vessel all the time and everybody bought, of course. We gave ten cents apiece for the pineapples. Several boatloads of white coral were sold down by the ship, too. Lovely pieces, some much larger than the piece you used to have, sold from 10 to 25 cents. I wanted some awfully but had no way of carrying it.

For the last four or five evenings the sightseers have been gratified by a sight of the Southern Cross, but it is not nearly so pretty or so bright as the constellations around the North Pole. Still, it is interesting to see.

We will make three or four stops on our way up. I know, in many respects, we are better off traveling this way than by land. All the children are more comfortable, but it is a long, long tiresome journey—too long for pleasure.

Mary is doing pretty well. She is so much a child, but I know we will get along much better when we are settled. There are some little girls here that Mary likes to play with. Several times I have left her by my stateroom door to watch Bess and have gone for a little walk around the guards with Doctor. She does not mean to disobey, I don't think, but I have found her, or seen her, running past me with the children at just the other end of the boat from where I had left her. Her excuse is, "I forgot," but she really seems to be willing and anxious to please.

June 9, 1874
In the Gulf of
Tehuantepec

Here we expected a rough sea, but it is about as usual. Our seasickness is all over, I guess, unless we have a storm or a big blow or some such thing, which we don't expect this time of year. We are due tomorrow at Acapulco in Mexico; it is the city our ship on the Atlantic side was named after. That will be our first stop. We are glad of it, for we are all tired of the water and want to see land.

There is one thing I forgot to tell you about this ship. We have Chinamen for waiters. They did seem so funny at first in their loose black pants, white coats, just like a shirt worn outside, their Chinese shoes, and their pigtails twisted into a knot on top of their heads. They talk funny, too, but seem to make very good waiters, though preserve me from having one in my house.

We are all sitting on the deck in front of our staterooms, a whole party of us trying to get cool, but it is awfully hot. We are not going to get to San Francisco for about two weeks and then it will be so long before we get to our journey's end and to housekeeping. On Sunday we saw a school, or shoal, of porpoises quite near to the ship. There must have been hundreds of them jumping and tumbling about in a most laughable manner.

We hear we will find peaches, strawberries, and all such good things in San Francisco when we arrive there. That is comforting. Bess is not real well though she isn't sick either, but she is uncomfortable with the heat and has two big double teeth coming through. No matter what day we arrive, we will have to wait in San Francisco until a Saturday, because the Portland boats leave only on that day. So you can think the

Saturday after you hear we have arrived at San Francisco that we are on our way north. Our thermometer stands above ninety degrees today and tomorrow we expect a hotter day than this. They say it is awful in the Bay of Acapulco.

Friday Morning
June 12, 1874

Day before yesterday we stopped at Acapulco. The Bay was lovely! Such pretty green land on each side of us as we went in, cute little houses, palm trees, and some other beautiful trees. We got up to the town, or as near it as the big ships go, about five in the evening. From that time until ten o'clock, the little boats of the natives were all around the ship, most of them full of things to sell. Doctor, nearly all of the gentlemen, and some of the ladies went ashore. I didn't like to leave Bess but enjoyed myself hanging over the guards, seeing the buying and selling from the little boats. They had bananas, limes, coconuts, shells, coral, baskets, hammocks, birds, fans, and all such things. And such a time the people in the little boats and the people on the ship had understanding each other. The party that went ashore were very much pleased. They found the town clean and lots of flowers in bloom. We did not make any purchases at Acapulco as our bundles are now more than we can carry. Doctor did get some limes to use for a drink because the water we get to drink is horrible and our ice will give out in a day or two, but they say we will be in a much colder region by that time and won't miss it. Sometime this morning we reach our second stopping place, Manzanilla. We make one more stop in Mexico — Mazatlan — and then stop for a few hours at Cape St. Lucas — then San Francisco.

Saturday Afternoon
June 13, 1874

We are a little cooler, so things all seem more comfortable. Yesterday we stopped for five hours at Manzanilla. It looks just like all the other little towns we have seen. One new feature struck me rather horribly — the quantity of sharks in the water. They say this southern water is full of them and they are found in enormous quantities near shore. I stood at the side of the ship and in the course of ten minutes saw as many as a dozen great, big fellows, all bigger than a man, and I live in constant terror of Doctor or Bess falling overboard.

I spoke of Mary in the first part of the letter. Bess goes to her now and will stay with her much more willingly than at first and I think, considering that she has never had anything to do with babies, that she does pretty well. I can't form much of an opinion living this way, though, and hope to like her very much when we get home. She has shown one propensity that worries me — she walks in her sleep. She has had two walks on the ship and gone into people's staterooms but, as yet, no one has been frightened, nor has she hurt herself. She seems rather pleased than otherwise at the notoriety it gives her and talks about it considerably, which Doctor says is the very way to make her walk more. I tried to impress upon her that it was a bad habit that might get her into a great deal of trouble. She seems to be perfectly contented to be with us and I think she likes the baby.

Bess has a great many friends on board; she is quite a belle. Our Captain, Captain Connolly, has had her up in his cabin playing, and he stops and takes her every time he passes. She amuses herself with his hat, his cigar, or anything she can get her hands on.

Sunday, June 14, 1874

This morning, before we were up, we had arrived at Mazatlan. It is on the eastern side of the Gulf of California, some little distance from its mouth. We stayed there until about noon; now we are steaming a little southwest and will touch Cape St. Lucas tomorrow morning. Mazatlan looked like a very pretty little town, though they say it is dirty. One thing I did not speak of that we noticed, both here and at Manzanilla, is the cactus. The hills are covered with it — a coarse, ugly, rough looking cactus of the tree variety — *Cactus gigantia,* Doctor says, and it bears a yellow flower. We see strange things in the ocean — sharks, swordfish, turtles, porpoises, etc. We don't often see any but the porpoises while the vessel is moving, but the other day while we were in clear water, we saw an enormous swordfish as big as the Doctor. Now we are in hopes of seeing a whale, as they are often seen a little farther north than we are this afternoon. Doctor and I are a little comforted today by the hopes held out by Captain Connolly that we may make San Francisco next Saturday morning and that will enable us to take the Portland steamer on the same day. We would like it so much better than to have to wait a whole week in the unsettled way we will be. My one wish now is to be settled and have a home. We will visit Frisco again when we feel more like it, so I do hope we will catch the first steamer.

Wednesday Morning
June 17, 1874

Now we are just as cold as we were warm this time last week. The hour after we turned around Cape St. Lucas we began to feel the need of our thick clothes. I like the cold much better than the warm, only I can't make Bess comfortable. There is no place warm for her to stay and she will run about on deck. I don't feel that she is warm enough, although she has had her waterproof knit cap and leggings on for the last three days.

Yesterday Doctor saw a whale blow; I did not have the pleasure. We have seen some very singular rocks in our visits along the coast. At Mazatlan there were a number of rocky islands, some of them just a large rock, almost a mountain, rising out of the water, and they all had great caves in them. Some of the caves seemed to go into the heart of the mountains and, as far in as we could see with glasses, they looked large and dark. Then just off St. Lucas there is a natural arch, quite a large one, with the waves and spray breaking through it. Cape St. Lucas is the most desolate, barren, God-forsaken looking place I ever saw. The vessel is rocking fearfully this morning. It makes me feel shaky, but I hope our seasickness is over.

The other evening I was standing with Bess in my arms. The people were promenading and everybody that passed stopped and spoke or made some motion or sign to Bess. She responds, says "Bye-bye," or shakes hands, or nods her head. I said to Doctor after we went to our stateroom, "I wonder if some of the other mothers don't notice it and think that their babies are neglected."

I am getting to feel a little uncomfortable and wish our journey was ended. My clothes feel heavy and I am very tender about that part of my body, and I have felt motion there for the last two weeks. I am very anxious to hear from you and know how you are, but I don't suppose I will until we get to Portland.

We are all having swollen feet. For the two weeks we spent in the tropics, I could not get my biggest boots on, and if I did pull them on, the buttons would not meet by an inch, and my feet felt like pin cushions. But for the last three days, it is different. Our feet are all right and the temperature now is about like what is felt on the Atlantic going to Europe. So I guess it is the cool weather, not the sea, that makes the difference. I got out our dirty clothes this morning to pack all together in one trunk. Oh, such a lot and such dirty ones, I am afraid they will never get a good color again.

Thursday, June 18, 1874

I guess I will finish up my letter now. The sea is awfully rough this morning and lots of people are seasick. I am not, but this constant rocking makes me dizzy. The sea and wind are both against our progress, so, much to our sorrow, we now expect to get into San Francisco just a little too late for our Portland steamer and that means a whole week to wait. Well, I will be thankful if we get in safely anyway. Four weeks is too long for a pleasure voyage. I am as tired as I can be of it and will never willingly take it again, though I can imagine circumstances that would make me take it rather than go by rail. It is certainly more comfortable for children, and if I had a family of small ones, I should feel it a sort of duty to come this way, for the children have room to run about. But the tropics and tropical fruit I pray to be delivered from. I never want to hear about them again. We have seen some wonderful things, to be sure, and if we arrive safely at Frisco I shan't be sorry we have taken the trip, but once is enough.

Doctor joins me in a great deal of love to you and to all the rest. I will write to Sallie and Aunt Annie from Portland or San Francisco.

Friday, June 19, 1874

We expect to get in about noon tomorrow, and I will send this at once. With lots of Love, I am,

Your daughter,
Emily FitzGerald

P.S. Several enormous whales were seen close to the ship this morning. Doctor saw them. I was not out.

San Francisco
Sunday, June 21, 1874
Occidental Hotel

Dear Mamma,

We missed our Portland boat by just a few hours! It was too bad and we don't quite know yet what we will do. Doctor talks of going overland rather than wait a week, but he wants to see some friends first and see about some freight before he decides anything. This is a rather pleasant hotel but we are enjoying it at the rate of 10 dollars a day. Doctor has been out all afternoon. Such a Sunday! The stores are all open!

Yesterday, soon as we arrived, Doctor went out and got me the first fruit he came across, a box of raspberries (they were lovely), some plums, and apricots. Then for lunch, which we had in our room, we had cherries and currants, and today Doctor brought me apples. They have fruit on the table every meal and apricots seem to be plenty — the streets are full of them. I have not been out at all, so I don't know anything about the city, though it is a barren looking place, judging from what we saw riding through, lots of sandhills and banks but no trees.

Bess is well but fretful today. She misses the host of friends that amused her on the boat.

Your loving daughter,
Emily

San Francisco
Wednesday
June 24, 1874
Occidental Hotel

Dear Sallie, [*Emily's Sister*]

We are still here and expect now to wait until Saturday and then take the Portland steamer. I am so tired of the water I hope to live the next four years out of sight of it entirely.

Doctor was greeted when he arrived here with the lovely news that he would most probably have to go to Sitka! [*In 1874, Sitka was the capital of Alaska.*]

Dr. Brook, who is in Sitka, is sick and wants to be relieved at once and they say Doctor is the only available man, that is, the only one they have ready to send. I was horrified and felt doleful about it until I found it is not certain. Nothing is decided, or will be, until we get to Portland. I felt a little comforted, too, to hear from some officers that it is not such a horrible place and is not unhealthy. The greatest trouble is its isolation, and just now there is going to be a larger and pleasanter garrison there than ever before — quite a number of nice ladies that I know of — but we still hope it will not be our fate.

I am thankful the warm part of our journey is over. I am wearing my winter clothes here and half the ladies are out in fur cloaks. We have had quite a number of calls since Saturday, mostly Army people. We have had to have all our greenbacks turned into gold and with a hundred or two we will have changed in Portland we lose just 70 dollars! Doesn't it seem too bad that our small amounts have to be cut down in that style? [*Dr. FitzGerald's salary as an Army Captain was $200 a month.*]

I have been out but once, when I took a little walk with Doctor to see the sights. The stores look nice. Almost every second building is a broker's, though, and there are banks upon banks. Tell Mamma I am so thankful for the redingotes, loose in front, that she disliked so much. I don't know what I would do without them. Nothing else I have will meet!

Friday Night
June 26, 1874

I meant to tell you a thousand things but have put this off until I have not time to finish it. Bess has been real sick all day. I have scarcely had her out of my arms. She seems better tonight, but I do wish I had her at Portland without the journey up there.

This scrawl is not fit to send, but as I really can't write another and want some of you to know, at least, where we are, I will let it go, but will write from Portland. We leave early tomorrow and now it is past bedtime. Let me hear from home soon. Tell Mamma that Bess is not at all well. Doctor says her teeth are troubling her and he is really anxious about her. She has four big double teeth and her eye teeth are all nearly through. I hope the change she will have in our trip up will do her good.

Good night and
love to all,
Emily FitzGerald

Portland
July 4, 1874

Dear Mamma,

Here we are this far on our journey and all is well. Bess is much better and has looked and been much more like herself for the last three days. She was really ill in San Francisco.

We left San Francisco Saturday in the *Orriflame* and were awfully seasick for a day and night. Doctor looked white, though he did keep up. I was obliged to be up and have my clothes on, too, for I was worried about Bess. Mary was not sick, but she is a child that is very much given to thinking she is dead if anything at all is the matter with her. Our trip up here, I think, was the hardest part of our whole journey. It was so cold and horrible and we were on the water for two days more than we expected. The winds were against us. Quite a number of enormous whales were seen. The part of our trip we enjoyed the most was after we had gotten into the Columbia River. Then we had pretty shores on both sides of us, which was such a comfort after the long stretch of water our eyes had been accustomed to, and we had another interesting sight — snow-capped mountains in the distance. They looked grand. We came in sight of Mount St. Helen just as the sun was setting, and the whole top glistened like silver.

We got here Thursday morning and went to the best hotel, the Clarendon, but oh, such a hotel! We had heard of a Mrs. Dolan's boarding house and yesterday Doctor looked it up. Fortunately, we got her to take us. So last night we came here and it is a thousand times nicer than the hotel. Mrs. Dolan is a very pleasant lady; she has two or three families and four gentlemen boarding here. The table is so nice, we hope we are fixed for the month.

But I have not told you yet about our destination. Don't be horrified. We are going to Sitka! I thought at first it was doleful, but we find the worst part is its isolation. We have only one mail a month, so Doctor and I are beginning to take comfort and think about our comfort there. The quarters are better there than any place else in the Department and, instead of being an unhealthy place, it is a good place for children. They always thrive there. Then there is going to be a much more pleasant garrison there than ever before. There will be half a dozen ladies there, one of them Mrs. Campbell, a sister of Mrs. Jack Davis whom you met at the Point. [*The wife of the Com-*

manding Officer at Sitka, Captain Joseph B. Campbell, 4th Artillery, Co. F.]

Dr. Bailey, the Medical Director here, tells Dr. F. that the first medical officer that reported in Portland just at this juncture would have to go, no matter who it was. Dr. Brook, who is there, has to be relieved, and they are particular to be prompt about relieving the doctor at Sitka. It is only a short two year's detail, often not more than eighteen months, so it won't be so bad after all. It takes us ten days from here in a steamer; the only bad part is we will be so far from our friends and hear so seldom. Dr. Bailey said to Dr. F., "You will have to go to Sitka sometime, and you never can go better than now when you are young and have a small family. When you come back, you shall have as good a post as it is possible to find." I have met quite a number who have served up there who tell me it is much better than some of the far away posts in Washington Territory.

Now what I want most particularly you should think about is that any little thing I want you to send by mail you will have to start off at least two months before I can get it. If you have one or two of the little shirts you were going to make me nearly ready, I would be glad if they could be sent to me here. Then I will be sure of them in time. I don't want him to come before his clothes! Sometime in the next six months, I want another dozen of those 12 cent handkerchiefs, the ones not hemstitched, but they need not come until we get to Alaska. Doctor has been put on duty here in the city for a month. Our boat sails the first of August.

We had ever so many calls at the Clarendon, among others, Dr. Alexander. [*Dr. Charles T. Alexander was married to Emily Houston, a distant relative of Emily FitzGerald. He, too, was an Army Surgeon, with the rank of Major, later Colonel, in the Medical Corps. He was stationed at Fort Vancouver.*]

He said Em would have been with him, but one of the little boys had hurt his eye badly the night before and she did not like to leave him.

The worst part of my troubles here is that Mary must be fitted out with new underclothes. We won't be able to get anything at Sitka and can't send for large things, so I must get everything she will need for next winter here now. Bess won't want much more and I think I will get one black alpaca dress. Do you know we are all in our winter underclothes? I never knew such funny summer weather. It is pleasant but cool, and they tell us Sitka is much like this. Of course the winters are rainy and, as one of the waiters told Mary much to her distress, our feet grow together and we have to swim. I am sitting up here now on the Fourth of July with my thick brown cloth dress on and am just comfortable.

Portland is a real pretty place. Such lovely little cottages covered with flowers. Nearly all the buildings are frame. I have seen some real nice stores, but things are high. The loveliest thing here is the fruit — so much and so cheap. The most delicious strawberries, a bit a box, peaches, plums, and everything. The cherries are very nice and the vegetable market is the nicest looking place I ever saw. There are some Chinese stores here I want to see; they have so many curious little things. [*The word "bit", as Emily has used it, means twelve and a half cents.*]

There are a whole lot of little things I wish I had gotten at home such as a lot of narrow ribbons to trim caps etc. for the babies, pins, buttons, and such. I have been so taken up with my own affairs that I have not mentioned home. I was so glad to get your letters when we arrived here. I found two from you and *The Spy*. [*The Columbia Spy, a newspaper which the family sent to Emily throughout the Sitka tour of duty.*]

Write often, and whenever you find any interesting reading matter that can go by mail, remember us in Alaska. We will be here a month, so direct mail here until you hear from us not to. Doctor has felt very badly about his detail on my account, but I tell him I would rather live in Sitka with him than in Paradise with any other man. We will be back at some nice post in 20 months. Then you will just be about ready to come and see us. Doctor joins me in lots of love to all.

Your loving daughter,
Emily

P.S. I will write every week while we are here and by every ship after we get to Alaska. Get some of the late works on Sitka. You will find it is not as bad as one thinks at first. Doctor read me the most comforting things from that *Alaska Coast Pilot.* [*A periodical published by the United States Coast and Geodetic Survey beginning in 1868.*]

The climate is good and the funniest part will be the long days and short nights — and long nights and short days.

Your loving daughter,
Emily

Portland
Sunday, July 12, 1874

Dear Mamma,

We have had no news from you since we arrived; hope I will get a letter this week. We have been doing all sorts of things since I last wrote, buying some furniture, getting some sewing done, making some calls, etc. I have spent, or will by the time I pay for the shoes, about 30 dollars for Mary. Her underclothes were all worn out and outgrown, and her dresses are in about the same condition. I am in hopes these things will do her a long time. I never want another child unless I can pay her money, though I think I can clothe Mary comfortably for less money than I would have to pay a little girl out here. If I paid her at all, I should like to be just, but it is a great trouble to me to be responsible for her clothes. She is very much a child and real noisy and rough, kicks things around and upsets chairs etc., but I think after we get settled she will get into our ways. She is quick and willing, and nice and clean about herself. People told us here we would have our greatest trouble at Sitka getting help. Doctor said he would use every effort to take a cook from here, but everybody told us we would not get one to go. But we have been fortunate enough to find a real nice-looking woman who will, and we are going to take her — wages 30 dollars a month in gold, but anything is better than having no cook.

Our steamer leaves about the last of this month, and we are very anxious for its departure. I am so tired being in this unsettled condition. Bess is real well again. The gentlemen boarders here make a great fuss over her; they are all middle-aged men and most of them are married. They send up for Bess on all occasions and she entertains them. One of them brought her a box of candy this week and a Mr. Townsand, an English gentleman who is here on business, brought her a dollie. I wish so much I had known we were going to Sitka, for I would have had nothing but little double calico wrappers for Bess — no white dresses at all. This week I have been sewing and have finished the white and flannel shirts for the "little brother."

Doctor has made another valuable investment here — a cow! I am very glad to have it, though everything costs so much, it leaves us poor. We did not invest in much furniture. We got a nice set for our own room, white ash faced with walnut, really a nicer set than we had at West Point, but we had to take that or a very common kind of cottage furniture. Both Doctor and I want our own room to be the nicest or, at least, the most comfortable in the house. We got some carpet for two rooms, some chairs and big rocking chairs for the sitting room, a table cover, some dishes, etc.

Bess seems so much older than when we left home. She is so much wiser; she talks more and knows more. She tells us nicely when she wants pot-tee; then everything she finds she comes to you to put in her pock-ee (pocket). She comes and stands by us and says, "Take-ee," and wants us to take her. Everything ends in *ee*; the gentlemen here says she is a little Chinese.

Doctor has gone to church with Mrs. General Davis who boards here and Mary has gone with a colored minister who lives next door. Bess is sleeping. General Davis is in command of this Department but is just to be relieved. Mrs. Davis is busy thinking of moving and changing, too. He is the General Jeff Davis of the Modoc War. The Davises are going to Fort Russell near Cheyenne. Mrs. Davis was in Sitka for several years and says she liked it much better than Portland. The thing really hard to bear is its being so far away, but it is only for a short two years.

We will have to depend altogether on lamps and candles for the next two years. Mrs. Davis says in the winter you have to have your lamps lighted by three o'clock in the afternoon. Then, in the summer months, the sun scarcely sets at all — just pops down and up again.

Bess has just appeared, caught the paper I was writing on, and swung if off the table, ink and all, and just about ruined the nice white wall opposite and my light dress. Her hands have been smacked and kissed, but that can't improve Mrs. Dolan's wall. Write soon.

Your loving daughter,
Emily FitzGerald

Portland
Sunday, July 19, 1874

Dear Mamma,

Sallie's letter arrived a day or two ago and I was glad to hear again from Columbia. Our steamer will reach here sometime this week and we will start a few days after. Nothing of any account has taken place since I wrote to you. We are just getting along and waiting to start. Mary and I are making her chemise. She is anxious to learn to sew and is trying to hold her needle right and use a thimble. She always sewed without one and she went down yesterday to get a brass one and had to pay a bit for it, much to her indignation. Just think of a brass thimble costing 12½ cents, but a bit is the smallest change they use here. Everything costs a little more than it does East. Mary wants very much to learn to sew and manage for herself so she can get wages. I tell her I will give her six dollars a month as soon as she is sure she can manage. Little girls out here probably get eight to ten; cooks get enormous wages from 20 to 30 dollars. I can't afford to give Mary enormous ones because we brought her out at great expense and mean to take her East again. She seems to like us and says she would not leave us to go back.

I went out yesterday to do a little shopping and spend the last few dollars I had. I got some very common blocks (the best I could get here) for Bess for Christmas. Then I wanted some muslin books, as she has gotten very fond of pictures. I could only find one that would do, *The Naughty Kittens That Lost Their Mittens.* I wanted to get *Little Bo Peep,* particularly. Bess thinks it the most beautiful song she ever heard. I wanted to get woolen stockings for her, too, but couldn't. Don't know what I will do unless I send East for them. I got a pretty silver thimble for Bess to give Mary for Christmas. Think of planning for Christmas in July! But this is the last chance I will have to get these little things, and I think we must make the most of Christmas way up here.

The medical director told Doctor the other night that he thought one year long enough for the medical officers to serve in Sitka and, if he could arrange it, he would make it a one year's detail instead of two. He says that Dr. F. should write to him by next spring and let him know whether he would like to change or would rather stay another year and, by fall, if he wants to change, he can.

I wish I had some money left and was on my way East. There are so many pretty things at these Chinese stores I would like to take home with me. The silk dresses are lovely and you can get a dress pattern of sixteen or eighteen yards for 15 dollars. Then they have such pretty carved little boxes and cabinets, pretty card baskets, and lots of other things.

Bess is pretty well, though I am anxious to get settled on her account, too. She feels the irregular way we have been living for the last few months and just now, while her teeth are troubling her, she needs to be at home, somewhere where she can have a fire when it is cold and particular sort of food. I have put on my winter flannel again. I got Mary a real nice pair of boots, a pair of high slippers—something like I wear, only stronger — and she is delighted with them. I thought they would do nicely for houseshoes. I also got her a pair of gum shoes. Her new waterproof is being made; it is a real nice cloak. She says she never had so many things at once before. I am going to give her 50 cents every month and with that she must supply herself all the little things: pins, shoestrings, etc. She is very anxious that her mother should write to her, so tell Barbara to write. [*Barbara, Mary's mother, worked for the McCorkle family in Columbia.*]

The city is full of Chinamen; you should see some of their names. Our washman is Lee Kee and there seems to be a whole Kee family on the signs I have seen. Our washing costs us from 3 to 5 dollars a week. They flute nicely but starch the clothes within an inch of their lives. Passing the washing houses, as we do every time we go downtown, I often see them ironing and sprinkling from their mouths, as we have heard about. Some of the Chinese girls are real pretty, though they all look exactly alike to me. They dress nearly like the men, only they wear more ornaments. They all seem to have silver bands or bracelets around their ankles.

We will have at least four ladies at Sitka, which is a great many compared with many other posts in this Department. I met a lady from Fort Lapwai who has been the only lady there for a year.

I hope I have not counted wrong about the time to be sick. As it is, I have just about time to get to Sitka and fixed up.

Doctor sends love. He has been amusing himself catching flies for the last half-hour. The room is full of them and they bother him so. He thought he would pay them back! He says he has over eighty in the wash basin. Love to all — write often.

Your loving daughter,
Emily

Portland
Sunday, July 20, 1874

Dear Mamma,

Your letter from Chestnut Hill arrived night before last. I am glad you are well and only wish I could see you a little while. We got some photos of Bess taken but they are such frights, I will not distribute them. I will send you one just to see what an ugly baby can be made out of a pretty one.

Bess is very well and so noisy. She talks a great deal, has a name for everything, and is so hard to manage. Mary plays with her and they seem to like each other very well, but Mary is not gentle, and, I am afraid, is rough with Bess often. She speaks to her in such a rough manner that I am continually correcting her. She gets provoked with the baby and talks to her just as she would to a child of her own age. She is a rough child, anyway. She uses her feet too much, kicks open the doors, and kicks over chairs, and always is swinging her feet and rubbing them along the carpet when I don't remind her of it. But don't tell Barbara this, for I have great hopes of her learning to behave nicely when we get settled. She is really fond of Bess, but she is very much of a child herself. She tells me she is sixteen years old. Is that possible?

Doctor says to tell you that he will write as soon as he gets to Sitka. Now, you will certainly expect your furs as he is going to Alaska. We will be on the steamer a week from today and will be in Sitka in about 9 days after, if nothing happens. So after this, direct everything to Sitka, Post Surgeon, Sitka, Alaska. Our mails are only monthly, but they are prompt and we will write home by every mail. I think I will write every Sunday. There will be nothing to do Sunday, and as I expect there will be very little Sunday reading to be found, I think I will break the Sabbath less by writing home than by any other way.

I am so thankful I had my old black and blue dress fixed up. It is just the sort of a thing I will want up there. Do you know I am wearing my winter flannel shirts now? Bess still wears her little, old long-sleeved ones, but they are very small for her, so you can send me some more soon.

Did I tell you when we first wrote that Doctor had taken out a three thousand dollar insurance policy in New York before we started? He concluded that after we got out here he would be able to pay the premium on a little larger policy, so he has written to Uncle Jim to have it made a five thousand dollar policy. I used to have a horror of those things and did not like Doctor to talk about it, but I feel now that it is the wisest thing a man can do who has a family and lives on a salary.

How I wish you could come out to this country to see us, Mamma. After we come down from Alaska, you will find us at some comfortable post, and it will do you good to come and hunt us up. I am sure it will do us good.

Mrs. Davis has so many pretty and interesting little things she got at Sitka. I am becoming quite anxious to collect curiosities. Hers are baskets made by the Indians, carving in wood, and some little Russian things, too. The Indians there are very skillful in basketmaking and make very pretty ones and carve wooden spoons, etc.

Write as often as you can and tell me all about yourself and all the family. The next letter will be from Sitka and you won't get it for some weeks after you get this one. Doctor sends a great deal of love. Tell Barbara that Mary is writing to her and will send the letter the end of the week.

I just asked Bess if she would give me a kiss to send Grandma and she came and kissed me at once.

Love to all.
Your daughter,
Emily FitzGerald

Portland
Sunday, August 2, 1874

Dear Mamma,

I didn't expect to write you another letter from Portland,

but we are not off yet. Our steamer does not leave for another week, much to our disgust. Then it takes all the troops up that are expected to relieve the garrison now at Sitka. At the mouth of the Columbia River, *The California,* our Sitka steamer, meets *The Ajax,* which will have two companies on board and they will be transferred to our ship. We will be a crowd, but we will meet and know all the officers and families we are going to live with.

Your letter written just after getting home from Chestnut Hill arrived a day or two ago — it just took ten days. The package and newspapers also arrived nicely. I am much obliged for all. The little shirts are lovely and the collars are just right. I am sorry to see by your letter you did not get the first letter I wrote from Portland. I hope you have gotten it, for I told you a great deal I will want to tell over, if you never receive it.

Doctor, Mary, the Baby, and I went over to Fort Vancouver on Tuesday and stayed until Thursday with Em Alexander. We had a very pleasant little visit. Her children are lovely little fellows and the Doctor is very, very pleasant. Em is a dear little woman. She is comfortably fixed over there and they like Vancouver very much. The Doctor is very popular and everybody speaks of Em as being lovely. We talked about Columbia and our friends until our husbands thought we had nothing else to talk about.

We are disappointed about our cook — she has gone East. Her child died and she departed. We don't quite know what to do. I am perfectly enormous and am afraid I have counted wrong. It is certainly twins if I haven't. Doctor says I could not easily have made a mistake, but the delay about getting on worries him very much, as I am so uncomfortable. Bess lets Mary put her to sleep now nicely; that is a great relief to me. I am nearly ready for the baby as far as clothes are concerned but hope so much to get our quarters all fixed and kitchen department started before it arrives. Yesterday I went downtown with Doctor for a walk. We went into the Chinese store and I could not resist getting a set of such pretty carved ivory jack straws. They were lovely — and only a dollar. I got them, though I do feel as if I ought not to spend even one dollar foolishly just now.

I am getting concerned about flannel shirts for Bess. I want them good and big — you should see how she grows. The little dresses I made for next fall and the little calico wrappers are above her shoe tops.

Monday, August 3, 1874

Doctor is just going downtown so I will finish this and send it off. Mary is counting out the dirty clothes for the Chinaman who will be here in a little while. Bess is not very well this morning and just now Doctor is sitting on the bed with her making her a cow, that is, drawing it for her on a piece of paper. She is delighted and says, "Cow-cow;" she says nearly everything.

Mary was very much pleased with her visit to Vancouver and I hope after we get settled Mary will tame down a little. Just think of it — last night I caught sight of her holding Bess over the balcony railing in her arms and swinging her, and when I hurried out to stop it, she told me she had held Bess the same way over the railing of the ship over the water and she didn't fall. She frightened me, I can assure you, and I made up my mind to keep them in sight until I was a little more certain of Mary. A few minutes after I spoke to her about holding Bess in such dangerous places, I looked out and Mary was running along the top of the narrow balcony railing and Bess looking on delighted. I just thought in a few more months Bess will be old enough to do everything she sees Mary do and I won't be comfortable if Mary doesn't tame down a little. She is quick and smart, but wild as a boy. Fortunately, when we get to Sitka, I can't help but have them under my eye all the time and Mary can be a great help to me.

Doctor joins in much love. I will write another letter from Portland if we don't leave this week.

Your loving daughter,
Emily FitzGerald

Portland
August 9, 1874

Dear Mamma,

I should have written to you several days ago to tell you the little packages had arrived and to thank you for them. The little nightgowns are as sweet as they can be, and I am so much obliged to you for them and the flannel for Bess. My baby things are all ready now. You don't know how much I have accomplished for the "little brother" these weeks we have been waiting here. Now I have six little dresses that Bess had, all pretty good, 12 new little nightgowns, six white shirts, four flannel skirts, six pairs of socks, four belly bands, and the knit shirts. Then I have the little flannel shawls Bess had and, a day or two ago, I made two new ones — stitched (or ran) that white silk flannel binding around them over the turned up edge and they look real pretty.

It's strange that Sitka, with all its rain, should be such a healthy place. They say children are always well there and it is a good climate for weak lungs, all owing to the evenness of the climate. There is no sudden change there from cold to hot, or otherwise, but from January to December, the temperature is nearly the same. [*Emily apparently had not been told that in Sitka two-thirds of the days of the year are cloudy, and that it either rains or snows about 200 days in the year.*]

We leave tomorrow afternoon and hope to reach Sitka some time next week. Doctor spent several days at Vancouver this week with Dr. Alexander and had such a pleasant time. Dr. A. is a very agreeable man and such a gentleman; you would like him very much.

I have been ever so much worried these last few days about Mary. Don't say anything to Barbara about it unless you think it best, for I am in hopes she will do better. But I find she deceives me in a great many ways and I feel so anxious about Bess. A friend of Mrs. Davis, who has seen Bess here and knows her, called Mrs. D. a few evenings ago. She told her that she had gone to her door (it is way uptown, too, where I never allow Mary to go) and saw Bess in the carriage which was standing out by the curbstone, and no one else was around. A drove of cattle was coming down the street and this lady stood at her door to watch the carriage. The cows walked up on the sidewalk and all around the carriage (think of poor little Bess) and after at least five minutes Mary came out of the house that Bess was in front of and started off. This lady called her back and told her she was going to tell me, and Mary was very impudent to her. Then only yesterday I had another worry. Two or three streets below this one we live on, a railroad runs through the town. I don't allow Mary to go down there with the baby at all, and yesterday morning I started her off myself and said, "Now, Mary don't go anywhere below Fifth." Ten minutes later, Mrs. Dolan met her two squares below the railroad on Third Street and said to me when she came in, "I met your baby downtown." When Mary came in, I asked her where she had been. She said, "That ill-natured old Mrs. Dolan told you I was in Third Street," etc. How can I trust her? She doesn't seem to have any idea of obeying me. I have had the greatest time about her calling out our room window to a nursemaid across the street. I forbid her doing it and told her she could go to see her, but she should not converse out the upstairs window in that loud tone. Twice, after talking to her kindly about it just before going down to dinner and trying to make her understand how much more comfortable we would both be if I could trust and depend on her and she would try to please me, I have been obliged to sit at the dinner table and hear the same sort of conversation from my window that I had just forbid, she thinking I was out of the way and would not know. The streets slope here and two people have told Doctor of seeing Mary sitting up in front of Bess in the little carriage and riding down hill. Just think — Bess might be killed! I am afraid all the time that Mary will hurt Bess, or that Doctor will whip Mary. Indeed, I think it would be the best thing for her, but I don't want him to do it. She is not one bit sorry about these things and I don't know how to make her.

After I scold her, or even object to her doing something she wants to, she is so cross to Bess that I am afraid to trust them together. Indeed I am sure she shakes Bess just because she is angry with me!

I tried to talk to her the other night and tell her how wrong some things she did were, but she had so many excuses and put so much blame on the baby and everybody else that I lost all patience and told her as soon as we got to Sitka I would leave the Doctor manage her just as he saw fit and that I would not correct her at all, for if she has one fear, it is of him. I will have to be head nurse myself and let Mary work. She is good and strong and I will keep her busy that way. I don't believe I will ever feel easy up there with Mary and Bess out of the house, for you know we will live on the beach with water all around us. Enough of Mary, I am worried about her particularly because I did trust her until now and felt that she would not deceive me and that her wildness was her worst fault. What would you do? How would you punish her if she would not obey?

Bess is well and so cute. She does the sweetest little things — sticks my hand with a pin and then, when I pretend to be hurt, takes it and kisses it all over. She has a name for everything and expresses her wants very distinctly. I wish you had her until the little brother is safely landed. I am afraid she won't be properly attended to while I am in bed. Poor Doctor will have his hands full, but he is so devoted to Bess, I guess she will get along.

We made our last purchase yesterday. Doctor got me a nice little eight day clock and we got 10 gallons of coal oil. Don't expect us to blow up, for we will be very careful. I am afraid we are going beyond the reach of Christmas gifts. You will have to wait for this year's gift until we come home. I may find some trifles I can send by mail but am afraid there are not nice things for Christmas gifts to be gotten at Sitka. Doctor says he will give me a 20 dollar gold piece. You don't know how hard it seems to spend these lovely gold pieces. I have over two hundred dollars in gold now that will all have to be spent tomorrow to pay Mrs. Dolan and help pay our way to Sitka.

Doctor joins in love to all. Write often. After this letter you won't hear from us but once a month. I will write on my way up and send a letter back in the steamer.

Your loving daughter,
Emily

On board the *California*
Saturday, Aug. 15, 1874

Dear Mamma,

We sent off the last Portland letter to you on our way to the steamer. General and Mrs. Davis went down on the steamer as far as Astoria where we met the *Ajax* with the two companies we were to take to Sitka with us on the *California*. I wish you could just know where we are today. We are going up what is called the Inside Passage, skirting all around the eastern shore of Vancouver Island and it is said to be a most beautiful trip in clear weather. Unfortunately, it is raining hard and we can only guess at the beauties or see them through the mist. The channel is not wider than a street in many places and the shores might be very interesting, if we could see.

There are five officers (three of them married) going up with us. Major Campbell, Captain Field, and Lieutenant Quinan are the married ones; Dyer and Goddard, two young lieutenants, are the others. Mrs. Campbell is a very pleasant little woman, very much like Mrs. Davis whom you met at the Point. You know they are sisters. Mrs. Fields is pleasant, and Mrs. Quinan is a bride of three months — very young, only about seventeen.

We have our cow with us, but I told you our cook disappointed us. I hope we will find something there. Mary is good and strong and quick, but I will have to keep her pretty busy and keep the babies with me, I expect. She is real cross to Bess, scolds her, shakes her, says, "Shut up, you," and altogether doesn't please me as a nurse. She gets cross and real impudent if I have her empty a chamber Bess has used anytime she doesn't feel like doing it. Doctor has taken the greatest dislike to her on account of her manner. She always answers back and looks and swings herself so impudently when he corrects her, I expect daily he will shake her. I don't believe she always intends it for impudence, but, indeed, she is a specimen. I am afraid sometimes I am not trying to manage her as I should, but, indeed I don't know what or how else to do. I have made her comfortable about her clothes, and in Portland tried to please her by letting her go downtown now and then and taking her to see things with me. But you can't imagine how particular Miss Mary is about the style of her garments. From the condition of the clothes she had when I got her, I imagined she would be pleased with anything, but do you remember the handkerchiefs I got in Lancaster? She greeted the getting out of those with, "Such handkerchiefs!" And I had a great deal of trouble with her about those striped stockings. Several pairs of them, in the washing, have run a little — not much. I certainly would not let the child wear anything that actually was not good enough, but she would not wear them and said they were disgusting to look at. I found she was wearing instead such a filthy, dirty, torn, white pair that I made her wash her feet and sit down in front of me and put on a pair of the "disgusting stockings." She was cross about it for two days, then seemed to forget, and now wears them without question. I told her I would always get her things she liked, if possible, but if it ever came to a question between us, as long as I was providing her clothes, she must wear whatever I thought best. Now, I will not write another word about Mary. I would not write this much, but I want you to know just what trouble I have so you will understand what comfort I have in her.

Write as often as you can, Mamma, and we will hope they will catch the steamer. I will be awfully distressed if one of our monthly steamers comes in without letters from home.

Sunday, August 16, 1874

We are nearly to Sitka. About 60 miles more and we are done traveling for a while and can have a rest. We have had a lovely trip — really the most beautiful part of our whole journey from New York. I never saw such lovely waters as we have sailed over, smooth as glass, and the shores close on each side, great high mountains for the greatest part covered with fir trees and the tops white with snow, and here and there a little Indian boat with Indian fishing. The first night out we had a rough time. It was in the open sea before we got into the narrow passages. Doctor and I were both awfully sick and tumbled into bed long before dinner time without strength left to say much more than, "Oh, dear," and each feel sorry for the other. But since then, the water has been so smooth, no one could be sick. And even though it is going to Sitka, Mamma, I am so thankful to get to the end of our journey and get a rest.

Bess is such a little darling. The old white zephyr cap has traveled all the way around with us. It is the only thing I have warm enough for her head. If you want to send your granddaughter a Christmas gift that will please her mother, too, I don't know anything that would be as nice as another cap like that one.

We expect to get into Sitka late tonight. Then tomorrow and for the next week we will be in confusion. I am so anxious to get fixed.

Afternoon

We got out to open sea again and Doctor and I both had to rush to bed after trying for some time to stand the rolling. It is about four o'clock now and we are nearly to the Sitka Bay and it is getting smoother. You can't conceive how comfortable I will be (in mind) when we get there. Doctor's rank gives him first choice of quarters, so we will be as comfortable as possible in body, too.

Monday Morning
August 17, 1874

Arrived at Sitka last night. We are going up to Dr. Brook's for breakfast. Everybody was down to the wharf to meet the ship, ladies and all. I will have a letter ready for the ship, so look for one in a month from the time you get this one telling you all about our likings and dislikings for Sitka life. Love to all. Doctor is on shore seeing about the cow. Mary and Bess are out on the guards. All are well. Write me all the home news. Love to all from Doctor.

Your loving daughter,
Emily FitzGerald

PART II

ISOLATION

Life in Sitka — 1874-75

The United States, which had purchased Alaska from Russia in 1867, had assigned the Army to administer the new land. When the FitzGeralds arrived at Sitka on August 16, 1874, Dr. FitzGerald reported for duty as Post Surgeon.

Sitka, Alaska
Sunday, August 23, 1874

Dear Mamma,

A week ago tonight we arrived here. The ship came in about ten o'clock. The Sitka people had seen her for hours coming up the Bay and turned out in a crowd to see, or, rather, to meet us. The officers and wives who were expecting to be relieved were all down and rejoicing. Dr. and Mrs. Brook insisted upon our coming up to their quarters at once, but I had Bess in bed and had some packing to do, so we did not go up until the next morning. The ship was only to wait until Tuesday night, so you can imagine the confusion the whole garrison was in — two companies of soldiers and all the officers to get off and the same amount to get fixed in the same places.

I like our quarters very much, or will when we get them fixed. As far as pleasant rooms are concerned, they are the nicest, but they were the worst off for paint and a few little fixings. Major Campbell said they could be fixed at once if we wanted, so rather than fix our carpets etc. only to tear up again, we concluded to live in confusion a little longer than the rest of the people. By this time next week, though, we hope to be nearly fixed. We have a little sitting room and two bedrooms in a row, then beside the last bedroom the dining room, and next, back of that, the kitchen, and then two real nice little rooms upstairs. We fortunately got the cook Dr. Brook had, and he does nicely. We put the washing out, even Mary's. No one is able to do their washing in their own house because they can't get anyone to do it, and besides it takes the clothes so long to dry some seasons. It is a great trouble; ours will cost eight dollars a month. I would have Mary do her own, both to teach her and because it would cost me less, but it would make it necessary for me to buy a whole set of washing things and it would take Mary so long. Noah, our man, is black and comes in the morning, gets breakfast, clears up after and goes away, then comes in the afternoon, gets dinner etc., and departs. He takes all the care of the dining room and kitchen, sets and waits on the table; so, you see, there is nothing left for Mary and me to do but the care of three small rooms. We give Noah 12 dollars.

I wish I could make you understand about Sitka. This is the pleasant season, of course, but today is one of the most beautiful I ever saw. It is not warm. We have all our winter-flannel on but are sitting with doors and windows open and it is mild and bright outside. Bess is out on the grass with her sunbonnet on, though this is the first day it has been warm enough for that. But with a different climate, this would be a lovely spot. The Bay is beautiful. Doctor counted 50 beautiful green little islands in sight this morning and about as many snow-capped mountains. He took a walk of a couple of miles yesterday and came back delighted. The woods are full of all varieties of berries and Doctor brought me home the most beautiful hanging moss — yards long. It will be dreadfully lonely here; the winters are so long, but I guess we will flourish.

There is a dirty little town scattered around the post full of Russians. Then, off to one side, is the Indian village. The Indians are not allowed in the garrison until after nine in the morning and are obliged to go out the gate again at three. I wish you could see them — the most horrible, disgusting, dirty hideous set I ever saw. Their faces are all painted and they have rings through their noses and chins. Some of them paint their faces bright yellow, some red, some blue, and some jet black. They come to your backdoors every day with things to sell: venison, birds, fish, berries, etc. One woman quite frightened me yesterday by stopping to speak to Bess. She saw her and came back and said, "Your papoose?" I said, "Yes." She pointed out the gate to a little Indian baby off on the grass and said, "My papoose." She came again this morning with some birds to sell and again noticed Bess. Just a little while ago she appeared again with the paint washed off her face and, with her, the baby also washed. Evidently she was bringing her papoose to see mine. She sat on the backsteps and Bess looked out the window and appeared very much delighted.

Bess is learning everything. She is the cutest youngster. Poor little toad, she has been neglected these last few days in the confusion and takes care of herself, but she is good as pie if I just let her trot around and keep me in sight. Yesterday, after Noah had departed, I went into the kitchen to make a pudding and Bess went too. I put some paper over my dish, and it scorched and fell on the pudding. I blew it off and shut the stove door quickly, for Bess was close by, and she wanted the stove door open. I turned to her a minute after, and she had her little face close to the stove door, blowing with all her might. She evidently thought the blowing opened and shut the door. Gentlemen have often told her to blow their watches open, etc.

Sunday, August 30, 1874

Two weeks at Sitka! I only hope we will be as comfortable in a week from now as we are now compared to last week. We have two carpets down and two rooms looking real comfortable. The paint won't get dry or we might be more fixed. We brought with us from Portland a carpet we hoped would be large enough to cover our sitting room and bedroom (the rest of the house we thought might do as it could) and we are delighted to find it does that and will cover the nursery. And if I leave out a piece under the bed and under the stove, it will give me enough to make a nice big square to put in the middle of the dining room. It is a bright ingrain and looks so cheerful down. Our room opens from the sitting room and, as usual, I have everything in green. My set of ash furniture looks very sweet and I have a little government crib fixed up for Bess. At my window I have a green calico curtain made with a ruffle all around it, and it looks real cute. This time next week we hope to be fixed, and if only the "little brother" doesn't arrive until his expected time, we will get along nicely.

This morning I went out with Doctor for my first walk. Everything is beautiful. The Bay is so full of lovely islands, the beach so pretty, the paths and roads through this pretty green fir (the only tree here) so fresh looking, and such lovely moss and fern, and all so new and strange, that though I know that life here after awhile will be dull and doleful and awfully tiresome, I did enjoy it this morning and know you would have thought it lovely too.

Bess has been out all day. She is well and eats everything. She is devoted to potatoes and molasses, I don't mean together, but she calls every hour in the day for bed and buttie, which is bread and butter, and she won't eat it unless it has molasses on it. Mary is not very kind to her and it worries me very much. I wish I could get another nurse and just have Mary for sort of house girl. As it is, I have to leave Bess to her some and have to depend upon her for certain nursely duties, and I know she is not gentle or kind. Bess doesn't like her. Just a little while ago I was showing her some pictures and Mary leaned over me, too. Bess pulled the book away and said, "No, no, Mary." Not very pretty for Bess, of course, but it just shows one of a hundred little things that both Doctor and I notice about Bess not liking her, and, I think little children don't dislike in that way without reason.

Mary is a good little worker. I put her to some window washing and floor scrubbing this week and she works fast and well, but she is a disagreeable child in a great many ways. She is so pert and has an answer for everything and likes to arrange matters for herself. She never does anything I tell her without suggesting something else first. I say, "Take Bess out riding," and she says, "Oh, not now." And if I insist, she jerks Bess up, and slams doors, and does all such things in the most indignant manner. Then her worst fault is she talks too much and makes so free with all the men around. I mean, in a certain way, she talks and laughs and quarrels with them. I have had to speak to her a dozen times a day about conversing with these painters who have been painting the house. She talks to and at them; then they tease her and she gets perfectly furious, but it is really her own fault.

Sunday
September 6, 1874

This is another lovely day though we have had a rainy week and our paint still won't dry. We are nearly fixed up and will be real snug and comfortable. The ladies here are all pleasant as possible, Mrs. Campbell particularly so. There is a contract doctor here, Dr. Boyer, who told Dr. F. the other day he is from Lancaster. He and his wife are both quite young; she is not more than twenty. Do you know any Lancaster Boyers? [*Dr. S. S. Boyer, Citizen Physician and Acting Assistant Surgeon at Post Hospital. Emily's reference to him as a contract doctor meant he was not a member of the Army but was hired for a specific period for a specific job.*]

As the paint would not dry and we could not do much towards fixing up this week, I got at the afghan that I have had on hand for so many years. It is nearly done and real pretty.

Did I tell you what furs you could get here or anything about them? In the first place, you can get robes of all sorts — fox, otter, bear, squirrel, etc. The squirrel robes are just as pretty as they can be and the handsomest only cost two or two and a half dollars. Then they can be made up, nicely lined, etc. for 12 or 14 dollars. They are soft and look like the Siberian squirrel and are so nice to put over the foot of your bed or to use for travelling to keep your feet warm. I was looking at some furs the other day down in the store of an old fellow who trades with the Indians and always has a supply of things of the sort on hand. Everybody gets baskets, furs, etc. from him, as trading with the Indians yourself is slow work, for you can't make them understand. The handsomest furs, of course, are the sables. The hair of the handsomest is long and dark. They are really a marten, but they are called Russian sable. Everywhere the handsomest cost about 12 or 14 dollars a skin. Six skins will make a muff and boa, but you can get lovely skins for 4 or 5 dollars a skin. The men-of-war that now and then put in to this port buy up most of the furs this old man sells. They take hundreds of dollars worth. Some of them are foreign ships, you know, and some belong to our own country. Then you can get lovely mink skins, darker and richer than the handsomest mink sets I ever saw, for only 2 dollars a skin. I would like a mink coat ever so much. A sable one would be almost too handsome to wear all the time for a wrap, as you would want to wear a fur sack, but a dark rich mink would be lovely. Doctor says I can't have a cloak; they are too hot, but he will get the handsomest sable to trim my velvet cloak. You can get all varieties of seal skins or otter, as handsome ones as you would want, but they, in the end, cost too much, for they have to be colored and can't be done nicely unless you send them abroad. Certain times in the year you can get ermine, and the little skins only cost 25 cents a piece, but then it takes a hundred to make a cloak. I don't know how many it would take to make a small set. In the winter the Indians make baskets and such things, and in the spring there is a fine market of those little matters, but, I believe, the fall is the fur time. They hunt among the islands north of this all summer and from there come the handsomest furs. Then in the fall they come in with them to trade.

Sunday
September 13, 1874

I must tell you this week about Bess and her smart doings. Indeed she is the funniest little thing and just knows everything. This last week she swallowed a penny (the only one I have seen since we came out here) and a pin. The penny we did not feel much worried about and she passed it in about 24 hours, but the pin Doctor felt uneasy about and it did not appear until after two days.

Just for fun, the Doctor put the penny she had swallowed in her wrapper pocket and took her down to a little store where she handed it out to a man and got a stick of candy. Since then, she is continually going downtown — she says it quite distinctly — "For tany." When her papa tells her he has none, she reaches out her hand and says, "Money, papa." The other day at the table I covered my face with my hand to ask a blessing. She laughed out loud, turned to Doctor, and said, "Mamma hide."

I told you we had been nearly devoured by fleas, didn't I? Poor Bess knows by personal experience about bites, but if she sees me pull open or up my garments, she looks up from what she is doing with the greatest interest and says, "Mamma bite?" as much as to say, "You are having your turn, are you? I know what it is."

Mary is the most dreadful pest that ever was. I don't trust her now at all, and I am uncomfortable about Bess all the time she is with her. She has not the least idea of obeying me. I have forbidden her taking Bess out of the buggy, as the ground is so damp and the little shoes so thin. Twice that I have gone to the gate with her and impressed that upon her, Bess has been found by some of the post people on the damp ground alone and Mary, with her back turned, talking with some Russian children. Mrs. Field met Bess one day this week being pushed along by some strange child, with Mary off in another direction. Mary told me herself, as if it was great fun, that she had been running along the boardwalk with the buggy, seeing how near she could go to the edge (the walk is three feet from the ground) and had run it off all but one wheel and had to get two people to help her get it on again. Nothing but the little strap kept Bess in. As the result of all this, Miss Mary's airings of Bess have been for the last week on the parade ground in front of the quarters where she is in sight. A few days ago I went out with Doctor for a walk and left Mary with Bess in the buggy out on the parade. The parade is a slight hill with an iron chain and posts all around it. When we came home, Mrs. Campbell came in. She said it wasn't her business, and I might think so, but, indeed, she had been so worried that she had sent out and stopped Mary. Mary and a little Russian girl that lives at Mrs. Quinan's had been starting the buggy at the top of the hill with a push and letting it run down alone, each time just missing one of the iron posts. If it had struck, poor little Bess would have been thrown out and most probably killed. I think Doctor could have pounded Mary with one of the posts in question, but again I interfered and kept him from whipping her, but indeed she shall have one the next time.

Day before yesterday I sent them out and told Mary to stay within the chain and to go up and down the walks for an hour. She thought I would be in the back of the house. In about five minutes, I went to the front door to look for Doctor and got there in time to see Mary's hat disappearing downtown. I was too angry for anything. If I could have found Doctor, I would have sent him after her and been glad if he had boxed her ears on the street, but I could not find him. So I took my hat and started myself. I caught up with her way down the walk and asked her if that was where I told her to go. She said, "No," so I brought her back and made her keep Bess in front of the house until the hour was up while I sat at the window with my sewing. Then I called them in and sent Mary right up to bed. Doctor said he did not even think I would do that because I have talked to Mary so many times and said, "If you disobey again, you shall be punished," that she thinks I mean to take it all in talking and no punishing. But, indeed, Mamma, she must obey or what sort of a time will we have the next time? Doctor may get a switch and use it over her shoulders until they sting, but I won't object.

I have Bess with me almost constantly and have put Mary to doing a great many little things. I always did such things as making my bed, sorting out the clothes, hemming towels, etc., but you see I must trust her some with Bess. I can't keep her in my arms or even in my sight all the time. She must have her outdoor airing, and I am not in a condition to take her out myself. Mary must be made to know I mean her to obey. Last week, I wished fervently she was in Columbia or Heaven, but thinking more seriously about it, she is too useful to me, in other respects, to let her go either place. She is a good little worker, though not the most amiable in the world and so noisy and giddy, but then she can and does do things I tell her. She brushes up and dusts my rooms every morning, does the chamber work and keeps up the fires, and washes the diapers etc. I have been looking for a good Russian girl, thinking if I could find one to help with my two babies, I would just have Mary do everything else, but they are a horrible set. They drink and steal, and are bad, entertain the soldiers, etc. The one most highly recommended to me has a baby that she boards out, and I don't feel that I would better myself much. So, if I once get over my confinement and get about again, I will just be nurse myself. Mary can do all else and can get my baby's bath ready, wash diapers, clear up after me, etc., as there are no calls of society upon us here that will interfere. We all live so close together that we can talk from our front and back windows, steps, and porches in whispers, and walk into each other's houses and hunt each other up and lend a hand to anything the other is doing. Mrs. Quinan runs into my room to see if I can't give her some of my sewing to do; she has not a thing left to read or sew. Mrs. Field came in the other day when I was just going out to beat up a fruitcake to send for the baker to bake for me. She took her hat right off and said, "I am so glad I came. I love to beat up eggs and I am going right out to help you." Mrs. Campbell comes right in, takes off her hat, and takes out her work and sits for an hour every day or two. That is all of us, so you see, there is no one here I could not see in my room with my babies. If one has to do without a nurse, this is a very convenient place.

Now about myself, I am very well but very uncomfortable and uncertain about how soon I will be sick. I have some indications that make me think I will be confined sooner than I expected (the middle of the month). I am all ready and have done all I could to make things go right. I hope I won't be sick before next month, as there are some little things I want to attend to—some mending and fixing for Bess and Doctor. My clothes are all right. I have had the new nightgowns washed and fixed in a drawer, have hunted up all the old muslin and rags I could find, and the baby's drawer is all ready. I even have the things for my bed all ready to put on. For the occasion, I have done the best I could, too, and it is much better than I ought to expect here and under the circumstances. A very nice woman, Mrs. Smith, one of the laundresses, will be with me for the occasion and will give me as much time as possible for some weeks after the event. [*Mrs. Smith was the wife of a soldier stationed at the Post.*]

Of course, she has her regular laundry work, which will take her part of several days every week, but she has no children of her own and, what is quite unheard of for one of them to do as they are not professionals, she will stay with me at nights for the first week or so. Now the only times to provide for are the days she can't be with me, and I know of another nice woman, also a laundress, who, I think, will come and stay with me those days Mrs. Smith is at her work. I told Mrs. Smith I felt much more anxious about Bess than about the new baby or myself and I want her to have an eye to her all the time she is here. She will, I know, and Doctor is so good about such things, I know we will get along nicely. And you may expect your next Sitka letter to tell you that you have another grandchild.

I wish you could send me by mail a couple pieces of diapering; that is one thing I forgot. I don't suppose there is any of my money left to pay for it, but will you pay for it and let me pay you? I would send you ten dollars in this but must wait until the paymaster comes to get some greenbacks. Doctor has nothing but a little gold and that won't do to send. I am going to try to send you some Sitka baskets. I hope they will go nicely. I can't get very pretty ones till spring, but I am going to try to get a workbasket apiece for you and send home before Christmas. They tell me a great many are sent through the mail and if they do mash, it won't hurt as they can be straightened out again. The Indians carve wooden spoons and forks for salad which are odd and rather pretty. I am trying to get one of those for Aunt Annie. Doctor joins me in love to all. Write often and long.

Your loving daughter,
Emily

Monday Night
September 14, 1874

Dear Mamma,

Yesterday I finished a scrawl to you that I fear you can't read and got it ready to send this morning. The steamer came in, in a pouring rain, but you can't imagine, though, how delightful it has been. It is actually the first mail or news of any kind, since we arrived, and everybody was alive and anxious for his share. Doctor's mail came up in a big box and I sat down until he went through it to see what was there. There was lots of official stuff, of course, that helped fill up the box, but we got lots for ourselves, too. He got a lot of letters from friends, and I got three from you and two from Chestnut Hill, and a package with the neckties and a lovely little dress for the "little brother." How kind they all are there.

Then we got some good things by the boat. Doctor has sent for some boxes of apples for my special benefit, and Mrs. General Davis sent me two boxes of lovely ones. Wasn't it kind of her? Then Doctor got a box of lovely plums from the steward of the boat which, though the cost of them broke my heart, I have been enjoying all day.

I wish you could be here with us. I know you would enjoy it and be charmed with Sitka. I said to Doctor a little while ago how I wished you could just look in on us this evening and see how cozy and comfortable we are. Bess is asleep in the next room with the door open so I can hear if she even moves. I am writing at the sitting room table and Doctor is enjoying the papers you sent us. Thank you very much for them. We get so little eastern news, they are really a treat, particularly to him.

Bess has been particularly well ever since we came up here. She is the brightest little body. Last night for the first time she had the little photograph album and in it there is a picture of Sallie which she seemed particularly pleased with. Doctor told her that it was Aunt Sallie. She has asked for it a dozen times today and finds "At Sallie," which she says very distinctly. Mary is out at the dining room table writing to Uncle Wes, whoever he is. She has been actually more amiable since I sent her to bed. We have a sweet little dining room, that is for the circumstances: a big crumb cloth of carpet, and pink chintz curtains with ruffles all around them at the windows, then my pretty lunch cloth on the table, and silver around on some little shelves, and tables with towels and napkins over them. Indeed, it all looks comfortable and sweet. Then there is a wood stove that Doctor says is worse than the fiery furnace.

Today I have been employing myself, after reading my letters and eating apples, getting some fruit ready for a fruit cake. I found the baker here would bake cakes very nicely and thought how nice it would be if I could have some Christmas fruit cake baked before I was confined, for I might go along until the last of October, and then it might be a long time before I ever felt strong enough to get things ready for a fruit cake. I had one baked last week and put Mrs. Field in the notion, so both Mrs. Field and I are going to have one baked tomorrow.

You quite comfort me about the money you have of mine. I think you get a great deal for a very little. Pay for Bess's stockings with it and I will be glad to have you get the diapering I spoke about. Pay the postage on these packages out of that money too, Mamma.

Cousin Henry Houston spoke of his probably visiting Portland some time. [*Relative of Emily Houston Alexander*] You come if he does. From Portland here is nothing and such a lovely trip, but you must not make it in winter. I want to speak of a great many things that are in your letters but must leave it for my next, as the steamer will carry off our mails tomorrow. Write often and Doctor will write by the next, if I am in bed. Give love to all our friends and tell me all about yourself when you write. Love to Sallie and Bep and tell them to write. [*Bep is Bethel McCorkle, Emily's brother*] My afghan is all done but the outside strip and is hanging over the sofa now looking perfectly gorgeous. Doctor says come out, if you can, and see how much better Sitka is than it has been represented.

Your loving daughter,
Emily FitzGerald

Sitka
Sunday, Sept. 20, 1874

Dear Mamma,

I just got your letters that came in the last steamer to read over again before I began to write my letters for the next boat. I think the next boat will find me in bed, but I don't know, of course. If so, Doctor will finish the letters and give you the news, good, I hope. Bess is playing in the nursery. I have had her with me almost entirely this week and had Mary doing some other work. Bess is so good and cute, but Mary isn't improving much. She doesn't try to do things nicely if she doesn't want to, and she gets herself so dirty. She blackened a little stove the other day and blackened the floor for a yard around more than the stove. She actually tramped it into my pretty new carpet so it won't come out.

Doctor is so devoted to Bess; he has taken ever so much more interest in her lately then he ever did before. Of course, he always loved her, but now he plays with her for half an hour at a time, and indeed, she does so many smart cute things, you could not help being interested in her. She seems to reason and think things out for herself like an older child. Yesterday she brought me a little round china knob broken off the top of my soap dish and pointed her little finger up to my neck, then put her two fingers up to her own, then pointed to the place this little knob or acorn had broken off and said, "Neck, Mamma, neck." It reminded her of a head, and she at once thought it was broken at the neck. Now you know she was only 19 months old this week and I do think she is knowing.

We have been enjoying the apples. I told you we had gotten some for ourselves besides those Mrs. Davis sent me. We are richer in apples than any of our neighbors. We have four boxes and I have been sending some to my neighbor, Mrs. Quinan, as she was the lady that did not get any by the boat.

Thursday Morning
September 24, 1874

I am busy this morning fixing some of Doctor's flannels over but am going to stop to write a few lines and tell you something I wish you would do for me, if you can. I am afraid every day I may be sick, so I am afraid to leave this for my Sunday writing for fear by Sunday I may be in bed. Doctor broke his brush, and his comb is not a nice one. We can't get anything of the kind here and I just happened to think I could have a nice one sent by mail and get it about Christmas. I wish the paymaster would come so I could send a little money, but by the boat he comes on I will send you a Post Office order for ten dollars. Guess that will settle up all my late demands. I wish you would get me a good brush, a fine tooth comb, and a toothbrush for Doctor — nothing very fine — but real good ones. Then I want very much a little brush and comb for Bess, and I guess I might send for them, too, at the same time. Don't you think you can send these by mail? I wish you could send me something else. I want a dollie for Bess — not a very big one, but one with a rag body and about as big as the gum dollie Aunt Annie got her. She has smashed all but the China dollie. I can't get any dolls here and the postage won't be very much.

Now, Mamma, I hate to trouble you so much, but if you send these things off after getting this letter, I will get them by the December boat. Mary's brush and comb are horrible, so I guess you might get me a good common one for her too, and I will give my whole family combs and brushes for their Christmas gifts. Now, Mamma, I want to pay for all of these things and the postage. I will send you ten dollars as soon as the paymaster comes, and if that and what you have of mine at home doesn't pay all, let me know by the next letter. I am out of the world, you know, as far as getting things are concerned, and so I have to keep troubling you.

Sunday, Sept. 27, 1874

The house is all fixed up and Bess is taking her nap. Doctor is at the hospital, though I expect he will be home in a few minutes. I wish so much and so often for you. The other night I said to Doctor, "I have the most awful longing for Mamma tonight." Doctor wanted to know if I expected my son to arrive and wanted you for that. But I just wished you could walk in and see how comfortable we could make you. I never dreamed we could be so nicely fixed at Sitka or any frontier post. Of course, it is our own little comforts around that make it so, but both Doctor and I are determined to take just as much as we have now. No matter where they send us, they can't possibly send us to a post any more out of the way. Mrs. Quinan, who is next door to me, has been sick for the last week. She has had something like a miscarriage.

I have been sitting with my sewing in the nursery for the last two weeks and we have all been getting along better. Mary, I think, will get into the habit of being nice with Bess in that way. Bess plays about, and Mary and I both sew. Mary has made herself some drawers that indeed are real nice. I made her rip out what was not just right and the bands are all nice and straight and the little gussets are put in as nicely as possible. It is good for Mary and good for me, too. I have forbidden her to sew when I am not about, for I don't want Bess neglected. But these last ten days I think Bess seems to like Mary much better than usual and I think it is a good sign.

Time passes rapidly up here. This month is nearly ended and before the middle of next, we will again look for the steamer with home news. Doctor says he expects "the little brother" will arrive as the steamer comes in. As the steamer's gun goes off, I will go off!

I am so much afraid I won't get the Indian baskets I want to send home in the next boat. The Indians are drying their grass now and won't make any until in the winter. There are some in the store, but they are old, not fresh and nice like the new ones, and to send so far, I want real pretty ones. I have one beauty for you but can't send it until I get some more, as I want to put one into another and make one package, but you may all expect some workbaskets or darning baskets of Sitka Indian manufacture as soon as I can get them. Old Whitford, the storekeeper, says they will be in by the hundreds before spring.

Doctor was quite sick for a day or two this week. I was very much worried. He has not been so sick any time since we were married. I began to think he would be seriously ill. I have been thinking so much about myself being sick and laid up and making all plans for that, leaving everything for the Doctor to do and counting on him for everything and mourning over my own pains and uncomfortable feelings, never imagining he could have any. I began to think I was going to be punished for my selfishness by having the worst thing in the world happen to me — my husband be ill. Doctor is so good to me in every way, besides being a good husband in the every day sense of the word. He does a thousand little things for me, relieves me of little cares in so many little ways, and makes our home, wherever it is, such a pleasant one for me by all these matters that count up, that I think I would be much worse off than many other women if I should lose my husband, but I hope that dreadful fate will never be mine.

The photograph of Bep I have standing on a little bracket in the sitting room blew down the other day and Bess picked it up. Doctor told her it was Bep. Now she comes in and stands under it, points up, and says, "Bep." She can't say F or any word beginning with F. A fly she calls a sy, and she goes all around the room catching sys; a flea is a see, etc. How much I would love to see you all. Doctor says to tell you to come overland to Portland, then up here on the *California,* and you will find it like sailing on a river and such a lovely trip.

Bess is up and is wiping up a drop of water on the carpet with a rag she has found. She rubs at it as if her life depended upon it. Her greatest delight is a brush and dust pan, and she plays with it for an hour. I wish I could get her a little one. About every fifth line in this letter is about Bess. I hope you aren't tired of it. I find I feel much more like petting her now when I know in a few weeks there will be another little one on my lap and I can't always respond to the, "Takee, Mamma, takee," which I hear any time she gets tired playing. She is only a baby herself. It does seem hard for her, but she is awfully devoted to Doctor and between us we still have enough laps — unless it is twins.

I have another want I believe I have not mentioned. Be thankful you only can hear from me once a month, as I expect every time I write I will want you to send something to me. Please get me 2 ounces of black Germantown wool. My afghan is all done but the fringe and I find I have not another thread of black, so I have to stop. Then please get me some narrow blue ribbon that will do for Bess. I don't want her hair banged anymore, so have been parting it and tying it back with a piece of ribbon around her head. It looks sweet but I have no more ribbon and can't get it here. I have a little pink left but no blue. Mary is not kind to Bess. The other day after Bess had been hurt through Mary's roughness, the Doctor said, "I believe if your Mamma was here she would want me to put Mary in the guard house."

Sunday, October 4, 1874

Doctor and I just came in from a walk. We took Bess and Mary with us, Bess in her carriage, and went down to the beach. There is the greatest fascination to me in hunting among the stones for shells, seaweed, etc. It seems so funny for both Doctor and me, who never saw the ocean in our lives, to take the awful trip we did and then to live as we do now — right on the water. I wished this morning, as I was dressing, that you could see the bay out my room window. All along the shore, the water was as smooth as glass and blue. Then, off towards the sea, you could see a long line of high breakers that looked like silver in the sunlight. This has been another beautiful day, though we have had lots and lots of rain for the last three weeks.

Doctor came in the other morning and quite delighted my heart by holding up two or three pretty, fresh-looking Indian baskets. A little steamer that belongs to one of the storekeepers here had been making a trip among the islands and Indian camps up North. Among other things, they brought down a few baskets. Doctor just happened to be at Whitford's when they came in and picked out the prettiest for me. So I will send them with this letter.

I went down to the store the evening after Doctor got the baskets to see some Indian things and wished Sallie could see some of the feathers and furs. There was one heron skin there that had half a dozen of the prettiest bunches of feathers I ever saw. If I wanted a pretty hat, or was anywhere that I could get a ribbon to match it, or was going home, I would certainly have wanted it. You know the color, don't you? It is a soft, blueish drab, something like a hat Sallie had sometime ago and this whole skin (the breast was lovely, too) was 50 cents. I expect Whitford gave the Indians about five cents. Then I thought of Sallie when I was looking at some grebe. [*A diving bird.*] They are plenty here sometimes in the year. He had several pretty skins for 25 cents a piece. Of course, they would cost more in the end, for they would have to be tanned and fixed, but really a grebe muff and trimming for a cloak would not cost much. I should think 10 dollars would cover everything.

Mrs. Smith has just been here to see me. I told you she is the woman who will be with me when the baby is born. I am sorry that she can't stay with me all the time, but she can give me certain hours every day and always the evenings and nights for some weeks.

Sunday
October 11, 1874

Certainly the steamer will be in before next Sunday, so this will be my last to write in this letter. I am still about but so uncomfortable that I wish it would come. I dread to put on my clothes in the morning. They are so heavy and tight, particularly my flannels. My flannel drawers are almost the death of me. I don't think I can possibly go longer than this week. I can scarcely walk and am the stiffest old thing you ever saw. Doctor says I am perfectly enormous and he guesses it is twins.

This week Doctor got me two knives and forks cut by the Indians. They are not exactly the things I have been looking for to send home. I am going to send one of them to Aunt Pace and I will send the other to you just for a curiosity, but I won't send it in this mail. Let me know how the baskets arrived, for I am afraid they will be mashed up.

Mary is the most terrible child I ever had anything to do with. She will be the death of me yet. She has such an ugly disposition, gets so angry if we speak to her, and dashes and slashes things around so, it nearly distracts me. She thinks she knows how to do everything, and when I insist upon certain things being done my way instead of hers, she gets cross as can be and is cross at everybody and everything. She speaks to poor little Bess in such a sharp, cross way that really I should be mortified to have anyone hear how a servant speaks to my child before me, but I tell her and tell her. Doctor says, "Get up and box her ears or I will break every bone in her body." I think she feels herself she is not trying to behave. I told her the other day that if this continued, I must find a way to send her home. She said she would drown herself before she would go home. I tried to make her see how happy and comfortable she might be with us if she just tried to please us and have me trust her, but I think she is too giddy to reason about anything.

I don't believe her mother has any idea how much she knows about men and such things. She is no child in her knowledge and worries me most to death and makes Doctor cross enough to kill her by already knowing the names of every soldier at the post by talking and laughing at and with them out the back gate and everywhere she gets a chance. All together, she is a specimen! I forgot to mention another of her failings. She thinks she is charming and that she is noticed by all the men when she goes out anywhere. If I make her wear her old waterproof in the mornings, she almost cries and certainly is cross. She goes upstairs to fix her hair and dress before she goes over to the carpenter shop (which is nearer than Grandpa's work shop) for shavings for her fires. The other day she put on her best plaid dress, and when I inquired why, she said there were "so many soldiers over there." Then another thing that provokes me just because it is so absurd is that she comes into the sitting room and surveys herself in the long mirror every time she goes anywhere. She asked me if I didn't think the pimples were going off her face and she said she wasn't going to eat meat for a month until her skin got smooth again. Another time she came into my room and examined her teeth in my glass and then asked if I didn't think her teeth were nice and that if she had such teeth in her head as Bess had she would go crazy. Enough of Mary! With Mary and Bess I fill up my letters.

Doctor and I took a little walk yesterday and I feel as stiff from it as possible. Our apples are almost done for, but the boat will bring us a few more and some pears. Now I wish I had laid in a small supply of those nice sour dried Fruits like you sent me at West Point. Doctor got me a jar of very nice looking tamarands a day or two before we left Portland which we have on hand, but we can't even get prunes here.

We have a roast of venison for dinner. How I hate it. It is a thing one will tire of soon, but for several days every week we have to depend upon the Indian market. The things are cheap enough, but I don't like game. We have mallard ducks and teal ducks often, and grouse, too. The nicest thing I have had was a pheasant I got, or Noah got for me, the other day for ten cents (silver, of course). The meat was as white and as tender as a chicken's. But I hate venison. We buy a hind quarter for 50 cents (four bits, they say) and often can get both hind and fore quarters for the same. Beef is only issued to us once a week and we can't get much more than 20 to 25 pounds. You know that won't last such meat eaters as Doctor and me a week. I believe they have fish in great abundance here sometimes in the year, but this is not the fish season.

I stopped writing a few moments ago to go out and wash a little tapioca to make Doctor another pudding. You know he is devoted to it. While I was doing it, an Indian woman knocked on the window and held up a snipe to sell. She said, "Two bits." I shook my head and then remembered something Doctor was telling me about snipe yesterday and called him out to see if this was the bird he was describing to me. He said he wanted it but would not give two bits for it. I had a half bit which he offered her, but she said she wanted a bar of soap. So Doctor helped himself out of my kitchen supply and gave her a bar of soap that costs 8 cents at the commissary for the snipe and she went away rejoicing. He wanted it to stuff. I told him I was afraid he wasn't as pious as I have been hoping. You know this is Sunday, but, oh dear, such Sundays! Indeed the only difference it makes to this family to all appearances is that Doctor is home more than usual, for on weekdays for the last few weeks he has been busy at the hospital, and, indeed, to some of the people here, I don't believe it makes even that much difference.

Oh, but it has rained this week; indeed, I should say this

month. It has poured and poured, but I don't mind it. I couldn't go out much anyway and we are comfortable inside. In this letter I asked for some ribbon to fix Bess's hair. Please get me a little flat gum, too. I will put little bows on gum and fix it that way. When you get my letters, always thank fortune you can't know any more things I want until that time next month.

Sunday
October 18, 1874

Another Sunday and I am still about! I think every night that certainly I will be sick before morning and every morning that I will before night. Mrs. Quinan has just been in to get a little toothpowder. We sat at the window and discussed our supply of meat from our butchers, as it was issued this morning, and wondered if the steamer would come today and let us enjoy Sunday because we would have our month's mail. Now what do you think of that for a Sunday at Sitka? Bess is so good; she just plays about me and amuses herself. I let Mary go down to the beach for the morning as it was a bright one and, indeed, I am always the most comfortable when she is out of the house and I know is somewhere safe for herself.

Our steamer is more than a week late. Why, we don't know, of course, as she is our only means of knowing anything. At first, I wanted very much to be sick first, but now, when I may be sick any hour, I wish I could get my mail first, for I don't want the boat and the baby to come exactly together. It would be real nice to be a day or so over it and be comfortable than have it come with its news and other things which Doctor has ordered for me, such as a box of fine pears, and have him sit by me and read me all our mail matter. But, I expect, as the boat comes in I will go off and poor Doctor will have his hands full and I will not be strong enough to see my letters for some days.

Doctor says I haven't told you two of the smartest things about Bess. He says she takes strongly after his mother's family in her love of talking. She comes into the room where we are all smiles, gets a big chair, pulls it up by us and climbs up into it, fixes herself in it and folds her hands in her lap, and then with a satisfied air says, "Now talk." We have to inquire about the dollie and kittie etc., and if we stop to speak to each other on a foreign subject, she says, "Talk. Talk." Poor dollie got quite mashed up and I did not know what in the world to do, for Bess won't sleep without it. I thought I would have to make a rag one but found in a box the old one with a China head that you had tied and bound up. So I dressed it and Bess is delighted. She calls it Lulu. She likes her Papa to sing "Lulu is Our Darling Pride." He sang it to this dollie, too, so she calls it Lulu and now, on all occasions, Lulu is called for.

She is a dear child but is not growing pretty, but she is well and smart and has good features and, I think, a good disposition which is more than all else. Her mother was never handsome and has about the best old husband in the world, so if Bess gets as good a one and is as happy, her mother will be satisfied for her.

I am sure about every hour that my pains are coming on. I have had some quite severe ones for several days. It is all coming on gradually, which is better for me, but I hope it won't last long when it does come and that I will soon get strong again after it. Everybody is very kind. Mrs. Campbell came in yesterday and said she was an excellent nurse and could quiet a little baby and, if Doctor would let her, was coming in the daytime to keep the baby and let me rest if Mrs. Smith was not here. Mrs. Field says the same. They have both gone through it all — Mrs. Campbell seven times. So you see, I have kind friends and neighbors. Then a Russian girl, daughter of the matron at the hospital, had done sewing for me and seemed so kind and good with Bess that I asked her if she had ever nursed children. I found she had lived with a doctor's wife — had gone to her while she was in bed and stayed all the time the baby was in long clothes. So, on the spot, I engaged her to come up to me in the morning and stay until the evening (when Mrs. Smith will be sure to be here) all the time I am in bed. She is about 20 years old and she can dress and wash Bess, can change and fix the little one, and do all such things for me that I would be a little afraid of Mary's being rough about. Mary can keep up the fires, wash diapers, and dust and fix up generally. So we will get along nicely.

October 25, 1874

Neither the boat nor the baby have arrived. The boat is anxiously looked for by all at Sitka and the baby by this family! I am well but stiff, and it hurts me to walk. We have looked for the boat hourly for ten days. It is more than two weeks late though we all hope nothing has happened to it. Probably it is being repaired, as the Captain said last month it was in need of some. We want our mail that we know is on it awfully — and now. I hope I will be over my trouble and be comfortable before the steamer leaves so Doctor can inform you of the fact in this letter.

Your loving daughter,
Emily

Steamer came in this afternoon. It had been delayed by the rough weather. I was ever so glad to get my letters and other mail matter, but the stockings for Bess did not come and I need them so much. I suppose in this long distance there must be delays in our letters and packages.

I have to make Bess an entire new lot of dresses by spring. She has not a dress that the sleeves are not nearly to her elbow and to see the poor child try to pull them down is distressing. I am writing this note tonight as I think certainly I will be sick tomorrow. The paymaster did not come on this boat but writes that he will come on the next in about three weeks. Of course we will get all the more money when he does come, but I wish I could send you some now as I am writing for so many things. If you have not the money by you or Uncle Essick, just wait to get my things until money arrives.

The steamer brought me a dozen letters and some magazines that Doctor had ordered for me — *Appleton's* in monthly parts, five letters from you, one from Sallie, and the others from other friends. [*A periodical published from 1869 to 1881. It is curious that Emily referred to "monthly parts," for it is generally believed to have been published weekly until 1876.*]

I was delighted, too, to receive a great box of apples, a box of fresh tomatoes, and a box of candy for Bess from a gentleman who boarded with us in Portland. Way up here we feel these things particularly and both Doctor and I, while we feel delighted to get the fruit, feel pleased to think the people we met and knew there must have liked us to remember us in this way.

Don't forget I want some little linen books full of bright pictures for Bess, some that cost 25 or 50 cents. The steamer leaves again tomorrow (Sunday) so I will just add this note and say goodbye. Write as you have been doing. I am so glad to get my letters. Doctor got a whole lot; he has not read all his yet. We had a great lot of West Point news.

October 26, 1874

I am still about! Doctor went down to the office a little while ago and found lots more mail for us and, thanks to your kindness, everything I expected — the little shirt, stockings, Bess's books, etc. The stockings are very nice and I think I will let her wear the cotton ones unless it gets very much colder. Those gray and white ones are beautiful and I am very glad to get the little shirt. Thank Aunt Annie very much for the book she sent Bess. Bess has been on the floor with it for an hour in delight and saying, "Kittie, kittie, kittie." I did not open *Little Bo Peep* until afterwards and I think I will keep that until Christmas. I can get so little for her here and she is old enough to understand that Christmas day is different from all others.

I will send you 20 dollars as soon as the paymaster comes, which will certainly be in November, and I don't believe even that will cover all the demands I have made. Please add them all up and let me know how much to send. If you sew up packages you send me in a piece of old muslin under the paper, they will be sure to carry better, for sometimes the paper bursts. I only wish I had muslin around these baskets, but Doctor had them all done up by a man at the hospital and says they are all right. Love to all.

Your loving daughter,
Emily

Sitka, Alaska
November 16, 1874

Dear Mamma,

I regret to tell you that my darling Em has been very, very ill. At the same time, I am very happy to add that she is now out of all danger and is rapidly gaining in strength and appetite.

I mailed you a letter by a passing schooner bound for San Francisco on the 10th inst. in which I duly reported the arrival of a grandson and of the good health of all. [*Herbert Fitz-Gerald was born October 30, 1874.*] Emily, having had a comparatively easy confinement and up to the 11th day after, had scarcely a thing to complain of in the way of pain or discomfort of any kind save weakness. She had been unusually smart, having been up on the 8th, 10th, and 11th days for a little while and even wanted to be about more than she was.

On November 10th (her 11th day), she suddenly was taken down with an acute peritoneal inflammation, and for more than 30 hours I watched by her bedside in an agony of dread, but hoping against hope that my darling would be spared me. I am pleased at the thought that my watchfulness was an important element in her recovery, with her youth, good constitution, etc. coming in as necessary factors.

Today (Monday) is the 7th day since her illness and she is sitting up in bed with a great appetite and anxious to be up again and without anything to complain of but the usual weakness incident to a confinement. I feared this recent illness would cause her to lose her milk and that Mr. Herbert would necessarily have to do the best he could, but I am delighted to find that the milk has returned in abundance, so much so, that the baby has a great deal more than he can make use of. We are looking for our steamer now daily when we will send off a mail. I will add a line from day to day reporting progress, etc. until then and, in the meantime, will endeavor to hasten Em's recovery by all reasonable means so that she may, at least, say a few words on her own account in a postscript.

November 19, 1874
9 p. m.

Emily is improving rapidly and will be able to sit up and read her letters when the steamer comes in, an event momentarily looked for. Until today, for a period of three weeks, we have had almost continuously fair weather, but this morning it was raining in a mild fashion but quite warm withal. At this hour (9 p. m.) it is raining steadily and bids fair to continue for a few days or weeks!

The only event of outside interest for us just now is a powwow going on at the Indian village between these Indians and a neighboring tribe to settle a little difference. The Sitka Indians, while out hunting seals recently, shot and killed a squaw belonging to the neighboring tribe, mistaking her for a seal (she being in the water at the time). Her friends have now come down in force to demand satisfaction which they are to have either in "blankets or blood." They arrived yesterday morning about 6 a.m. in their war canoes and had (from their point of view) a grand time. It is said they demand one thousand blankets for the loss of the squaw, but it is not possible that the Sitka Indians will comply with a manifestly unreasonable demand, and war may be the result.

November 30, 1874

Since the 19th there has been nothing of interest to record excepting the continued improvement of my precious wife. She has already begun a letter to you, has been up now a week, and began this A. M. to wash and dress the boy who is a perfect stunner and flourishing serenely. I do wish you could be here in a few hours' notice, in which case I am sure you would come if for nothing else than to see him grow.

Our steamer has not been heard of for more than a month. She was due here since the 20th and we are truly disgusted to be so long without a mail. In the future, if you should not hear from us for 2 or 3 months, you need not be alarmed, for we have 6 or 8 months' supplies of provisions on hand and our principal trouble would be the absence of mails and consequent privation of news from absent friends.

Our Indian pow-wow came to a peaceful termination and the friends of the unfortunate (?) squaw departed with increased stores of blankets for the mourners. Our first snow to speak of fell last Thursday and Friday, but it has mostly disappeared at this writing under the influence of warm, drizzly days.

[*At this point, Emily continued the letter*]

Doctor began this letter to you just after I had the attack that sent me back to bed and nearly put an end to me. It makes me about sick now to think of my poor little babies if I had not gotten well. I can imagine the sorrow it would be to Doctor to lose me because I know what it would be to me to lose him. But what would my poor little babies do? Here there is actually no one that could have been gotten to take care of them. Now that I am so much better, I can scarcely realize how ill I was and can't bear to think about it. Our steamer is still missing. How I wish it would come and would bring you to us. I got to wishing the other night it was possible you might walk in and got to feeling as if I could not do without seeing you any longer. Babies are both well.

Your loving daughter,
Emily

Sitka
November 28, 1874

Dear Mamma,

Our steamer is not here yet. Of course no one knows why it is delayed, but we all hope nothing has happened to it. I suppose I ought to be glad it is late as I will be all the better able to enjoy my letters when they do come.

I have had my clothes on and been up now for a week and am so comfortable though weak, that I can't realize how ill I have been. Doctor has been so good! He has done everything for us all, babies and me, and has been so patient and thoughtful I wonder any man could think of doing all the things he has done in the way of taking care of us. Mrs. Smith had left us when I was taken sick, that is, she was only coming to wash and dress the baby. Doctor sent for her again (she has a great deal of her own work to do and could scarcely give us as much time as she did) and she came back and stayed at nights until a week ago. She is coming tomorrow to bathe the baby for the last time. I dread undertaking it myself, but we can't get help here for love or money. I hope I will never have any more babies where I can't have some of my relations with me to look after the other children and a nurse to look after me.

Doctor looked as if he had been sick himself. The night I was so ill he never left me for a moment. Everytime I opened my eyes I found him watching me, and for days he fed me and even got all I ate ready for me himself. Fortunately, the baby slept all the time. He is a real good little fellow; my only trouble is he is too big. His little knit shirts will hardly go over his shoulders and in another month's time he won't be able to wear the little night slips at all. Bess is real good, only she is beginning to think he takes up some of the time and attention she ought to have and whenever I get him on my lap says, "Please, Mamma, take Bessie."

Sunday
November 29, 1874

Six weeks ago today I finished your last letter, I am thankful I am alive and well enough to write again. I forgot to tell you we have had Bess's hair cut short. It was so pretty and I did not like to cut it off, but it was all in her eyes, and, when I was sick, no one could attend to it so I asked Doctor to have it cut off. She looks real cute and I do believe she is going to grow up pretty. I will send you a little lock of her hair in this. I wish you could see both my children. I know you would be proud of the boy, too. He is so big and such a good little fellow. Everyone who sees him exclaims that he is a splendid baby. Dr. and Mrs. Smith say that he has the broadest chest and shoulders they ever saw for a baby. Doctor says he noticed it when he was born, that the head was born and then it took another hard pain to bring the shoulders into the world. I did not suffer nearly so much as I did with Bess, though it was awfully bad anyway, but as soon as I had the first bearing down pains, Doctor gave me chloroform and I did not feel another until the last one. Mamma, it made it so much easier. I did not have any tired worn out feeling after the baby was born but felt as if I had had a comfortable sleep. I got sick about ten in the evening, just as I did with Bess, and was awfully disappointed that it did not come more quickly than it did. Most everybody has a much shorter time with the second baby, but I suffered dreadfully from about eleven to four. I begged Doctor to give me the chloroform, but he doesn't approve of giving it until later, as there is no knowing how long a time a woman will be and he was afraid to have me under the influence of it long. I took it again the Tuesday I was so sick. I was suffering, so Doctor kept me under the influence of it more than an hour. How many times I have wished for you these last weeks, particularly since I have been up and about a little. I want you just to sit and talk to me and admire the babies.

I never write that I haven't some wants, so I won't make an exception of this letter. Mrs. Quinan wants to send East for some Germantown wool and wants to know what colors she can get. Does it come in plain colors, gray, drab, etc.? Sometime when you are at the store, won't you get me scrap ends of the colors there are and Mrs. Quinan can send for it.

Bess talks a great deal. She says everything. I have been telling her about Red Riding Hood and she insists upon connecting you with Red Riding Hood's grandmother. She calls the baby "Buzzer" and it is real lovely to hear her talk to him.

"Mustn't ky, Buzzer. Hush by." If she is out of our sight a moment, we have to rush, for we are sure to find her up on the bed beside the sleeping baby patting him with all her might or kissing him. I am delighted that she likes him but afraid she will hurt "Buzzer" with her violent loving. They are nice babies, both of them.

Mrs. Smith has just been down to bathe Herbert. She has been telling me about the Doctor while I was sick. She thinks he is a wonderful man. She says she never saw such patience in a man in her life and she tells me that the days I was so ill he never ate a mouthful — one time he went from one breakfast to another dinner time and sat up all night, too. No wonder that when I got better I thought the dear old fellow looked as if he had been sick himself.

Sunday
December 6, 1874

We have had no steamer now for nearly two months. We hope no disaster has been the cause of it. The steamer may have had to lay over for repairs but everybody feels anxious for mail matter etc. Did you hear, or do you remember, the fate of the steamer *General Wright*? It was the mail steamer to Sitka from Portland; the *California* (our steamer now) has taken its place. It was lost coming up and never has been heard of, no survivor has ever been heard of, and its fate, whatever it was, never has been known. That was not quite two years ago. One Army officer and his wife were on board. At any time if you don't hear from us for several months, don't be worried, but remember the steamers are very irregular. We can't send this letter to you until our steamer does come, so I will be able to tell you why we had none last month.

Such a place for a military post! I wish some of those big guns at Washington would come on and try themselves to see how they liked living out of the world. The little papers you sent Bess got mixed with someone else's mail and they were sent up to Doctor while I was in bed. They could not have come at a better time, for they amused and kept Bess quiet when we wanted her to be. Thank you for them.

Do send me some diaper pins! Here they are ten cents a piece — a silver ten cents, too. Sometime when you are sending me a little package, I want a little tape, too. I want it for straps on little petticoats. If I send home the measure of Bess's bust, length of arms, etc., do you think you could have one or two little yoked dresses made for summer? I will have to make her everything, as she has entirely out-grown all she has. I have some percales and calico that I thought would make her half a dozen dresses for summer on that box pleated pattern, but she ought to have at least one or two nice white ones. Let me know how much over the 20 dollars I send in this letter the things I have sent for amount to. I can't spend all my allowance here; at least I need not. So I believe I will send home to you what I want to keep when it amounts to 50 dollars or so and get you to put it in the bank for me. I can send it in checks. Will you attend to it for me?

Wednesday
December 10, 1874

Still without a steamer! If it doesn't come before the 15th, there will scarcely be a doubt but that something in the way of a disaster has occurred. I am better every way than when I last wrote and have had the entire care of both my babies for two weeks. Bess is so cute and does so many sweet little things —as well as bad ones. The boy is the biggest thing you ever saw. He is six weeks old today and is a real good baby. He sleeps all day and all night but will stay awake all evening. Doctor says my greatest trouble now is that I can't show my babies to my Mamma and he says he does believe he would be even more pleased than me to see you walk in for a visit.

I keep Mary busy with housework and her sewing. She is well enough about her work — sweeps, dusts, keep up fires, washes the diapers, etc., but she is too rough and giddy to trust with the children. When the baby is awake at mealtimes I have her sit in the room next to us and hold him on her lap. That is all she has done for him since he arrived. She was pretty good about her work while I was sick and I think tried to be kinder to Bess, but she ran off from the house several times to see something that was going on. Twice she left me entirely alone (in bed, you know) with the children. Doctor had gone out somewhere for a few minutes and left her in the next room so she could hear me call. She never does think she has to obey unless she wants to. But I could not get anyone else here that I could have do the things she does, and though she worries me and gives me considerable trouble, I am glad I have her. But it is a lesson to me. I will never take another child away from her home so far that I can't pack her back if she doesn't behave.

December 16, 1874

Everybody here at the post is now worrying and wondering about the steamer. Some of the oldest inhabitants do say that in very bad weather the steamer has been known to make one trip do for two months, but all last month and until last week the weather has been lovely. The contract with the government calls for twelve trips a year, so we fear its not coming is caused by some accident. Everybody feels particularly interested and anxious, for, you know, it is our only means of knowing what is going on anywhere, and as it is the only breath of the world we get, its comings and goings are the events of our lives here. We know the entire crew from Captain Hayes to Tommie, one of the cabin boys. We are beginning to feel its absence, too. There is not a potato in Sitka — has not been for two weeks and though we could not quite starve up here, as fish and game are plenty, we might soon be pretty short if the boat doesn't come. They try to keep about a six months' supply in the commissary but the flour is low and is to come on the boat. There is about 20 days' more supply of flour on hand; the corn meal gave out last week. Little by little we are getting short and may have very scant Christmas dinners if the boat doesn't come. We are all short of money, too, but as there is nothing to buy, that is the least of our troubles. The paymaster is expected on the boat and when he does come, we will all be rich, for four months' pay is due. Another cause of anxiety to the post people here is about Mr. Dyer, one of the lieutenants. He went down to Fort Wrangell (so called, a little place on the way to Portland) with a little company of men to settle some trouble about the people (only a dozen or so there) selling whiskey to the Indians. The "Wrangellers" are miners and a pretty rough set. Lt. Dyer and his company had only 40 days' rations, as they expected to come back on the next steamer. How they are getting along is a question that is worrying Major Campbell. They are so much isolated and dependent upon the steamer as we are that if the boat doesn't appear this week, Major Campbell means to send a little steamboat that goes about among these islands down to Wrangell to see about Dyer and his men.

Sunday
December 20, 1874

The boat at last! I was washing the baby yesterday when someone rushed in and said, "The boat is coming!" The Russians and Indians began rushing in crowds to the wharf and the soldiers and even the dignified officers got to rushing around in an excited manner. I bathed my boy, put him to sleep, and then took Bess to the front window. Mary was almost standing on her head. In about an hour, I saw the steamer coming around the corner of the island and everybody was out on the parade ground using glasses to see what boat it was. Soon she came near enough for me to see it was not the *California* and I could read *Gussie Telfare*. I felt my heart sink, for it was the same boat that had been sent out by the company to hunt the wreck of the *General Wright* two years ago and I thought the *California* was lost, of course. By this time all our husbands were on the wharf and we had no one to ask news of. Mrs. Quinan came in awfully excited and said she could not wait until Will would come up to tell her, so we opened a window and hailed a soldier who comforted us by telling us the *California* crew were on the boat. Pretty soon Doctor came and told us that all was right. *The California* sprung a leak going down and had to be repaired. This boat made the trip in her place.

Our mail soon came up and I was so glad to get letters from home. Your last is written on the 6th of November. This boat has been nineteen days out from Portland, an awfully long trip. We must not expect to get our letters regularly. It is awfully hard, but the steamers are not prompt and there will be all sorts of delays, but no steamer or vessel of any kind shall leave our wharf bound south without a letter for you, and you write as you have been doing to me. I heard, too, from Em Houston Alexander in this boat. The two pieces of diapering arrived; thank you for getting it. It is very nice and I needed it awfully. Doctor went to see if something that would do for diapers could be found in the store here, but nothing could be used. I was in despair when the boat brought me this. I am going to put a Russian girl to hemming them tomorrow. I am not quite strong yet and, with my care of the two babies, could not hurry them up much, and I need them at once. The little white zephyr things arrived too, and thank you very much. The little white caps and sack are lovely, but Bess at once took possession of the red cap and insisted upon wearing it around all evening. Whenever Doctor or I would suggest taking it off she would hold it on with both hands and say, "No, no. On Bessie." Tell Aunt Annie I won't keep this little cap she sent for "Annie", for fear it would be old-fashioned by the time she arrives, but I am obliged for it anyway and will lend it to "Annie's" brother. [*If the baby had been a girl, it was to have been named after Aunt Annie.*] Those are the only packages that came by this mail — you told me to let you know what bundles I receive.

The paymaster came on the boat so, in this letter, I will send you a check to pay my debts. I think I will send you a check for 75 dollars — 25 of it to pay (if it will) for things I have sent for. The other 50 I wish you would get and put in the bank in my name. I will make it the beginning of my savings. I have made up my mind to lay by 10 dollars every month until my children are grown up. I got to counting the other day and found if I did so, that by the time they are ready to go to school (if anything should happen, or if we were not any better off than we are now) I would have a sum, nearly enough to school them. Of course, Doctor puts by what we can, but generally by the time it is five or six hundred dollars, we make a big move and spend it all getting fixed up again. I always feel that the hundreds that he pays on his insurance policies is that much saved, for sometime the children will certainly get the benefit of it. Anyway, my savings will be my own and I think I can easily lay by that much. I will send 50 dollar checks to you whenever it amounts to that much and you attend to it for me. I don't believe I know anything about banking. If you put any amount of money in a bank, what proof of your having done so do they give you? Whatever it is, you take care of it for me and tell me what bank you put my small amounts in and what interest they pay. If this is going to be any trouble, I won't ask you to do it.

Monday Night
December 21, 1874

Doctor has just brought me in the check I wanted. I don't believe you will have any difficulty getting it cashed at one of the Columbia banks. They all know you well and will know it is all right. Please write and tell me when you get this. I will be so glad when we get stationed a little nearer home. It takes so long now for our letters to get to us.

I wanted to tell you about what furs I think I want. Do you know what sea otter is like? The skins are expensive but are large and will never be common, as they are not plenty. Mrs. Boyer told me she had secured that for her handsomest fur, but I did not know anything about what it was like. I find it is considered a very valuable fur. The skin plucked is almost black, thick and soft like sealskin, but for ladies' trimmings and furs they leave in the long hairs which are a silvery color—very rich and beautiful. The skins cost from 50 to 150 dollars according to their darkness and size. A hundred dollars or even eighty will get a beauty and one skin will make two sets of boas and muffs. I think I would like it on my velvet cloak. It will be handsome and, as they are scarce and getting to cost more every year, in a few years it would be handsomer still. Doctor likes silver gray fox. Some beautiful ones have been gotten here. Doctor saw a very handsome skin at the furriers in Portland; it had cost 50 dollars. I don't believe one skin would quite make a muff and trimmings. The cheapest thing is bearskin and, indeed, some of these northern bearskins are a lovely jet black, long and soft, and look exactly like the black fur that was worn so much last winter. I am thinking of having a common thick cloth sack made this week and trimmed with bearskin and a little matching muff. Mrs. Field is going to have one, too. They will always do for common wear and for travelling, and then when we come home from Sitka, anything, even bearskin, will be rare as everybody can't get it. I forgot to say I think five dollars will more than buy all my bearskin. There are some beautiful cheap furs here; a great many are bought up by English vessels. There is a gray hedgehog that would be taken for silver gray fox by almost everyone. Mrs. Field wants that on her common sack, but she is afraid people will know it isn't silver fox if she wears it for common. Like you, I like dark sables and think a sack of them would be handsome. Doctor will find out all you ask about them. I know it takes six skins for a boa and muff. There is a beaver skin up here that is not very expensive and looks exactly like seal. It is a dark rich brown. Mrs. Campbell saw a cloak that had been made here and took it for seal. I don't know exactly the cost of it.

Mary is still a dreadful trouble to me. She is very useful in many ways but is so giddy and so rough. Bess gets a great many bruises and hurts playing with her and I can't keep Bess by me all the time. She runs out to Mary to play and always ends with a bump or hurt of some kind. Only this week Mary has tramped twice on her poor little fingers and once right on Bess's foot. Then the other evening (we sit with the doors open all through the house and Bess runs all about) we heard a scream and Doctor went out to the dining room and brought Bess back with a lump as big as a walnut on her head. She had been running about playing with Mary and Mary had thrown a diaper over her head and jerked her back with it. Of course, the bump was the consequence. Mary said, "I meant to jerk her back but didn't think she would hit her head." The polite Doctor FitzGerald informed Mary that the next time he would break her neck. The worst of it is I have never yet known Mary to express any sorrow, or regret, or even pity for Bess. She behaves as if she thought poor Bess got hurt on purpose. Of course Bess tumbles about herself sometimes, but really most of the hurts she gets through Mary. But as I said before, Mary is useful to me in a great many ways. She likes to work and works well. Someone who had no little people about, who could learn her rough ways, ought to take her in hand. She might be made a good, useful girl but, indeed, she is a great trial to me. The other night she went out about nine o'clock without permission. Major Campbell told Doctor he saw her. I inquired about it, found that she had, and punished her for it by deducting from the little money I give her every month to spend herself. It is the only way I have of punishing her — that and keeping her Saturday afternoon. She said this morning she wished she had another dollar for Christmas money and that she would have more than she had if the "horrid Major Campbell" hadn't told the Doctor. She wasn't sorry she went out that night, but was awfully sorry Major Campbell saw her. Proper spirit, isn't it?

I forgot to tell you of our short days. We breakfast at half past nine with a candle and by half past three in the afternoon it is too dark to see and we light up again. I think it's disgusting! Mrs. Campbell says as soon as we light the lamps she feels as if it was evening and begins to be sleepy by five o'clock.

I am glad you have a dollie for Bess. I suppose it is on the way some place now. She is devoted to her babies. Poor Lulu has neither head, arms, or legs, and it made me feel real badly to see poor Bess's devotion to the remains. The other morning she came in with the old rubber dollie rolled up in a piece of carpet and singing "Hush a by Darlin" to it. I put one of Herbert's little slips on to it (he scarcely can get his arms into the sleeves of them now) and she has been playing with that ever since.

You know the Indians here all wear blankets over their heads. Bess walked into the sitting room the other night with a diaper (her principal play thing) over her head and said, "Bessie In-In" (Indian).

Wednesday
December 23, 1874

Doctor says the steamer will leave in a few hours. He has just rushed in and out again. Lots of love goes home to you all with this letter. Mamma, don't give up the idea of coming out to us. I know I will think of a thousand things I want to write you as soon as I have closed this but Doctor says I must hurry.

Ever your loving child,
Emily FitzGerald

Sitka
December 27, 1874

Dear Mamma,

This is very early in the morning to begin writing but I want to begin my Sunday writing again and, as I can't count on any time certainly, I am going to write any time, just when I can get both babies disposed of. Bess is watching inspection out the window, baby is asleep, and we are all waiting for Papa and breakfast. Christmas is over. I wonder how you all spent yours. We had rather an anxious one as both baby and Bess were suffering with colds. Bess was really very sick. She is so much better this morning than she was yesterday that we feel relieved. For the last five days we have been very anxious about her. She is growing so fast that she is quite thin and this cold (she had fever with it) pulled her down in such a little while that until yesterday she has been almost too weak to talk.

How I have wished for you these last few days. Bess wanted to be nursed all the time and my poor, patient, good little boy would cry a little and then lie with the most patient look on his face, as much as to say, "When will my turn come?" Indeed, when Doctor was busy I had my hands full. I felt that if I was only near you, you would take the same interest in the babies that I do, and I would take such comfort in having you with me.

Tuesday
December 29, 1874

I believe I was going to tell you about our Christmas. Doctor went down to the store and found they had just gotten a box of toys on the boat and he wanted to buy all he could get his hands on for Bess. I had to stop him, for he was going to buy her things that would have lasted about five minutes (it was a small box of toys and a miserable assortment, of course). At last he bought her a set of dollie furniture (that would have lasted her less than five minutes, for she *would sit* on the chairs until I put it away), a set of wooden dishes (he gave a dollar and something for them), a dollie, and a tin horse. The furniture has little upholstered chairs, etc. Such a thing for Bess! But Doctor was worried about her being sick and felt he wanted to get her all he could in Sitka. I got a box of blocks and a little book for her in Portland and I gave her the *Bo Peep* book you sent her on the last boat. Mr. Goddard brought her two Indian dollies which are such funny things that I am going to send them home as curiosities when she gets tired of them. Poor Bess was too sick to enjoy her things, but she is pretty well today and we feel easy about her.

We filled Mary's stocking. Bess gave her a silver thimble. I made her pulse warmers and a pretty little pin cushion with M on it and stuck full of pins. Then we put in the usual filling of nuts and candy and a big candy and gilt heart that I saw downtown and thought would please her. I have had a laugh about the heart since. Christmas morning Mary asked me who gave her the different things. I said Bess gave her the thimble, etc., and that Doctor gave her the candies and filled up her stocking. In the afternoon I heard her telling someone about her nice Christmas things and that she got a beautiful, elegant heart from Doctor FitzGerald with friendship's offering on it, etc. Poor innocent! Doctor was quite indignant when I told him, for he was so cross at Mary for behaving so badly he declared she should not have a thing.

Doctor and I mourned together over not having anything for each other, but when I got up in the morning I found an envelope pinned to my pincushion with a twenty dollar gold piece in it. What pretty things they are! I have two now and mean to keep them to buy something pretty with.

Sunday, January 3, 1875

I have not had a minute of time to write this last two or three days, though I have often wanted to talk to you. The babies have both had such awful colds that I was very anxious about them. They are better now, indeed almost well, and are the two nicest babies in the world. Doctor insisted Bess was not warmly clad enough, so this week I have put her into canton flannel drawers. They are the funniest looking little things. Doctor made me make Bess's longer than the pattern so they would cover her knees, but they certainly are an improvement on the diapers, for Bess is nothing of a baby anymore. You would be very much surprised to see how much older she seems than when we left home. She says everything and speaks very correctly and uses the pronoun I these last few weeks. She is delighted today over a new pillow. Her little pillow was too small for her and I wanted to use it on my lap with Baby, so I got a new one a little larger for Bess and had some pillow cases made. Bess is charmed with it and has insisted upon having it in her lap nearly all day.

I did not tell you how I manage about my sewing. My time with the two babies is entirely taken up and I don't get many minutes to spare, so any sewing I want done I give to a Russian girl who does it nicely and it doesn't cost but a little. I am going to have Mary sew for me some — but plain sewing. My trouble is to find enough to keep her busy. I said to her the other day, "Did you used to behave this way at Mrs. Jackson's?" She said, "I didn't get time there to do anything but work. I didn't get time to think about being cross." So it gave me an idea. I will rush her! When I think I may have to keep that little vixen for four years I get distracted. Indeed she is the most trying imp I ever came across. I told her the other day I would do a great many more things for her than I had done, would fix her up nicely, and would get her some nice things if she would be obedient and kind to Bess, but if not, she should not have a new stitch of clothes or a cent of money. I would see that she was not hungry and had something to put on — but nothing more. I wish she was in heaven!

Wednesday
January 6, 1875

We are all better this week of colds and all such things. I have been out every day. I had not been out since before Bertie arrived, but Doctor declared I must go out if I left both babies yelling. So now I put the boy down for his morning nap, rush on my rubbers and blanket shawl, and rush down to the end of the boardwalk and back. I generally take Bess with me or else leave Bess and Mary at the sitting room window to watch for me, and I always leave special instructions not to take baby up even he does cry, which the dear little fellow doesn't often do. I enjoy getting out and Doctor says he sees a lot of improvement in my color, appetite, etc. I wish you home folks could take my walks with me every morning. The boardwalk runs down through the Russian town, which is vile, but every few steps you can see the ocean and the tide and great white breakers rolling in or out. Then on all sides are the mountains, one above another, the highest ones always snow covered. I just wondered this morning if I would ever see anything as grand again and could not help but wonder if this was me standing there with the roar of the surf in my ears and those mountains all around me. While I was looking, the sun was shining on them and they were sparkling beautifully. But you should see the Indians. I met about fifty or a hundred in my walk this morning. Such wretches! They are the most horrible looking things you can imagine. They crouch down in a corner somewhere or on some steps, six, eight, or a dozen in a bunch, each rolled in a dirty blanket or squirrel robe. Their faces are painted every way imaginable — some just the cheeks, some the entire face, jet black or red, some in smears or spots, and some in streaks of two or three colors. The women all have rings in their noses and their lower lips pierced with a silver pin about as thick as an ivory knitting needle. They all go barefooted over the ice and snow and the children that are too young to hold blankets around them are almost entirely naked. I saw a little fellow about eighteen months old, I suppose, sprawling over the floor of Whitford's store with a little fur robe down his middle with holes for his arms and open in front — and that was all! The poor child's face was painted the most hideous black. He looked like a little devil.

New Year's day and your birthday have passed. I expect you had some gatherings at home. Mrs. Quinan came in here New Year's morning and we received five calls together — our five officers of the garrison. I had some fruit cake and egg nogg and I received the gentlemen with my baby on my lap. Primitive, aren't we? Another thing I forgot to tell you. The four ladies that are here, as we are out of the world, have renounced the vanities of the world, among others "store hair," and we go about with the meekest looking heads you ever saw, mine in particular. I never did have the faculty of making my hair look much.

Sunday, January 10, 1875

This is such a lovely morning. The ground, the hills, and the little islands in the bay are all covered with snow and the sun is shining brightly. All the trees around are fir and you know how beautiful they look covered with snow.

Bess has a kittie that is the best natured little kittie I ever saw. Bess pulls it around by the tail, or the leg, or anything she can catch first, and Kittie takes it all as if she was born to it. Mary, much to my disgust, teaches Bess to tease and worry the cat. She ties paper to its tail, ties it all up in a towel, and then throws it about and does all sorts of things. I wish Mary was in heaven! Doctor says Bess is learning Mary's ways every-day. I do so want Bess to be a little lady but she has learned all sorts of rough things. Really Mary is about the roughest, noisiest girl I ever saw. Bess is not with her much, but it is impossible not to have them together sometimes.

Mrs. Campbell expects to be confined in March. Hers will be the second Sitka baby. I made some gelatine this week. It was very good but too awfully sweet. Did I make a mistake when I copied your old receipt, or is it 2 pounds of sugar it calls for?

Wednesday
January 13, 1875

I have just been down to old Whitford's to see a devil fish that was brought in yesterday. It is perfectly horrible. Doctor says it is not an octopus at all but a cuttle fish, but it is bad enough anyway. It attacked and almost pulled an Indian canoe to the bottom before the Indians could tumble out into shallow water and attack it. The body is about as big as old Jack (our old red dog) or bigger. Then it has a tail, broad and flat, larger than the body, and around the head eight of those arms (this one's arms are about a foot and a half long), and two longer arms or tentacles or feelers. Way in among all these (Bess just came for my handkerchief to wipe Kittie's nose) is its head, a long, sharp beak like a parrot's only much larger. Each of these arms of the horrid thing has a double row of suckers. They are hoof shaped and about as big as a penny. Inside of each of them is a row of little bony spikes which would enable the monster to hold on so much better. Doctor says it is the most wonderful and powerful contrivance to adhere to a flat surface that can possibly be imagined. It is to be sent to some museum, I forget where.

I went behind the counter and looked at all sorts of furs and Indian curiosities. The store was full of Indians, indeed it always is, with things they bring in to trade to Whitford for whatever he will give them, from a gold piece or a piece of calico to sugar, tobacco, or even a piece of bread. I wish you could have been behind the counter with me. If you could have stood the awful Indian smell, you would have been interested in the medley of things — furs, skins, feather, Indian dollies, Indian rattles, wooden carvings of all sorts and painted all colors (hideous things), little dollie hats (about the neatest thing there), and lots of table mats made like the baskets. Doctor got a set to send Mrs. Compton. You remember he lived with the Comptons before we were married. I will get some when I find some nice ones for you home folks.

I was looking at some mink furs and I believe you would like that as well as anything else. I had my old muff with me and it looked bright red beside the skins. They are not a red brown at all but a dark drab or slate color about as thick, soft, and long as our old mink furs but so much handsomer, for they are so dark and just like marten (what is called Russian sable) only not such long fur. The marten costs from 10 to 12 dollars a skin and the mink, which is plenty here, only costs two to two and one half dollars. I asked old Whitford if he knew how many it would take for a cloak. He said he thought about 22, but he doesn't know. Doctor will write to a furrier in Portland and ask him how many skins it will take and how much he would charge to make a cloak. So in my next letter I can tell you definitely. The Russian sables that are considered most valuable here among the dealers are nearly black, long and soft, and cost from 10 to 12 dollars a skin. There are some here not quite so dark and therefore not so expensive. They cost five or six dollars. Doctor wants me to get these for the trimming of my velvet cloak and then get a muff of the handsomest. I am not going to be in a hurry, though, as I won't need my cloak here.

Did I ever tell you what a time we have had getting a cow? They cost awfully out on this coast. We brought one from Portland with us and as soon as it got here it went dry and is almost dried up by this time. The horrid thing has just had a calf, too, so there was 75 dollars lost! But Doctor thought he could better afford to send for another one than do without the milk, so he sent, but one thing and another prevented the boat bringing it to us and we are still buying pale blue milk at 20 cents a quart. Last month our bill was 13 dollars. I am afraid we won't save much, but we must have some milk for Bess and now for "Buzzer," too. Thank fortunes we have no debts hanging over us.

Friday Evening
January 22, 1875

This evening the steamer came in and leaves again tomorrow and my letters are not ready. It is after ten o'clock now. You can't imagine how full my hands are with the two babies. When the baby goes off for a nap, I feel that I must pay a little attention to Bess who wants her lunches, head combed, hands washed, etc., for when he is awake I can do little for her.

Mary is not improving much and is so noisy and rough. Doctor whipped her this week for the first time. I felt sorry about it, but I don't see how we can manage her unless she knows she will be punished if she doesn't do as we want. She was changing Bess's drawers and Bess wanted to play a little. She kicked her feet about and, I suppose, shook her hands about Mary's face, all in good humor. Mary has not a particle of patience with Bess and told her in a very rough way to stop. Doctor was writing in here and heard her say, "Stop now, or I will. See if I don't." In a moment there was a scream from Bess and violent sobbing. Doctor went out and found Mary had bitten Bess's finger. Mary said, "I didn't bite it hard enough to make her scream that way," but the poor little finger was blue from the bite and Bess doesn't cry much if she is not hurt. I picked Bess up and Doctor took Mary by the shoulder and shook her and gave her two or three slaps. She has bitten Bess's fingers two or three times before, but not to hurt as much as this. She doesn't do it in play, either. Every time she did it, she was angry at Bess for playing or teasing and really wanted to hurt the child.

Aunt Annie's letter and Sallie's arrived today, too. I was ever so glad to get them and will write to both this month. I wish you could be with us to enjoy the arrival of a steamer and our mail coming up. This one brought me five letters from you and I guess *all* the packages — the calico and wool, combs and brushes, and the dollie for Bess. She is delighted and has gone to sleep with it in her arms. Tell Aunt Annie that Bess and I are both ever so much obliged for the books. They are lovely and Bess enjoys them so much.

I am sorry the baskets got mashed up. You can dampen them and press them out and I will send some more when I can find nice ones. I wish you could see my boy. He is such a comfortable looking baby and so good. Mamma, I would like some more of those knit bands. I would get at some myself but can't get the yarn.

I have just written a letter to the Portland furrier for Doctor. I will let you know about the prices when I get his answer.

Our cow came on the boat. I hope she will do better than the other one. It will be such a comfort to have milk. I hope she will pay us. She cost 85 dollars in gold, but I told you how high milk was here and Doctor thinks it best for us to get her, as the children must have milk.

Doctor has gotten very fond of chocolate caramels and I have been boiling him some on the nursery stove every Saturday for some weeks. Ask Aunt Annie to send me word how she makes that white sugar candy.

The Indians make hats (sundowns) as they make the baskets, and I have heard of some that were very much admired away from here. I will try to get you hats next summer. These Indians don't talk anything, Mamma; they grunt. I believe their language is called Chinook and Siwash. It is just striking twelve and I am going to bed. If the boat doesn't leave early, I will add some to this in the morning, but, as it may, I will say good night. With lots of love to all,

Your loving daughter,
Emily FitzGerald

Sunday
January 23, 1875

I forgot to say the blue ribbons are just what I want. Bess is playing around with her new things. She insists upon having her new brush and *will* brush the dog, kittie, and the floor. I wish I could get her a little dust pan and brush like we used to have but guess I will have to wait until we get East. One of those books Aunt Annie sent, "Alphabet of Country Scenes," is lovely. Isn't it wonderful how many things can be sent by mail? I am so thankful for it. I just looked at the things that came in my packages yesterday and thought how glad I was to get them. It is a lovely thing to get a big mail and I think there is always a fascination about opening bundles even if we know what is coming out of them. I hope you get my last letter and the check for 75 dollars. Pay my debts and put the rest in the bank. I am pleased with the idea of saving all I can and putting it to draw interest, no matter if it is a small amount. I hope, Mamma, it won't trouble you to attend to it for me.

Bess insists upon everything she has having come from "Gan ma." About several things we told her, "Grandma sent them to Bessie," and now we hear her tell her dollie about almost everything she picks up that "Gan ma" sent it to Bessie. I wish "Gan ma" would send her a pair of scissors with blunt points. She gets my scissors on all occasions and frightens me to death, and when I take them from her, she nearly breaks her heart. I forgot to say that her dollie and everything arrived in good order.

Doctor had Mary's hair cut last week, much to her indignation. It stood straight out almost five inches from her head, looked like a brush heap, and was always covered with dust. She could not help it, for it was so woolly. Doctor declared he would not have such a looking head about. I believe Mary is pleased about it now, for everyone has said to her, "How nicely your head looks," and she is quite delighted. She is such a little fool. She says she is never going to work any more when she get home again, is going to be a lady and wear dresses with trails. She wants me to have her calicos this spring made into wrappers that touch the ground. She says she is much better educated than her mother and the rest of them, that she speaks correctly and they don't and says her mother often says she ought to have been born a lady. I am afraid the education she does have doesn't amount to much. Someone gave her a prayer book on the ship and she was mourning the other day because she had not brought *her* prayer book with her; she wanted to read the prayers (I wish they would affect her a little.) I said, "Why don't you read the one you have?" and she said, "Oh, that is a common thing." I said, "It is just like the one you have at home," and she said, "It isn't at all, for it says so in the back. It says common prayer."

I would like two of those little black testaments like I got from Uncle Essick if you could get them for me. I think I gave only thirty cents for them. Bess has completely used up the one I have, and I hate to have a shabby one. It is too funny. She conceived the greatest liking for this little black book way back on the ship and would cry for it. I gave it to her and then she would sometimes amuse herself with it for an hour. I can't imagine why, for it has no pictures or is not bright at all. She calls it now, "Mamma *tes mon* book."

I think I had better get you to send me two or three neat, dark calicos for Mary. I will need them in the spring and there are only a few hideous pieces here and cost 15 cents a yard in coin. I think 9 or 10 yards will be an abundance for a dress for it. It only took seven yards for the plaid dresses I got her in Portland. I don't mean to get her anything but nice calicos while I am dressing her. She is very anxious to have wages this spring but she spends the money she does get so foolishly, I don't think I will give her wages at all. (I wish she was in heaven.) Doctor says I shan't give her a cent and, if I am distressed for fear I have not given her enough, I can give her mother a little money when I give Mary back to her. I wish to goodness I could give her back at once. Mary is very angry because I won't let her go out at all in the evenings. There is no place for her to go and no one here but soldiers and bad Russian women; more than two-thirds are prostitutes. Mary likes to race around and talk to the soldiers and I will not let her go out after dark. She informed me this week that next month she would be sixteen. Then she would go out in the evenings and no one should keep her in, but we will see. She certainly is the greatest trial I have ever had to put up with.

I sent by this mail an Indian dollie. You can keep it for your little Case grandchild. The little papooses here play with these charming dollies. [*Emily's sister, Sallie, had married Brainard Case.*]

I only meant to add a few lines today but I want to talk to you about so many things I don't know when to stop writing. I began this in the morning and have written in all my scraps of time. Now it is eleven o'clock and I am sleepy. I don't keep such late hours, only when the steamer comes in. Lots of love to all of you.

Your loving daughter,
Emily FitzGerald

Monday
January 24, 1875

The steamer has not been able to pull out yet and I always keep your letter open until the last moment. The sea is so rough that the steamer has to wait until the wind falls to get out of the Bay. We are all well and only wish we were nearer our friends. My baby sucks his little, fat thumb, but John says I must stop it at once. Isn't it lovely that I have such good babies? They are little darlings but Bess is actually, as Doctor says, more than we both can manage. Lots of love and good bye.

Your daughter,
Emily

Monday night
February 8, 1875

Dear Mamma,

By this time I do hope you have had our letters and know about your grandson. He is nearly four months old now and such a good baby. Every morning I dip him into a basin of cold water, and do you know that in all his life, he has never cried but three times while he was having his bath. His face comes out from under the washrag or the towel with the sweetest little smile on it and he is ready to laugh out loud if you speak to him. But he is the biggest little fellow. The six little nightgowns you made I have had to put away. His arms won't go into the sleeves and they span around his body. He has kicked out three or four pairs of socks, heels and toes. All together he is a buster!

Isn't money a nice thing to have? I see so many things up here I would like to get and send home for you to see and use in the ways of furs and Indian curiosities, but it takes more money than my pocketbook contains. I don't believe we will be able to save any more up here than we did at the Point. The difference between coin and greenbacks and the big wages we pay our servants over balances the cheapness of meat.

Wednesday
February 10, 1875

I have just sent Bess out for her ride. She would rather walk, but I am afraid to let her. The ground up here is so soft and damp. Once or twice I have taken Bertie in the carriage and let Bess walk on the boardwalk.

I got one Indian basket this morning and I am looking for four to send to Chestnut Hill. This one is right nice. I hope I get the others as clean. The Indians come to our back doors with things to sell and it is real interesting to see them. Noah, our cook, has to do all the bargaining, for I can't understand a thing they say or make them understand me. "Sitkum dollar" is 50 cents. That I do know, for their price for almost everything is a half dollar. "Cleck" means you don't want what they have and they must go away. Mary delights in having them in the backyard and I find her several times a day, when I am patiently waiting for her to do something for me, hanging over the porch rail trying to talk to the Indians.

We are going to have a good opportunity of getting furs in another month. A little schooner that belongs to a dealer here is going to make its yearly trip among the islands to the North, Kodiak, etc. When it comes back, we will have the best furs to select from that we have seen yet. I don't believe I can afford to get mine this winter but Doctor thinks if we see anything remarkably fine we had better try to get it.

I do wish you could come out here to us. It will cost twice as much to go overland as by water, so make up your mind to be seasick. Since the boy arrived, the time between mails has not seemed nearly so long; it is because my time is so taken up. I scarcely have time to long for it.

Bess is so hard to amuse. She wants a thousand things in a minute. She says everything she hears anyone else say. A few minutes ago she picked up something she did not recognize and said, "Oh, mercy, what is this?" I wish you could see her sew. Her sewing is a piece of muslin and a big darning needle with the thread doubled so she can't get it out. Then do you remember the little, long thimble I had when I was a child? She found it in one of my boxes and took possession at once. So after she finds "my sewing," she inquires for "my cimble. Where is my cimble? I can't sew wis out my cimble." She sews for half an hour sometimes.

Friday
February 12, 1875

I am going to start out with my two babies in a few minutes to go to the hospital for the Doctor. I invested in a lot of grebe skins and am going to see if I can have some trimming made. I thought perhaps Sallie would like some for a cloak if it would match or nearly match her muff. Bess has the broom which Mary brought in to use and she is trying to sweep, but the handle catches in the chairs. Everytime it gets caught she says, "Oh, mercy!" What shall I do with her?

I am delighted with a new arrangement about officers' leaves that has lately been made. Officers are entitled to 30 days a year, that is, they could never have a longer leave than that without expecting their pay to be cut, but they could not take two months if they waited two years. But now they can have as many 30 days at one time as they wait years. Isn't that a nice thing for us? We won't want any leave out here and when, in the course of the next two or three years, Doctor is ordered from this department, he can get three or four months leave. I am going to put my babies under the influence of chloroform and have a good time. I expect by that time I will have a dozen. I am busy all the time. When Bertie sleeps, Bess always needs some attention. I never count on any particular time for myself. If a third puts in an appearance, I must secure a woman for a nurse.

Sunday
February 14, 1875

The boat will be in and I won't have my letter to you finished. We look for our steamer this week. I hope there are lots of home letters on her for me. I have been looking over the clothes I have for Bess this week and planning for Bertie's short clothes. Bess has outgrown all her dresses but the little single calico wrappers, and the sleeves in them, I am afraid, are short. She has been wearing only the double ones this winter. I wish I had ever so many more for her. There is not a sewing machine in this place but Mrs. Campbell's and I can't have any wrappers made here as there is no one to do it. I wish to goodness I was near you and you could advise me as to what was best to do about clothing Bess. I thought once of having you get me some wrappers made and just letting Bess wear them right along, but it is so far away and will take so long that I decided just to get along this summer as best I could. I would like you to plan for her clothes next fall. I want her to have about six little bright plaid or worsted dresses. About the fall clothes, I only write about them now so I can have time to hear if you think it is a good plan before it is time to get them.

I always allow three months to get an answer from home. That is, this letter will be answered in the May boat.

Mrs. Campbell expects to be confined early next month. It is a dreadful thing to be sick here so far from all our friends and with so little help. I hope and pray I won't have any more here. I think to go to bed to have a third, not knowing who would look after Bess and Bertie while I lay sick, would be enough to put an end to me at once.

The babies and I have taken several quite long walks, at least Bertie is the only member of the party that doesn't walk. A few days ago we went down to the beach when the tide was out. You should have seen Bess; she was perfectly happy. We could walk out nearly a quarter of a mile on the hard, smooth tide-washed sand. Bess ran up and down, backwards and forwards, picked up every shell she found and insisted upon Mamma carrying it home. The tide began to come in while we were there and she was delighted with that, would stand looking at it with the most pleased expression you can imagine, then would look at us and say, "Water comin in," and laugh. out loud as if it was the funniest thing in the world.

Yesterday morning when Bertie went to sleep, Doctor and I went out for a little walk. We heard a great noise and commotion over in the Indian village and climbed up on some rocks to see over the stockade. The Indians were having some sort of a pow-wow. I wish you could have seen them in their bright colored blankets, all jumping around, talking and gesticulating in a violent manner. They all had spears and every now and then would fire off guns. I am awfully afraid of the Indians. I wanted my glasses but was afraid to stay while Doctor went to get them for me. So I went myself (it is only as far from our front door as you are from the foot of the hill) and we watched them for half an hour. Every now and then one of them would fall down and be picked up by four or five more and carried off. What the performance means is hard to tell. Probably some sort of sham fighting, but they always have something going on in the village. If they are not quarrelling with some other tribe, the two ends of the village are quarrelling or peacemaking with each other.

Wednesday
February 17, 1875

This is Bess's birthday. Her cold is better, but it doesn't seem possible to me she is two years old. Bertie is almost 4 months. Does Sallie ever mean to have any? I wonder how and where you spent Christmas. Just think, I have not heard any news from home for more than two months. Your last letter was dated December 12th, but we look for our steamer in the course of the week. On the Christmases and birthdays that we are out here and you want to send us anything, we will be delighted with anything! Bess (at least her mother) will be pleased with such things as a dress, some aprons, stockings, shoes, or any such things. I will like best to have about a thousand things that you will have to choose between — table cloths, towels, or any of those house things will always be nice. You would be repaid for sending Bess the dollie if you could see how devoted she is to it. Poor Lulu with the broken head has been in disgrace ever since Fannie, as she calls the new one, arrived. I bought Fannie a hat yesterday and trimmed it. By the way, these little hats are about the cheapest thing you ever heard of and they are real cute little straw hats. They are made like baskets and only cost five cents, in silver, of course.

Friday
February 19, 1875

How I wish I could show you my babies. I believe I love you a great deal more than I ever did before since I have had these babies of my own. When I think how much these little people are to me and then know you have felt to me just as I feel about them, it seems to me I have never loved you half enough and I just want you right away to show you what a good daughter I am going to be to you for the rest of your life and mine. When I think how far you are from me and how short life is even at best, I get frightened. I am afraid I am very wicked, Mamma. I know I could not say, "It is all for the best," if you should die, or the Doctor, or one of my babies. When I think sometimes of the changes a day may make in my life, I get sick and cold all over. I am not going to write in this horrible style any more. I don't know what has gotten over me.

We are looking for the steamer daily now. I hope she will come tomorrow. Doctor came in this morning to get some money and told me to wait a moment and he would show me a sight. Pretty soon he came to my room and held up the most horrible things — three arms of a devilfish, each about a yard and a half long. They tapered, were large at the top, small below, and were covered with enormous suckers as big as a big morning glory. They are very different from the arms and suckers of the other fish I told you about, which Doctor says was a huge cuttlefish. Doctor bought these arms from an Indian and he is going to alcohol them. The Indian said the body of the fish was as big as Doctor and that there were many of them about the rocks on the shores of their islands. Horrors! I hope none of my family will fall into the water.

Sunday
February 21, 1875

Yesterday morning I went out for a walk to the hospital. I thought I would escort Doctor down. We go out in the rain as much as in the shine up here. I have an old black hat without any feathers in it or anything that rain could hurt. Nobody carries umbrellas; the rain is not a pour. As we passed Whitford's, I saw a right nice looking Indian basket that he had just gotten in. I secured it at once. On our way down to the hospital we met Captain Field with a package. He stopped us to show Doctor a skin and ask if Doctor thought it a fine one. It was one of those lovely gray foxes he had gotten for Mrs. Field. It cost 25 dollars, and that is very cheap. The furrier in Portland told Doctor not to hesitate to pay 40 dollars for a silver fox skin. Aunt Pace wrote me asking about furs. I did not tell her about silver fox, which may be just what she would like. Are you tired of hearing about furs and devilfish? I should think you would be.

I expect when the steamer comes in I will hear from the Portland furrier and I will send you his letter. If you get your mink sack, I am going to get you handsome skins enough for your muff. I want to do it and you must let me. When you first wrote about a mink sack, Doctor told me to tell you he would make you a present of the skins and you could have them made up, but I did not tell you because I didn't think he could afford to do it now, though I think it is very probable next winter he will.

I am getting to be quite expert at doing things with baby in my arms. Mrs. Quinan came in the other day and found me weighing out stuff for some cakes with him in one arm. She said I looked quite interesting. I often sew with him on my lap, and yesterday I made Doctor some caramels with the baby in my arms.

Mary has been trying to be more gentle and more respectful this week and she has done very well. Doctor says, "Don't say a word, or she will break out afresh tomorrow and I will have to box her ears." She is such a good little worker I wish some-one else had her and I had some one who could help me more with the babies. She enjoys working, is always glad to scrub, wash windows, and do such things, but she is so noisy and rough. She cleans and fixes up very nicely and quickly but that is not all that is necessary for me to have. I want someone that I won't constantly be worried about and that I can trust to be kind to the little people if I have to leave them with her. I don't think she knows how to be gentle.

Bess is such a wise little thing. Do you know she can go out and get me a dry diaper and hang up the wet one. She does it often. I told you in this letter to use your judgment about what to get Bess for the fall. Doctor says, "Dress the babies here as warmly as you can and plain. No one but ourselves will see them. Then when you go East you will have all the more money to spend on nice little fixings for them to appear among their friends." I think he is right, so I don't want to spend any-thing more than is necessary for them while we are here. I want them to be comfortable and neat but I don't want to get them any of the pretty little trimmed things I would like them to wear if we were still at West Point or at Columbia. As for myself, I am going to be like the pious missionary woman who preached to the Timbuctooans or some other heathen for 20 years and then came home in the same bonnet she had departed in. Think of not seeing a new hat for two or three years!

With lots and lots of love, I am,

Your loving daughter,
Emily

Sitka, February 25, 1875

Dear Aunt Annie,

I was very glad to get your letter. I have heard of your travels from Leavenworth and I do hope the trip will benefit Uncle Essick so much that my next letters from home will tell me he is feeling entirely well. Let me thank you, before I forget it, for sending me *The Spy*. I am ever so glad to get it, for it tells me all sorts of home news that folks never think of writing. I have got just the two nicest babies you ever saw in your life and it breaks my heart to think I can't have them at home when you could all admire them with me, for I know they would get enough attention to satisfy even me if I had them at Grandpa's. Bess is growing so fast you would not know her for the child that left Columbia in May.

You are such a devoted wanderer about woods, climber of hills, etc., I wish you were here to explore these wonderful forests that lay around us. Doctor says he would not believe it when we were told in Portland that it was actually an impossibility to get through the forests or to climb the mountains, but he finds on trying that it is the truth. It took him several hours to go a few hundred yards. Then he was as tired as if he had walked miles. It is the dense underbrush that makes it impossible to get through. Doctor says you cannot imagine what an intricate mess it is unless you see it — logs and fallen trees covered and matted up with that long moss. The fir trees are nearly all covered with the long hanging moss that looks like what I have seen brought from the South. The climate, the continuous warm (for it is never very cold here) rains are supposed to account for the condition of the woods. The foliage that does grow here grows luxuriantly and the rains keep the ground soft and marshy even on the mountains. This is a most wonderful country. You know Alaska consists of a chain of islands. All along the coast there is a chain of these impregnable mountains. Stories are brought by the Indians that beyond lies a beautiful country — flat, mild, and warm — and that corn and other things grow well, but no one knows. Some day, I suppose, it will be opened up and all sorts of wonders discovered. This island has had several gold mines discovered in it and other valuable minerals have been found. Some miners who had gone far up the Stickeen River, farther than white man had ever gone before, in search of gold veins tell of a most wonderful waterfall. They are reliable men and among the better class of miners. They say they could not see the top; it was lost in the clouds even though they climbed a great distance to discover it, and that long before the water reached the basin below, it broke into spray.

Enough of Alaska. I began to tell you about some ferns but got off the subject. Quantities of ferns grow here, nothing very different from what we find at home. If anything, they are coarser and not as pretty. We heard before we came here that we could get most beautiful varieties of seaweed but we have not seen any yet. I said to Doctor, "I am writing about wonderful Alaska." He said, "Tell Aunt Annie the most wonderful thing is this boy of ours." He is sitting up in the rocking chair now crowing and talking to his Papa and Bess in the noisiest manner. He is the purest, sweetest, plumpest little fellow. But I don't believe I want any more, not even "little Annie," for I am afraid we won't be able to educate them and bring them up as we would like to unless Doctor falls in with his gold mine. You and Uncle Essick are such travellers you might come to see us. You need not bring any of your good clothes.

Write to me often. Lots of love to Grandpa and Uncle Essick, in which Doctor joins me.

Your loving niece,
Emily FitzGerald

Friday
February 26, 1875

Dear Mamma,

We expect a steamer in about two weeks so I must have my letter ready. Bess walks out every bright day now and enjoys it ever so much. She doesn't want anyone's hand — likes to go it alone, but it is rather slow travelling. She stops to look at everything and wants to pick up every stick and stone she passes. The little Indian babies interest her very much. They are funny little things with their painted faces and hair trimmed off with feathers. I saw an old Indian the other day that gave me an idea. He had his hair, or rather his head, all covered with swan's down. You can't imagine how pretty it looked, ever so much prettier than powder on the haïr. It would be real pretty on a head dressed for a party.

I have done nothing, as yet, with the grebe skins I got, but I am going to have it made into trimming, if possible. Mrs. Campbell is expecting to be sick this month. Speaking of her reminds me of her furs. She has a handsome dark mink cloak, a long sort of cape. She wants this altered into a sack. A furrier she went to in New York told her there must be new skins for sleeves and he would not fix it for less than 150 dollars. So I guess the terms of the Portland furrier are not so high.

Sallie told me of a watch Uncle Owen got for a niece for 30 dollars. I never heard of such a thing. Do you suppose the works are perfect? I would be glad to give twice 30 for one, ever so plain, if the works were real good. I took my velvet sack out the other day, ripped out the sleeves, and folded it away again. I won't need it up here. My old blanket shawl is my greatest comfort.

March 6, 1875

I won't have much of a letter to send off if I don't hurry. I have just washed and dressed both babies. Bess looks so pretty; she is going to have a very good complexion. I think she looks very well now and has regained all the flesh she lost with her colds. Bertie is growing and is now old enough to want to be answered and to reach for everything he sees. I want to put him in short clothes in June.

The little steamer that belongs here just returned from another trip. Whitford told Doctor he had a lot of Indian curiosities and furs. I am going down to see after he gets them all off the boat. He has some fur seals. They are the first seal skins that have been here since we came.

Major Campbell is in Portland this month. He was ordered down by the last boat but will come up by the last of this month in the March *California*. Mrs. Campbell was in a dreadful way about his going. It was too bad, for she expects to be sick by the last of this month at the latest. We hope, though, that Major will be back before the event.

Monday
March 8, 1875

Bess is bothering the life out of me, but I am going to try to write a little, for I am afraid the boat will be in and my letter not ready. Bertie is asleep and Bess is amusing herself pulling me and everything else to pieces. She does something awful and I say to her, "Isn't Bessie going to be Mamma's good little girl?" She always says, "No," and then I say, "Doesn't Bessie love Mamma?" And she says, "No." Then I have to put her in a corner and she sometimes stays there five minutes before she will say she will be good.

Do you know I will be twenty-five tomorrow? Doctor handed me a five dollar gold piece yesterday and told me it was for my birthday. I think he must be getting rich. I don't know where all his gold pieces come from.

I was so glad to get the tape and pins you sent. Those things are so useful and I can't get any of those little things here unless I pay about five times as much as anywhere else and then they are very common. The little stores here don't have much to sell but bright calicos, ribbons, beads, etc., for the Indians. This will be a very uninteresting letter. Everybody here has been mourning over the little we have to tell in our letters. After the first letters in which everybody told all about Sitka, there seems to be little more to say.

You speak of sending Mary to Em Alexander. I wish I could. I had thought of that before. Em said while I was with her that if I got tired of having Mary she would take her off my hands. I thought some months ago of writing to her and asking if she was in earnest. If I was any place else, I would send Mary off home, even if it cost me all I had. But in spite of all the trouble she gives me, she does a good many things about the house that I would have to do myself and my hands are just as full as it is possible for them to be. If I was in Portland where I could get anyone to take her place, I wouldn't keep her with me an hour if Em Alexander would take her, but up here it will not be possible for me to get anyone. There is not a girl to be had on the whole island. The Russian girls are kept by the soldiers and positively refuse to work. If I sent to Portland for a girl, as Doctor has threatened to do several times, I would have to pay her passage up, which would be about 50 dollars (in coin, of course) and pay her the usual price for servants out on this coast (25 or 30 dollars), and then run the risk of getting some girl that would not be good to the children after all.

Mary is the greatest trial I ever had. Doctor says she is the devil, but, indeed, she is the most aggravating child I ever imagined there could be. I am never comfortable about her, never feel that she is doing as I want when my back is turned. She doesn't seem to feel at all that she must obey or try to please me. It is just a constant drag, drag, drag to keep her doing what I want and I am so tired of it. Why I wouldn't keep anybody in my house an hour that gave me so much trouble and so many heartaches (for I could cry about her often) if I was anywhere near her mother. She is so ugly to Bess. I really don't believe she knows how to amuse a child or take care of one. She gets so angry at Bess if Bess runs off or attempts to play a little when I send her (Mary) to do anything for her. You can't imagine how ugly she talks to her, right before me, too. If I tell her to stop, she makes a show of obeying for a second and then goes on as usual. Doctor says I am a goose to stand it. I should do as he does, box her ears good, he tells me. But I could not do that, so I send Mary out of the room and fix Bess myself. But see what trouble that gives me, for I most probably have the baby on my lap to begin with. I don't think I have ever sent Mary to put on Bess's things to take her out that she has not pulled and jerked the poor little toad until she has made her cry, "Hurtie, hurtie! Mamie hurtie Bessie." Bess does wriggle and twist sometimes and wants to turn her head when she is having her hair fixed and she doesn't hold her fingers all as stiff as she should to have her gloves put on. But to have this little vixen in my house that gets furious at my child and actually hurts her for doing such childish things as that makes me just boil over.

If I send Mary to do anything and say, "Mary, hurry," I sometimes have to tell her three and four times. Then when I do get her out of the room, I am just likely to open the door suddenly in four or five minutes and find her hanging out of the window or leaning back in a rocking chair enjoying herself — indeed, much more likely than to find her gone. To show you how impudent she is, she whistles ferociously and has come through the halls two or three times whistling noisily when there was company in the sitting room. You can imagine how it would sound in these thin-walled houses. I spoke to her about it and she did it again. Then I forbid it and said she should not whistle in the house. After that, she forgot and came in whistling. I said, "Mary, stop that. Don't you mean to obey at all?" She scarcely waited for me to finish talking, turned around, went out on the step, and began whistling vigorously. I called her back and said, "Mary, what do you mean? Didn't I tell you to stop whistling?" She said, "I wasn't whistling in the house." I will not write anymore about her. It is not any use and we are too far from each other for it to do any good.

March 9, 1875

Just as I expected, Mamma dear, here comes the steamer and I have not half as long a letter ready as I would like to send. Dr. Sterling just looked in a few moments ago to say it was in sight. [*Dr. F. S. Sterling, citizen physician, who relieved Dr. S. S. Boyer.*] I went out with the glasses and could see it way out on the Bay, a long line of dark smoke rising from a little black speck. The speck is the steamer! I am glad it is coming, for I will have some late news from home. I hope it will be good news. If you could only see Bess with her *Mother Goose* book, I know you would be pleased. She knows every picture, can find anything you ask for, and knows part of all the rhymes. "Little Pollie Flinders" that "sat among the cinders" is one of her intimate friends.

Someone tells Doctor the paymaster won't be up again before June. In that case, I won't be able to send the money I want to add to the 50 dollars until the paymaster comes.

Later in the day

Doctor has come up from the office with our mail. Two letters which I have just read are from you, the last one mailed the first week in February. I am glad you are all well and will be very much obliged for the shirts for Bertie. They will most probably come in our regular March boat which we expect in a few weeks.

I have told you so much about furs. I am afraid you are tired, but as you mention them again, I will too. I sent you by the last boat a letter from the furrier in Portland. I think I have told you all I know about the prices of furs up here. Silver fox, sable, and sea otter are much the handsomest but are all scarce, so any we want we must be on the look out for. I tell you this so if any of you should send for skins, you will understand that there may be some delay about getting them.

After you make up your mind that you want furs and what you want, I don't think you had better try to send any money.

I want to send all I save home and we can manage in some way to settle matters without sending so much money back and forward.

I hope when this letter reaches you that you will be feeling better than when you mailed your last to me. I pray with you, Mamma dear, that we may all live to meet again. I wish we could be sent over the country and the waters, too, by telegraph or in some other special manner. I want to go East again so much, but I dread the long, long journey. I don't think I was made for an army woman. I don't like change and travelling. Now I will say goodnight and will finish this in the morning before the mail closes.

Morning
March 10, 1875

Baby is tied into the pot chair so I will finish. I just wrote a letter to the furrier and asked him everything we care to know, so let us await further developments. I have not counted the number of packages as they came but have mentioned them to you by their contents. We are fortunate again in having someone send us a box of apples. I don't know who sent it, but it is a lovely box. The *California* will be up by the 25th. I wish we had two steamers every month. Did I tell you our cow is doing so nicely? We have plenty of milk and cream and I send some away almost daily. Ever since we got her, Doctor has fed two very ill men at the hospital on the milk. I am so glad she is a success. Milk is such a comfort.

Tell Sall to hurry up and have some babies. I am always seeing some little trifles everywhere that I think would please some little children. Up here I could pick up dollie hats and rattles and I have several little baskets that would be cute for a "little Case." Bess uses one for her workbasket and carries it around under her arm.

The baby is not as pretty a baby as Bess was. He looks rather heavy, but he has the loveliest eyes — great, dark, bright ones, and when he looks up at you, you can't help but see how sweet their expression is, for they are so bright. When he laughs, they twinkle and his lashes are much longer than Bess's are now and are very dark. I am thankful, if I have to have babies, that they are nice looking ones, though not handsome. Love to all. Doctor is waiting for this. The mail closes in less than an hour. Write often. We all join in love and kisses to you.

Your loving daughter,
Emily

P. S. Doctor is sitting in a big rocking chair with one baby on each knee. They seem to be having a merry time.

Sitka
March 14, 1875

Dear Mamma,

Don't you want a chapter on Indians? Maybe it will be interesting because these are the Indians we see every day and you can think of them in connection with us. This Sitka tribe lives, that is have their village, close by the Army Post. Most of the year, most of the tribe are away hunting and fishing. The village is a wretched looking place. I have not been in it yet because Doctor says it is too dirty, but I have looked over the stockade. It is just a collection of low, log cabins without windows or chimneys. A hole in the side answers for a door and a hole in the roof for a chimney. They build their fires in the middle of the house under the hole. Mrs. Campbell has the best view of them. One of her bedroom windows looks over the stockade and every morning she sees men, women, and children attending to the wants of nature on and among the rocks. They don't hesitate to hold up their blankets and expose all that is going on. They all wear blankets. The men and women have some sort of a garment under it; the men, a loose skirt coming about to the knees or a loose pair of drawers; the women, a loose dress; and the children wear nothing and all go barefooted the year round — now it is over snow and ice. Every morning the men take the children out and throw them into the cold water. The water is bitter cold here, so cold that none but Indians ever venture to bathe in it. They think it hardens them.

These Indians are more given to being industrious than any of the Southern tribes. They do a great deal of hunting and trapping, both this tribe and those North of us. There are stories of rich men among them (rich for Indians) who have gotten their wealth by trading and selling furs. They reckon their wealth in blankets as we would in greenbacks. Such a one is worth so many blankets, etc., whatever the number may be. Some of these Indians are bringing in wood now from the mountains around for the man who has the government contract. Anytime you go out at high tide you can see them at work, their canoes pulled half out of the water and filled with wood. Then the whole family — squaw, children, and slaves — carry these huge pieces of trees from the canoe to the place where they are to be piled. They can carry the most enormously heavy things you ever heard of. Even the girls and boys can shoulder and walk off with a log of wood that a big soldier would stagger under. All the rich men have slaves. Some are bought, but anyone among them who is friendless, has no blankets, no house, gun, etc., is made a slave by the nearest of his connections.

They burn their dead. I guess I have told you that. One of their customs is that the body must be taken up out of the hole in the roof. They never take it out the door. I have asked why they do this but no one seems to know. Then the body is taken up to the hillside back of the village, laid on a pile of wood, and the friends gather round and somebody lights the pole. The performance is, more or less, according to the rank of the fellow that's getting burned. The hill is quite covered with little wooden houses like dove cotes where they put the bones, ashes, or whatever is left after the cremation. The old Eastern Indians with their Great Spirit and happy hunting grounds had a much more exalted idea of the hereafter than these do. These tribes don't seem to have much of an idea of religion of any sort. The hereafter they expect is an existence much like the present, only without labor and with much feasting. They believe in evil spirits being able to interfere with them and have performances to propitiate these same. Then they worship some half dozen things. The whale is one, and the crow, I believe, is one of their evil spirits. They are a fearfully dishonest set and think it is a credit to them to be able to thieve successfully. Those that come around to our backdoors selling things carry off everything they can lay their hands on. Mrs. Field has had three hatchets carried away. They have taken a dipper, coffee pot, and tea cup from here. All were out on top of the water barrel (it stands just outside the kitchen door and we use big dippers with it). We got a new dipper, and one afternoon while Doctor and I were sitting here, Mary rushed in out of breath and said, "A squaw picked up our dipper and is running with all her might." Doctor dashed out the front way, which is the nearest to the gate of the stockade where a guard stands, and called to the guard to stop the squaw who was just rushing for the gate. He took possession of her and Doctor says a half dozen squaws gathered around gesticulating and talking at a great rate and some little Indian baby from the Indian side of the gate set up a yell. But Mrs. Squaw was marched off to the guardhouse and our dipper, which she had in her hand all the time, was brought home.

The great chiefs of the tribe are Ahnahoots (Ah-na-hoots) and Skinnie Eye, both warriors and, fortunately, friendly to the whites. They know of the fate of the Modocs! The greatest tyhee (rich man) of the tribe is Captain Jack, or Sitka Jack as he prefers to be called. He is worth four hundred blankets and has authority in the tribe on that account. Another of their customs is for the rich men of the tribe to give away all their wealth — distribute it among the rest of the tribe. If they do this, they become whatever is the Indian for canonized, and are sort of worshipped all the rest of their lives. Old Jack is about to go through this performance. He has built a little new house which is nearly finished and, as soon as it is done, he will have a grand *shin dig,* to distribute his blankets etc., and be immortalized for evermore. All the great chiefs of the tribes around are to be here and quite a number of Chilcat Indians. Jack is not a warrior; he is only a great tyhee.

They have a great many singular customs which, you know, are as law to them. One is about collecting debts. If a man won't pay his debt, the one he owes can watch his house early in the morning and when the first member of the family comes out for wood or water, he goes in and sits in the place where the fire is to be made. He must watch his chance and slip in before the second person comes out, or the charm is broken. He must watch, too, that no one sees him, or the family won't come out. After he has once gotten into the fireplace, he has things in his own hands. Their law won't allow his debtor to disturb him and he can starve the family out, or rather starve them in to settling the matter in some way, for they can't build their fire or cook their food and the neighbors won't help them.

A Chilcat chief with an unpronounceable name and a bullet hole through his cheek has been visiting these Indians for some weeks. He asked the Commanding Officer for a cap like this. Major Campbell, thinking to please him, got him a soldier's cap with all the fixings — crossed cannons, pompon, etc. — and it was presented, but the Chilcat was very indignant. He saw at once it was a soldier's cap and he wanted one fixed like the officer's. He took up one of the officer's caps and pointed to the bullion crossed cannons on it and then to the brass ones on his and was highly displeased. The officer (Mr. Quinan) whose cap he had asked him if he would like those on his cap. The chief said he would. So Mr. Quinan took them off and sewed them on the Indian's cap, much to his satisfaction, and he went off delighted. But I hear he has come back again for a blouse!

March 19, 1875

A few days ago some miners came from some of the islands to the North and reported a man missing. It was a miner who had built himself a cabin at a little place about 16 miles from here called Warm Springs where he meant to winter. These miners stopped to see him and found him gone. They feared he had been killed by the Indians or, perhaps, had been frozen while hunting in the mountains. Mr. Goddard, with a couple of soldiers and men, went up on Tuesday to see if anything could be discovered of his whereabouts, but they were unsuccessful. Mr. Goddard says the springs are hot and that they found, some distance from the cabin, a parcel of burnt human bones which they thought might have something to do with the lost miner but which turned out to be a cremated Indian. Among the bones was one they did not recognize, but upon examination it proved to be a clay pipe.

This morning Doctor went over to the Indian market which is just inside the stockade gate. While he was there, he heard a great screaming and talking farther up the village and he saw one of the traders here going up, so he went with him. An old Indian man had cut his throat. Some Indians, who had been fishing, had found washed up on some beach between this and the hot springs the pieces of a canoe and some other things that belonged to the lost miner. So it is probable that these three Indians (brothers), who had started up in that direction a few days ago in a canoe, and this miner, who was on friendly terms with them, had started for here together and the canoe had capsized. The old Indian father, when he heard his three sons were drowned, ran out into the rising tide and cut his throat.

Doctor says I would be amazed to see how they live in those little Indian cabins. They only have one room in them with a fire in the middle and they sleep in the bunks around the sides, thirty and forty in one cabin. These Indians call all Americans "Boston Man," and all English (Hudson Bay Company men etc.) "King George Man." I will finish this letter with an Indian story.

The wharf here is built over the hulk of an old sunken ship and this is the story. Some years ago a Boston built whaling vessel went up north of this, somewhere about Cook's Inlet, and the mate, for some reason, went on shore where he was cruelly murdered by the Indians. The captain of the whaler was determined to be revenged for the loss of his good mate, so he went out to sea, rigged his vessel differently, made all the changes in its appearance he could, armed his men, and loaded everything on board in the way of a gun up to the muzzle. Then he put back for the region they had just left and where they had lost their mate. When he came near the shore, he made signs to the Indians to come out and trade which, not recognizing the ship, they were not loathe to do and soon came around him, canoes full of them to a great number. Then came the revenge. Every gun on board was fired into them, again and again, killing, wounding, sinking the canoes, and putting an end to them generally. Then they sailed away and left the remaining Indians to ponder over the matter and decide whether it would be the wisest plan to dispose of the next white man that trusted himself among them, as they had done with the poor mate of the whaler. The captain brought his ship here and sold it to the Russians who used it for various purposes. It was turned over to our government at the time of the transfer but, by that time, the stout Boston built vessel was beginning to feel and look the worse for the wear. When a foundation for a new wharf was wanted, no one hesitated about taking the old ship that had taken such an active part in a tragedy and filling it with rocks and sinking it to build the new wharf over.

Emily.

March 18, 1875

Dear Mamma,

This is such a lovely morning. I wish you could see Sitka on such a one. We are waiting for breakfast. You can imagine what a lazy cook we have when I tell you that we wait every morning and that I bathe the baby before breakfast every day. Our man won't come early in the morning and we have to bear it because we can't get anyone else to take his place. Isn't it too bad? And we give him such enormous wages!

Bertie is growing and Bess is just as full of mischief as ever. She can't let things alone. Bertie had a bad fall yesterday. We tied him into the pot chair with a diaper and, leaning forward on it, his weight must have made the knot slip. It gave way and he fell suddenly flat on his face. Poor little dear, I thought his nose was broken, but he did not seem hurt much. His lip is still a little swollen. The blow came on that. He is certainly the best baby. He sleeps so well at night and sometimes goes off to sleep sitting up in my lap. He is really an easy baby to take care of. I would be awfully hard to please now in getting a nurse. I know no one could care for either of them as I do.

After breakfast

Bertie is still asleep so I will write on. I am going to treat myself to some books, *Chance Acquaintance* and *A Foregone Conclusion* by Howells. I see them so highly spoken of in Appleton's and other magazines and I like all I have read by him so much. His style is so refined and aristocratic, if that word will do to apply to books. Doctor gave me a 5 dollar gold piece on my birthday and I am going to send three dollars of it by this mail to the publishing house for the two books I mentioned. I would so like to gather nice books around me, but I am always thinking of their weight and the room they take up in packing, crowding out actually necessary things. I am going to have some standard books, the books that one often wants to refer to. I have a pretty copy of Longfellow and am going to get one of Tennyson, bound plainly, and will gradually get enough to fill a nice little shelf which I will carry with me.

Last evening I had our small garrison spend the evening with us. Bess and Bertie went off to sleep and we had a pleasant evening. Between nine and ten o'clock I had fruit cake, sponge cake, some lovely coffee with real cream, and some candy (little lady apples) too. We expect the steamer now in less than a week; that is the one event of our lives, as you know.

Bess is a specimen! For some months she has been playing "Turn Out The Guard," a cry she hears from the guard house fifty times a day. When the officer (whoever it is) doesn't want the guard turned out, he calls out, "Never mind the guard," which Bess, with a stick over her shoulder, abbreviated to "Mine gaud." Doctor said her grandmother would be shocked at her profanity. She would go around crying out at the top of her voice, "Mine gaud. Mine gaud." Lately I have been teaching her "Now I Lay me down to sleep," but she evidently gets things confused, for the last week or so she has been singing to dear Fannie, "Turn out de gaud my soul to keep."

Sunday, March 21, 1875

Today everybody is on the lookout for the steamer. I do wish it would come, for I want some letters so much. We are going to have for dessert today that Bavarian cream you sent me the recipe for at West Point. I couldn't make such lovely things unless we had a cow. When you have to buy milk it would cost too much to use up cream by the pint, but the Bavarian cream is splendid. I made it yesterday evening and Doctor and I ate one dish full before we went to bed. Some of these days soon, after I send you some more money, I am going to get you to send me some gelatine. We have to pay 50 cents silver for the little boxes that I gave one dollar for 4 at West Point, and that was greenbacks, too. The mail will bring them safely and the postage will be very little, I know. When I send for them, you might get the storekeeper to put them up for you to save you the trouble. I never knew how much I loved jelly. Some German Jewish wine dealer here, a nice old man, who (sensible man) thought Doctor did not charge him enough for medical attendance, sent him a lot of fine brandy and old, old "London Club" sherry wine. I wish I could send you a bottle. I remember you have a fondness for sherry. I think it is horrid unless in fruit cake or jelly.

March 22, 1875

We have just come in from dinner. While we were taking our coffee, Noah brought in a little girl who said she wanted to see me. It was the Russian tailor's little girl and she had a fur collar her father wanted me to buy. Such a collar! It would have done for only great-grandmother, but the fur was lovely and was beaver. I never dreamed of it being so handsome. It was very dark, sort of lead color, very thick and soft. I exclaimed at once what a lovely fur sack it would make.

I asked Doctor to go to see the tailor who had sent that cape around and ask him what he would charge for making a beaver sack. I believe he can tan and do the work nicely enough for a common fur. He told Doctor half in Russian and half in English that he would find furs and silk and make a sack for 45 (coin) dollars. Doctor says it would be handsome in a sack but thinks too warm, as it is a closer, thicker fur than seal skin.

Morning
March 24, 1875

The steamer came in this morning. Mary (who, by the way, has been doing better for the last ten days than ever before so that I have hopes of better things) came in before I was up and said the boat was in. Doctor got the mail before breakfast, but he got me a brandy punch first, though, for this waiting for Noah's time for breakfast is awful. We will have a grand end up soon. This morning I got up with the babies at half past six, as I always have to, and did not get breakfast until nine.

I will try to go on now without any more wanderings off. Major Campbell came back on the boat. I am so glad. Mrs. Campbell was so much worried and expects to be sick now any hour. Mrs. Quinan heard, or rather I don't know whether she has heard it yet, but news has come of her mother's death. Her mother had been ill for a long time and we have been expecting to hear for months that the end had come. Still it is sad, sad news to get way out here where there is no possibility of getting home, no matter what the news is. I got two letters from you and the little shirts. They are so nice and I think I can do without any more. Thank you very much.

I must hurry up this letter. The steamer only stays until evening and I want to write a note besides. I began writing some weeks ago and started to tell you about the Indians and found I had so much to tell that I began this letter independently so as not to mix up the Indian stuff with these little home matters. I must tell you about Bess's blocks. She tore up one of those books of alphabet pictures Aunt Annie sent her and I saved the pictures, for they were so bright. Doctor got one of the men to make a lot of blocks just the size of the pictures, about an inch and a half high. Last night we pasted the pictures on the blocks and you can't imagine what a nice lot they are. Bess is delighted. They are such nice building blocks besides the pictures.

[*Doctor FitzGerald continues the letter at this point.*]

Em had to leave just here to pacify the babies and prays me to finish. The steamer got in this morning and will leave tonight, so we are all in commotion and already tired of it. I have nothing to tell you but of the splendid babies we have. Emily is in the best of health. If anything, she is better even that at any time since our marriage. The babies both have colds. Bess is as smart as we could wish her to be and Herbert is still the best baby I ever knew and one of the finest specimens one could wish to see. I am very sorry we can't exhibit this compound of McCorkle and FitzGerald.

Please remember me to Sallie and Brainard. We hope if they go West that it will be to the satisfaction of yourself with the rest. I have long been intending to write to Brainard but somehow I have failed without being able to say why.

I join Emily in love to you all. We would be very glad to hear from Bep.

Yours very sincerely,
J. A. FitzGerald

Sitka, March 31, 1875

Dear Mamma,

Two such babies as I have got. They are specimens! Bess is dreadful and Doctor and I hold daily consultations to know what to do with her. She is so cute and so little that we hate to punish her, but she hasn't the least idea of doing what you tell her. She takes anything she wants to take, no matter what we say, and holds on to it until we actually start to go to her. Then she drops it, or oftener throws it away, and says, "Don't pank me." I am afraid by punishing her so much we will make her afraid and tell stories when we ask what she has been doing. Indeed, this part of having babies isn't any fun. I never thought about my responsibilities in this direction before. I am so afraid of doing something or leaving something undone that would influence her disposition in the future. I hope you will pray that your children may bring up your grandchildren in the right way in everything.

Friday, April 2, 1875

We had Bessie's hair cut short again last night. She looks so cute. Long hair is pretty on children but they don't appreciate having it fixed or keeping it fixed. Bess actually fights when we fix hers, so I mean to keep it cut short until she is eight or ten years old. Anything but a head full of long hair all tumbled up.

Quotations from *Mother Goose* are always in Bess's mouth. She knows everything in it. When she gets awake in the morning, she says her favorites in bed before I take her up. Yesterday Doctor lectured her about something. I took her up to comfort her and said, "Papa loves Bessie dearly." With her eyes full of tears she said, "Thank you, kind sir. I hear very clearly."

Buzzer is the biggest thing you ever saw. He is nearly six months old now and I will put him in short clothes as soon as I get some shoes. He has entirely kicked out all his socks. The last pair are rags. I can't send for more, for by the time I could get them I wouldn't need them. But for number three I will provide more. Little bare toes up here in the cold (this is the coldest month we have had this winter) are not very comfortable. When Bertie's socks gave out, I thought I would put the little stockings on him that Bess wore with her short clothes. I got them but found they would not go on his toes and, would you believe it, the little white stockings you bought for Bess last summer just before we left Columbia are small for him.

Bertie is devoted to Bess's dollie and it breaks her heart to have him eat it. He is big enough to want something to play with. The next time you are in the city near one of those knit dollie stores I wish you would get me one of those little knit boys dressed like a Zouave. It would be nice for him if you could find one.

Mrs. Campbell has a little son three days old. It is the least little mite of a fellow. She is doing nicely but misses, as I did, the attention of home friends while she has to lie in bed.

April 3, 1875

Doctor has gone and done it! Last night he came in and said, "There is the loveliest silver fox skin downtown I ever saw in my life. Just the one was brought in this afternoon. Now, if you say so, I will get it." I did not say so, for I don't know whether I want silver fox or not and I told him we could not afford it now and all such things. But he was in love with it and said that I might get what I pleased but he would give me a muff and boa of silver fox, for we would not be likely to get such a one again. But 30 dollars seems so much — that is nearly 34 in greenbacks — and I said, "No." I thought the matter was decided, but before I was dressed this morning he came in and said, "You possess a handsome silver fox." It is hanging up in front of me now. It is lovely, so long and soft, and looks just like silver grey hair. I guess now I will have my velvet sack trimmed with it instead of sable, though I believe I like the sable best. I don't know what I want!

By the way, Doctor thinks a little muff of otter with a trimming for cloth cloak would be so pretty and serviceable for Bess. Otter is real dark, soft fur and cheap. There is an otter skin down at the store now that is large enough to make Bess a muff and trimming, and also a muff and trimming for me. The skin is worth six dollars, as it is a very large one. The ordinary price is 4 dollars.

April 6, 1875

Baby is getting two teeth. He is a little fretful but, indeed, you never heard of such a good boy as he is. He never cries while I am washing and dressing him and I put him into a tub of water every morning. Then when he wakens from his naps he is so good. He lies in his crib and plays with his feet and sometimes I leave him lie for a half hour before I go near him. Mrs. Quinan says, "What makes him always smell so sweet?" I expect he will be as great a mischief as Bess is when he can walk, but I am so thankful he is good now. I am constantly busy with them, but Doctor said the other day the trouble they give me arises from their overflowing with health and spirits and is much easier to bear than if I was worrying with sick, ailing childen.

Mary sent her mother some little baskets in a package and three dollars in a letter by the last boat. Tell Barbara to write to Mary as soon as she gets them, for Mary is anxious to know if they are received. You will be delighted to hear, as I am to tell you, that I think and hope we have at last found Mary's sphere. She has been cooking for two weeks and is much pleased with kitchen work and we are pleased with her. I told you of the trouble we had with Noah. It was breaking us up to pay him what we did and he was so lazy and dirty. His clothes (and self) smelled so, that when he came in to change the dishes on the table it would spoil our dinner. Mary said she could cook and often said, "Mrs. FitzGerald, I wish I could cook instead of what I do," but I never thought of it in earnest. Her sitting around worried me not a little and I was often bothered to know what to give her to keep her busy, for I long ago relieved her of all care of the children except at meal times and she is much easier to manage if busy. Noah got worse and worse, breakfast at ten o'clock, etc., and Doctor said he could stand it no longer, so we concluded to try Mary before looking for a Russian woman. She does very nicely and I do believe is happier and I have to correct her less than I ever have before. She cooks meats and most of the things we can get here nicely and is anxious to learn more. I have been showing her about some puddings and things and I think that she will make a nice cook after a little while. Of course, she has a great deal to learn and gets things in confusion occasionally, but it is such an improvement on Noah and so much better than we expected from Mary that we are happy. Then we are so nice and clean. You know dirt is not one of Mary's failings. She likes to clean up and keep clean. I told her I would give her a five dollar gold piece every month and go on clothing her as usual. She can save the money and she is delighted. I don't think she expected I would give her anything, but she is kept pretty busy and deserves the money. She sweeps our four rooms once a week, cooks our two meals, and washes the diapers. All our family washing and ironing are done out. The wood and water are brought by soldiers to the back door, so none of her work is hard, but it keeps her busy. She is anxious that you and her mother should know how well she is doing and how much we are pleased with her. So won't you make it a point to see Barbara and tell her? Indeed, it is such a relief to have her do so nicely. I am getting along with the babies but get very tired and am looking for a nice little girl to play with Bess and hold baby at meal times. Now the good little fellow sits in the carriage like a little man and crows at us all through the meal.

April 7, 1875

Mrs. Smith, the nice laundress that was with me when Bertie was born, was with Mrs. Campbell just as she was with me for the nights and the baby's bath, etc. She got sick the other night at Mrs. Campbell's, could scarcely be gotten home in morning, and is now quite ill. Mrs. Campbell can get along much better than I could have done, for she has two children, ten and twelve years old, who can help and play with the baby. She has also had Linda, a nice colored girl nurse, for years, though Mrs. Smith says that Doctor was worth all Mrs. Campbell's helpers put together. So Mrs. Campbell can get along; her worst time is over. Mrs. Field, who has no little babies of her own, has been attending to the baby's bath and feedings, but Mrs. Smith has no one to stay with her. There is no woman she can get and her husband has been excused from soldier's usual work to stay with her. Mrs. Campbell would pay anything for a nurse just now. I would be glad to do anything for poor Mrs. Smith, but here I am — tied to my babies. I can't even get up to see her unless Doctor stays at home, and I know his going to see her does much more good than mine. Mrs. Campbell, who has known her for years and would nurse her herself, is laid up in bed with a baby. This is a dreadful place!

I have been worrying all morning about the baby's clothes. He ought to go right into short clothes but he has no socks and his clothes are all too small for him and he has no shoes. I went to every shop in the place this morning and can find nothing. When those I asked you to send do come, I am afraid they will be too small, for his feet are so fat. What shall I do? Even that question you can't answer for more than three months. If I even send to Portland for shoes by the next boat, I can't get them even from there until the last of May. This place is too far from everything and every place. I wish the President and Congress would sit a term here and have one mail a month. Furs don't compensate! That reminds me of my silver fox. Captain Field and Mrs. Field came in this morning to see it. They wanted to compare it with theirs. Mrs. Field's cost eight dollars less than mine and I think Doctor was a very extravagant man to buy the one he did. But I am tired of hearing so much about furs. Doctor says I have written you so much about furs, and every time I have written I have told you I liked a different one, so that now you don't know what in the world to decide on for yourself. Whatever you do want, he will do his best to get the finest of the kind and I am going to get your muff.

Friday, April 9, 1875

Mamma, I want a whole lot of things but I don't have the money ready to send for them. The paymaster has not been up since December, so there is lots due. But that doesn't help me any now when I want some things. At the shortest, I can't get them for ages, for if I wait until he does come, it will be ages more. He won't be up on this boat, but we hope on the next and then I will send you 25 dollars more than the sum I want to put in the bank. If that doesn't pay for all, you must straighten matters up and cut off my list and wants until I can send you some more.

Later

Now I will tell you what I want and you can get them when you can and make out my bills. I want a pair of dark corsets. I think I take 22 inches. Nothing very nice, for you know I am nursing. I guess you might send me two pairs, if they are cheap. Then I want some gelatine. If it is cheaper by the dozen, get me a dozen. If not, invest about 2 dollars in it for me. Then I want lots of things for the children — shoes, stockings, shirts, leggings, mittens, and dresses for them both. Now, are you horrified? But indeed I am so thankful that I have you to send to, for I would not know what to do about them out here. I don't want these things only in time for fall. You know we always have damp, chill weather here, though it is never very cold, but I will have to keep the children in warm clothes all the year round.

I want you to be on the lookout and get me half a dozen pairs of woolen stockings for each of them. Yon can't imagine how cold our floors are and, of course, the chill goes right through the shoes and stockings to the little feet. I guess it always pays to buy the best woolen stockings you can find, doesn't it? Also send me something to darn them with. I will send the length of both little feet in this letter. Then allow for four months' growth. Doctor says, "Don't send for short stockings. They should come up over the knees."

Mamma, I am troubling you a great deal, I know, but I am perfectly helpless here and I do want the children to be comfortable and nice. Thinking over what I have written for, I am sure my bills will be much nearer 50 dollars than 25, so I will send more than I intended at first.

Morning
April 10, 1875

I wrote that last with about a thousand interruptions, but I hope I have been definite. That is all I need to say about the things I want, only you know the children don't need any best clothes up here. All that is necessary is that I have them nice and comfortable for home. There is no chance to dress them up for any occasion. When they go out, I have to think only of their being warm and dry. No one will see them but a few Indians and Russians.

I forgot I want a pair of slippers for myself, a big size 3½. Then I want some big, white common buttons to button Bessie's drawers. They cost 25 cents a dozen here and I have gotten cards of them for that in the East.

April 16, 1875

This long letter has been entirely about my wants and I have troubled you with a thousand. I won't mention another one for fear I set you wild.

I take Bertie out every pleasant day and Bess is quite willing to let him have the carriage. She is delighted to walk. Two old squaws stopped us on the boardwalk the other morning and made signs to let them see the baby. We stopped and they were mighty tickled by the way he was dressed up. His little mittens seems to please the most. They would point to them and laugh and talk to each other about them, and then point to them again and smilingly nod to me.

Sunday, April 18, 1875

Much to our surprise and delight, an hour ago the steamer was seen coming in. It is the first time since we have been here that it has come in before the 20th. I told Doctor that I was going to tell Mamma the steamer was coming in. He laughed at me and said you would enjoy hearing about it in three months.

Evening

I have just read your letters and find so many things in them to speak about I will have to let it go over to the next boat. First, I must thank you for the packages. The books for Bess, the dresses, little skirt band, and mittens arrived. The books are very lovely, too pretty to let her play with for common. I will put them with some of the others that I have rescued and let her have them on state occasions. She was delighted with them tonight and said, "Grandma sent them to Bessie," but the delight of her heart is the pair of red mittens. She put them on as soon as they arrived and on no account would allow them to be taken off until she went to bed. And I know they will be the first thing asked for in the morning. The little dresses are lovely. I did not expect them, and meant to let Bess get along with what she has until fall, but these fit her nicely and I am glad to get them. When the money I send doesn't pay all, let me know at once.

This boat brings the news that the next steamer (May) will bring the paymaster. So, if nothing happens, in my next letter I will send a check for 140 dollars, the 100 to put in the bank and the 40 for you to pay for the things I send for. If that doesn't cover all, I would still rather not touch the hundred dollars but will send 25 dollars more in the next boat.

Monday Morning
April 19, 1875

The steamer leaves today, so I must say all I have to say now. Thank you very much for all you have sent me. The packages of papers arrived.

You loving daughter,
Emily

Sitka,
April 22, 1875

Dear Mamma,

The boat just departed a little while ago but I have some more things I wanted to tell you, so I will begin my letter for the next. I did not tell you in my first letter that I had received a letter from Bep. I will answer it soon. I heard from Aunt Pace, too, by the last mail.

Mary is in the notion of saving her money to help her mother. I hope she will keep in the notion, for when she spends, she buys such foolish things. She is doing much better in the kitchen than in the nursery, but it is an awful trial any place. A year from this time when we go back to Portland, if

Em Alexander will take her, I will be glad to hand her over. I can't well send her down now for a great many reasons. She can do what she is doing now pretty well and I hope will soon do it much better.

April 30, 1875

We are having long, long days now and short nights. At eight in the evening we can read fine print on the porch and long before four this morning it was as light as it is now. Bess has been playing out of doors quite a good deal lately. I have let her out even when it was damp and rainy, for she gets nearly frantic if I keep her in. She is well bundled up in waterproof and rubbers. Her chief delight is to dig in the sand with a couple of little old tin pans she has. If I send you the money in this letter as I expect to, I wish you would send Bess half a dozen little patty pans in the next package you send me.

Mrs. Field says Bess plays like an older child. I wish you could see Bess eat. She so insisted upon having a fork that I got out my little old one marked *Emily* and she performs with it over her potatoes and meat. But she has the most singular appetite for a child. All milk and foods she should take she won't touch, and to feed her is force work. She is such a mischief. Indeed, she is dreadful. I just thought yesterday afternoon I would go wild if she didn't grow up soon and behave herself. Doctor had gone out. Mary was doing some fixing up I wanted done in the dining room. Bess was restless and I had to speak to her a thousand times. Soon I thought from some sounds I heard that Mary wasn't doing what she should in the dining room, so I laid Bertie on the bed and went to see. Bess broke as soon as the hall door was opened and ran out the front door into the rain. She would not come back and I had to go out for her and carry her in. Then after a little while I had to speak to Mary again and opened the door with Bertie on my arm. I scarcely had the knob turned until Bess was out again. I ran after her and caught her on the porch, came into the sitting room dragging her and carrying the baby, and sat down, a little out of beath, to nurse him. She ran on through

— out into the nursery. So I soon called, "Bess, what are you doing?" There was no answer so I called again. Still no answer. Then I said, "Bess, do you want Mamma to whip your little bottom hard?" Then she said, "No." I said, "Then you come to me this minute." "I'm coming," said Bess, but she didn't. Very indignantly I called again. Then a little voice just at the door said, "I am coming." I looked up and there she was peeping around the side of the door at me, the most comical little laughing face you ever saw with the baby's little lace, pink-lined cap on top of her head with the pink side out.

I had to stop writing a while ago to go to her. She had emptied my work-basket of its contents and was filling it with the dirt Mary had just swept in a pile in the hall. I was too indignant to laugh at her. It meant all the little sacks, caps, and such fixings that I keep nicely pinned up in towels, etc., were spread out on the floor. So I told Miss FitzGerald to go stand in a corner. She went quite willingly but in a moment danced out and said, "Tain't a nice corner. I go nuzzer corner." I made her go back and then such a performance began that you would have had to laugh yourself. She put her head against the wall and tried to see how far she could run her feet out. Then she danced up and down, and at last got to spitting to see how big a pile of spit she could make on the floor. Between all these performances she would say, "I be good girl, Mamma. Come out a corner."

May 4, 1875

This is a lovely day, the first pleasant one we have had for a long time. I took both the children out this morning. Usually Bess asks to go down to the beach the first thing after she is awake in the morning. She delights in picking up clam shells and filling them with sand.

Bertie is such a nice baby. I am in so much of a hurry to see how he will look in his short clothes, I can scarcely wait. He was six months old last week and has two little teeth just through.

The boat will bring six or seven officers for a court martial and I expect they will have to be entertained. I only hope some married men who have babies at home will fall to my share. One of the officers here has been getting into trouble half a dozen times lately and this Court, I guess, will settle him and he will be dismissed from the service. He is such a handsome fellow. I feel sorry for him, but he is so given to drink. He would as lief be court martialed as not.

May 6, 1875

This is another lovely day. I have been out with the children all morning. We went down to the hospital for Doctor and he walked with us out the road. One of the storekeepers here got a wonderful (?) supply of goods and you ought to see the excitement among the Indians and boys over the unpacking in front of the store. In our walk today I could scarcely get past the boxes and Indians. I was in hopes he had gotten some nice things I want, like a nice, plain table cloth, some little shoes for Bertie, and two or three more things, but there is no hope of getting such things here. I wish you could see the shoes the storekeeper thought would be lovely for my baby — velveteen with high heels. The table covers looked like some printing I have seen on balmoral skirts.

Doctor made an investment the night the goods were first unpacked — a little China cup and saucer, a cream jug, and a sugar bowl about as big as a walnut — and he paid 50 cents for the three pieces. I said, "Doctor FitzGerald, I could get a whole tea set as big as that for 25 cents in the East," but he said, "They will please Bess, and it is all he has for her." But he made a worse investment than that yesterday. He came in with his arms full of poles and things and said he had gotten something so nice for "Buzzer,' and then displayed a baby jumper, or rather a baby swing, for it does nothing but swing from poles fastened at the top. A little upholstered seat or chair swings from the middle. It is a horrid thing and he paid 10 dollars for it. I succeeded in making him think he had made a very foolish purchase. Then I felt sorry I had said so much and told him it was lovely!

May 9, 1875

This is a most beautiful Sunday morning. I have had a little walk and feel quite spring-like. Such an important event has transpired in our family that I must tell it. Mr. Herbert Fitz-Gerald is at this moment in the care of a Russian nurse! I am a little pulled down and tired fussing with the children. Doctor got concerned and started off, determined to find someone who could hold baby and run after Bessie, and he got a woman who has just come this morning. She seems like a pleasant, clean woman and both children take to her. Bertie was not a bit strange. She is a married woman and has a little girl of her own whom she leaves at home with her husband. But she can't speak anything but Russian. I hope she will do. I am awfully tired worrying with the babies. It is such a horrible feeling to think that there is no one to do things but yourself, and that you can't do anything you please, or count on any certain time. Bess is more trouble than Bertie, for she is into everything. I expect both the children will be talking Russian soon!

Yesterday we got two lovely swan skins, the biggest I ever saw. I will have enough swan's down to trim you all up when I come home. I don't think it is so awfully pretty, but it is cheap and will trim little sacks for the children prettily. I do hope our spring weather has begun. How I hate the rains, not so much because they keep me from going out, but because everything is so dreary and makes one feel blue. A lovely silver fox skin was offered yesterday but they wanted too much for it — 50 dollars! The same men told Doctor that the one he has is a finer skin than theirs. I want marten and I don't feel like investing any more in silver fox. I am awfully tired of Sitka and won't be sorry to move if my babies are well.

Everything is so different from what we are accustomed to in the East. Bethel would enjoy it, too. I thought of him when I was on the beach yesterday. How he would enjoy wandering about when the tide is out! We find so many funny, curious things: little fish in the pools of water, rocks just covered with limpets, clam beds, sea worms, shells, etc. The shells are not pretty and do not have the bright colors the shells found in Southern waters always have, but I have a handful put in a little basket to send you, not because they are worth having, but they are Alaskan shells and Bess and I have picked them up for you. To see how much better they did when we got them than they do now, you will have to put them in water.

May 13, 1875

Bess plays out of doors all day these pleasant days. I keep the front and back gates shut or Miss Bess runs off. She is not afraid of anybody or anything. I put Bessie's old blue waterproof, leggings, rubbers, and red mittens on her and she is in for a romp and tumble. She and Robbie Field are out on the front porch playing with what Bessie calls her "Baby deer." I wish you could see this "baby deer." It is a little fawn stuffed with grass. Doctor says it has never been born but was probably found in some doe when they had killed her. It is beautifully spotted, about as big as a cat, but all legs. I bought it from an Indian because Bess wanted it. Doctor declares it is disgusting. He and Bess have lots of discussions over it. She thinks it is lovely. He suggests she call the pups and throw the "baby deer" over the fence to them if she wants to see some fun. The pups are three bull pups belonging to the young officers and are the terror of the post. They tear everything up they get hold of: chickens, robes, door mats, etc.

Last night I saw sea otter for the first time. Doctor is in love with the fur, but I am disappointed. It looks to me just like a beautiful soft, black seal skin, only thicker and longer, but it is not what I expected. The animal is enormous, is shaped something like a beaver, and is more than two yards long. The man has four skins, but he asks 75 dollars a skin for them.

My Russian woman continues to be nice with baby. She isn't much use to Bess as she can't understand what Bess wants, but it is such a help and relief to have Bertie held when he wants to be, instead of taking him myself. And she does seem real kind and gentle.

May 16, 1875

Our boat arrived yesteday and leaves this noon. I have not had a minute to write this before. A Doctor Smith came up to relieve Dr. Sterling and he has his wife and baby with him. Of course they had to come here until they can get their quarters fixed. We liked Dr. Sterling. I can't tell how sorry I am to lose him. This sort of thing is always such a pity at a small post.

I did not even get to read your letters, which I always read first, until after ten o'clock last night. I pulled the packages open and, much to my distress, found there were no shoes for Bertie in it. But if ever you saw or heard of a delighted child, it is Bess with her dust pan and brush. She took it to bed with her and asked for it the first thing this morning. Now she is sweeping up the pieces of string and paper on the floor. And, Mamma, the little dresses are lovely. They all fit her, just as nicely as possible. The little wrappers are so cute and fit beautifully.

I am so distressed to have to wait for another boat to send you the money. The paymaster did not come and Doctor can not get me any money in Sitka. You know there are no banks here or any place to get money. Don't get any more of my things until you get the check, and let my money, when it comes, pay you for all you have spent for us in the meantime. I would never write for all these things, Mamma, without sending the money right along, but you see how we are fixed.

I am glad I received Sallie's letter and will write soon. The steamer came before I had Bep's letter written but I will send it next boat. I have not heard from Em Alexander for some time but hear indirectly through this Dr. Smith, who was at Vancouver, that they are all well. Thank you for the papers you sent us.

Later

I have a headache and I want to lie down, but I heard Doctor say the mail closed at five, and it is after four, so I will send my love and say goodbye. Lots of love to all. Write soon and often.

Ever and always,
Your loving daughter,
Emily FitzGerald

Sitka, May 23, 1875

Dear Mamma,

Last Sunday we were taken up with the boat's departure and the Smiths. Today we are calm again and I will begin a letter. Russian Mary is just putting Bertie to sleep. He is in short clothes and has been for three days. I am still in distress about his feet. I have an old, half-worn pair of Bessie's shoes and I brought them downstairs thinking I might tie them on to his feet in some way. They were twice as long as his feet but, would you believe it, the buttons would not meet by a good inch around his ankle! I never saw such puddings as his feet are. Now what will I do with him? Even if the shoes do come on the June boat, they won't go on his feet! Now he is flourishing moccasins! Doctor says it is a reversion. Bertie has just gone into Bessie's old clothes. You would be amazed to see how the things Bess has just left off fit him.

The Russian woman I have is really very nice. She is only useful to me about him, though. Bess doesn't understand her or she Bess, so I have to do all Bessie's wants myself. Mary (the Russian — I am bound to have all Marys) is particularly kind with Bertie and he evidently likes her very much. Bess is growing so fast. She can't keep clean to save her life. She must handle everything she sees, and the fires we are obliged to keep up all the time are so dirty. You can't imagine the dust and black coals we are sweeping up all the time. Bess gets dirtier than other children, I think. For one thing, she has no nurse, no one to look particularly after her. Another thing — the washing is badly done and expensive.

Sunday, May 30, 1875

We have been very dissipated at Sitka this last week and I feel sleepy this morning. Doctor has gone to inspection, and I expect you are all at church. Bertie is sleeping, and Bess is wandering about seeking what she can reach, and what she can't, she gets with a chair. Mrs. Quinan has been nearly the death of us this week with poker playing. She and Mr. Quinan came in here Monday evening and Doctor and Mr. Quinan got to playing some games of cards. At last they suggested we come and learn to play poker. Mrs. Quinan was so pleased and excited with it, she would not go home until twelve o'clock. The next night, after the babies were asleep, she almost dragged Doctor and me into Mrs. Field's. The next night she brought Captain Field and Mr. Quinan in here. Then last night she wanted us to come to her house. Doctor said, "For heaven's sake, give us a rest. Let up on poker," but about eight o'clock she ran in and said they were all coming. So about nine o'clock Doctor and I went in for a little while. You must remember it is light enough for us to read on our porches now at ten o'clock, so it doesn't seem so late.

Soon after we went into Mrs. Quinan's, Mrs. Campbell was sent word that her baby was crying, so she bid us all good night and left. A little later she walked in again and said she just came back to see how it would feel to be walking about after ten o'clock. Then this morning Doctor wanted to be wakened early. As the light wakened me, I got up to see the time. The sun was shining brightly and I found it was twenty minutes past three!

For the last two weeks I have been drinking Stout and am getting quite fond of the bitter taste. Doctor Sterling gave me three flowers when he left which, for barren Sitka, are quite a treasure — a big pink, a rose geranium, and a fuchsia. My window looks fresh and green.

We are expecting all sorts of excitement in the next few weeks. First, General Howard is out on an inspection tour and has his whole family (his wife and five children) with him.

Then we expect Major Rucker, the paymaster, with his wife and baby. We know they will all be so disgusted with the ship, though they expect to stay on it, that they will have to be taken off and entertained. Next, the Court that did not come on the last steamer is due to arrive on the June boat. Nine officers are expected, and Dr. Bailey, the chief of our Corps in this Department, is one of them. Then, the last boat brought rumors that a new company is on the way here. We heard that a new Commanding Officer will relieve Major Campbell. If this happens, we will all have to move. Major Campbell will probably take our quarters. If so, we will take those next door. The Quinans will move to the next house, etc.

Then another thing I am concerned about now is disposing of Mary. I am going to write to Em Alexander by this boat and see if she will take her, Doctor insists that I do. Indeed, she is a trial. She cannot cook enough for us to depend upon her, but then you never can depend upon her. She talks too much and thinks she knows everything.

Monday, May 31, 1875

I did not finish yesterday. Doctor wanted me to walk with him and after that I was tired and did not feel like writing. I was going to give you a chapter on Mary. I hope this will be the last, for if Em Alexander will take her, I will send her down at once. Indeed, she gives me more worry than she does help, and I believe the relief of mind when she is off from us will be the most comfortable feeling I shall have known for months. Don't tell her mother about what I am writing, for if Mary goes to Em, she may improve, and it will save Barbara's feelings. Mary has quarreled with so many people that she has come to contact with since we left home, and it is just because she talks too much and is so silly. She screeches and screams like a hyena and Doctor declares she is the "missing link." She is really the noisiest person I ever heard. I did not think anybody could make the hideous sounds she can. But my greatest trouble now is her not being reliable.

I have told you the sort of place we are in up here, and

Mary has never proved herself to be a girl I can trust to go where she pleased. So I do not allow her to go out anywhere without me or Doctor. But she does not mind me. She runs out for a few minutes whenever she thinks I won't find out. I have gone to the kitchen two or three times in the last week, after the work was done, to have a little milk heated for Bess, or something of the kind, and Mary was missing. Every time she was off, out of sight and call. One time I heard her voice way up by a post where there is a guard. She was screeching and screaming at this soldier; I felt I could whip her myself, but it would not do any good. She doesn't take all her expeditions when the work is all done either! I went out to the kitchen a night or two ago. The things were all standing and Mary was gone. I looked for her and saw her way up the road jumping rope with my new white clothes line. Then she went out one night when we thought she was in bed. Doctor locked the back of the house (it was before the evenings were light) and after nine o'clock Mary came gently in the front door. I called her in, questioned her, and found she had been down the road all evening talking to some men. Doctor wanted to whip her, but I would not let him.

These things may seem little and absurd, but they are constant, and I am always in terror for fear she will do something that will ruin her. And I know Doctor would turn her out of the house then, no matter what I would say. Not one of all these men here is too good to get her into trouble. She is not bad that way, I am sure, but she is a fool. And she does try in this silly, giddy way of hers to attract the men's attention. She calls them by their names and throws things at them and stops them. You know there are soldiers constantly coming to the house for various purposes. Doctor has told her so many times that these men would take all she says and does to them as encouragement to get her into trouble, but Mary knows more than anybody else. She was very indignant at Doctor for scolding her because she talked to the men. Several times he came upon her very suddenly when she was doing that.

Last week something happened that proved Doctor was right. I hoped it would give Mary a lesson, but these last few days, she is as bad as ever. A week ago, a soldier (rather a better man than the common run of soldiers — he was also a barber) came to our kitchen a little drunk and talked to Mary in a very ugly manner. He offered to keep her, told her she knocked about with the other men, and if she stuck to him alone, she would not want for anything. He tried to catch her and hold her. He came back a second time, but it was not till then that she came in and asked me to make him leave the kitchen. I told Doctor, who was home at the time, and he was indignant that a soldier should come into his house in that condition. He had the man arrested at once and put in the guardhouse. This little fool of a Mary would not tell me what the soldier had said or done to her until I threatened to punish her if she did not. I believe she thought it was all fun, for she said she could take care of herself, wasn't afraid of the men, etc. Well, the soldier, who is quite popular among the men and officers, was tried the next day by the Court, and Mary was sent for as a witness to prove he had been in the kitchen and interfered with her work. Then, to weaken her testimony, some soldiers, the barber's friends, came forward to prove that she was a bad girl and encouraged the men. The soldier himself said she came to the gate and invited him in on the afternoon in question. I am sure, and so is Doctor, that Mary's story is true and that her doings are only wild and silly — not bad — but see how it looks to the men. It came out at the trial that she has been down to the soldier's barber shop at night. (I never knew it; how she has deceived me!) One man, a clerk in the office where I have sent her sometimes, said she put her arms around his neck and said she would like to get married. Another said that she had caught hold of him. And there were similar stories.

I am so disgusted with her, for though the stories are exaggerated, there is some foundation for them all. I told her she should not leave the yard for six weeks, and if she did without permission, I would not give her one cent of her money this month and Doctor should whip her. Doctor got me a man to go to the baker's and for the other matters that would take Mary down among the men, who all tease and joke with her. But instead of being pleased, she is very indignant and thinks me very hard to keep her in that way. I wish she was in heaven! I will miss her in some ways — fixing the fires, washing the windows, etc., — and it will cost about 50 dollars to send her down. But if Em will take her, that is wants her (I won't have her take her unless she really does) I will tell Em the truth. I think she would do much better for Em than she does for me. This is enough of an unpleasant subject. If Em wants her, she will have her before your answer to this reaches me.

Sunday, June 6, 1875

For the last week we have had such lovely weather that even Sitka seemed charming. Today it is beautiful. Bess is out playing on the parade ground. I got her a little Indian sundown and trimmed it with a dark piece of blue ribbon which you sent me for her hair. She thinks it is lovely and is wearing it now. Today looks summerlike and pleasant. The whole month has been a delightful one to me. Russian Mary has relieved me in taking care of Bertie, and I have been out a great deal with Doctor.

About two weeks ago he had a croquet set made for me by some old Russian. It is a real nice set, and as it is the only set at the post, we have enjoyed it ever so much. Doctor says, "Anything to get you out of doors!" Yesterday afternoon Mr. Quinan, Doctor, Mrs. Quinan, and I played all afternoon and had a real merry time. We played down in the hospital yard and I have been taking Bess down with me, as I could not well leave her at home.

I have had some of the most beautiful walks this last few weeks through these wonderful woods. I enjoyed them so much because I have been out so little and I always did like hunting about in woods and brush. Then this place is so different from anything I ever imagined. The ground is like a sponge when you walk on it. But for the most part, we are climbing over and along old tree trunks and stumps, twice as big as the old poplars, and all covered with moss. Every now and then we would find ourselves in the loveliest little place, dark as could be from the dense fir branches and the long hanging moss. The fallen tree trunks are piled up one on another. I think it is very wild, but Doctor says this is notning compared to the forests a little beyond and on the mountainsides. The object of our walks has been to get to Indian River, the loveliest stream you ever saw or can imagine. I never did see such clear water. It is from 30 to 40 feet wide and not very deep, but it is so clear that you can see through it and count the stones on the bottom. Wild flowers are scarce, but we find lovely mosses. I have been so delighted with one variety that I have gone twice to one particular spot in a damp, dark place out by Indian River to get it. It has a stem three inches long and a big leaf of lovely fine moss. It looks like a little tree, but it is only pretty when wet. It dries fast and then looks horrid. I have a little, deep dish full of it on the table, and you would be surprised to see how it sucks up the water — capillary attraction, I suppose. The stems are in the water and the moss leaves keep wet all the time and even drip. It is the coolest feeling stuff I ever came across. I thought first I would try to send some home, but I fear it would not be a credit to the Sitka moss by the time it got to you.

June 10, 1875

I must add a line, though Doctor laughs at me, to say that the steamer is (there goes its gun) coming. It is so lovely to hear, though I always have a little heartache with my delight for fear my news will not all be good. You should see the condition we are all in. The post people are all talking to each other and looking at the steamer, and the entire population of Sitka is lining the street and wharf. It is nearly nine o'clock and I am writing here at the desk comfortably.

June 11, 1875

We have had such a time! The boat came in last night about half past nine. On it were the Court (nine officers), General and Mrs. Howard and their five children, Captain and Mrs. Wilkinson and their two children, and another officer. I did not get to open my letters until 11 o'clock and then only opened your last one to see if you were all alive and well. I did not read them until today. The people prefer sleeping on the boat (much to our delight), but they are in and out all the time. Thank fortune the paymaster has come. I will send you money by this letter.

The trimming and shoes arrived. The shoes are nice and just what I sent for, but the little buff ones will have to wait for *number three!*

Monday, June 14, 1875

I have been so busy, I have not had a moment to write. We have all had lots of company. The people all came off the boat and had to be entertained. The paymaster, Major Rucker, (Doctor knew him very well in Portland) has been with us ever since the boat arrived. Also, Captain Wilkinson, Mrs. Wilkinson, and their children spent yesterday with us, so we had to have dinner for eight. With my babies and poor help, I have had my hands full. Four gentlemen will lunch here today, two will dine, and then, I am happy to say, we will rest. The boat leaves tonight and Mrs. Campbell is going to finish up by having all twenty-three people at her house this evening. She has just sent to me for napkins. This having people every meal makes the napkins scarce.

I send in this letter a check for 450 dollars. Please put 400 dollars in the bank in my name. Ten out of the other 50 dollars Mary sends to her mother for a present, and 40 dollars I send to you to pay my bills. I hold another 10 to send you if you want it, and I think you will need it.

Your loving daughter,
Emily

Sitka, June 27, 1875
Sunday Morning

Dear Mamma,

I thought I would write a long letter today and speak of half a dozen things I forgot in my last, but I guess I won't accomplish it, as I have a perfect hospital. Doctor is very uncomfortable with a cold, and Bess and Bert have the worst colds I ever knew children to have. Bess coughs dreadfully, and poor Bert's nose is almost wiped off.

Miss Mary has been performing again. Doctor gave her a whipping, the second, a few days ago. I believe she would be better if it had been the second hundred. I wanted to put it off, hoping I could get rid of her and wanting to bear her until then, but she is too impudent and disrespectful and is altogether horrid. The morning she got punished she was as impudent as possible and actually laughed at me, as much as to say, "You can't make me," when I told her she must come back and say over to me something she had said in a very disrespectful manner. Then she vented her anger at me on poor Bess and spoke to her right before me in a way I would never speak even to a servant. I told her if she did a certain thing again I would have Doctor whip her, and she deliberately did it under my very nose, comforting herself, I suppose, that she had often been promised whippings (as I am goose enough to have been afraid she would be hurt and, as I usually do, interfere and save her). But Doctor came in just then, fortunately, and did whip her good. He was awfully angry at her and declares he will keep it up until she is conquered.

The scene after the whipping was too funny, if it had not been so dreadful. Doctor gave Mary a few slaps and she ran away from him and slammed the door. He called to her to come back and shut it without slamming. She would not come, so he walked after her with Bertie on his arm and gave her a few more slaps. Her howls were awful. Bess nearly broke her heart, and I could scarcely keep her out of the room. As soon as Doctor came in Bess rushed at him and, with tears all over her face, said, "Please, Papa, don't go to Mamy again." Bert set up a cry at the commotion and I felt so sorry, I almost cried, too. I sent Mary up to her room and she went up, wailing at the top of her voice, "Lord, have mercy on my soul." Doctor said, "That's right, Mary, only you need not make so much noise about it. He can hear you if you whisper." After a while I went upstairs, expecting to find her subdued and to offer a little consolation, but I found her rebellious. She sat on the bed and swayed backwards and forwards and would not listen to me at all. She said she wished the Lord would take her (so did I) and then she wished the devil would take her. Then she said she was going to write to her mother this minute. I told her I wished that she would write and give her mother a true account of the morning, but she need not expect any sympathy from her mother in her disobedience, as she had told us to whip her if she did not obey. Miss Mary's answer was, "Darn my mother. Darn her." So I got up and said I thought the Doctor had better come up and speak to her. That had some effect, for she knew he would whip her again. So she came to. If Em Alexander doesn't want her, what shall I do? She is too big to whip and I am afraid the poor, misguided fool will do something desperate — like running away. I don't believe I mentioned it, but the Russian nurse I have, who is so kind to baby, has left once and almost a second time on Mary's account, but she has come back when Doctor has promised her that she should not be troubled again. Mary teases her.

June 29, 1875

We had such a time with the Court! I was going to tell you about it and General Howard, but though I could tell you lots, it does not seem worth writing about. The officers on the Court were all very pleasant; we knew some of them before. Major Rucker was with us all the time, and Captain Wilkinson and several others came to meals. The Indians were so interested in General Howard's visit (they call him "The Big Chief from Washington") that they did not bring us as much game as usual and we, of course, wanted more. So now and then we were quite exercised to know what to do. One afternoon Mrs.

Field came in and said that her gentlemen were all going to Mrs. Campbell's for dinner and she was going to save the dinner she intended having that night until the next day. I said one of my gentlemen would be at Mrs. Campbell's but Major Rucker would be having dinner with us. She exclaimed that he was invited to the dinner at Mrs. Campbell's. She knew, because they meant to dine the whole Court and Major Rucker, being president of the Court, certainly was invited. She said, "Indeed, I know he is going there. Mrs. Campbell mentioned his name, so you better save your dinner as I have done." On the strength of this, I went out and had the venison roast put away and said we would have sort of a tea — bacon, and omelet, etc. A few minutes before tea, in walked Major Rucker for his dinner. I said, "Aren't you going to Mrs. Campbell's?" But he had never heard of her invitation, so he dined on bacon, etc. The next day he found he had been invited. Mrs. Campbell had a big dinner and only two came to eat it.

General Howard has come to command this department. He is just fresh from that investigation in Washington into his doings in the Freedmans Bureau transaction. Some people think he came out of it with glory, and some don't. I have heard the officers discuss him and he is not very popular among them. It is owing to his ferocious religion. He is one of those unfortunate Christians who continually gives outsiders a chance to laugh and have something to make fun of. He says himself, "You know, I am a fanatic on the subject." He is an ordained preacher and preaches and leads meetings on all occasions — on street corners, steamboats, etc. General Howard is an excellent speaker, has a charming voice, and uses beautiful language, but he does all his good in such a queer way, he gives people something to smile at. About eleven o'clock the night the boat came in, Captain Hayes, the old Captain of the *California*, came in to the steps to shake hands with me. I said, "Well, Captain, you brought us a crowd this time." He said, dropping his voice, "Mrs. FitzGerald, the knees are worn out of every pair of pants I got praying."

Wilkinson also leads religious meetings, but he does not have General Howard's brains. On the boat on the way up here, he felt called upon to give his experience. One night on deck, he rose up and said someone had asked him how he had found his saviour, etc. He wrung his hands and wept and went through a performance that Major Rucker, who is a good church member himself, says was ridiculous. Captain Wilkinson said to me, "You know, I am a ranting religionist!"

July 1, 1875

The colds are all better, but the poor babies have had awful sieges. Bess is so hard to amuse. Her dollies are the only things she doesn't get tired of. She has a perfect hospital corps of them.

Mrs. Field is expecting to be confined in a few weeks. I feel so sorry for her, as there is no help to be gotten here and I know what I went through. Mrs. Campbell's boy is growing and mine is an elephant. General Howard saw Bess and Bert on the floor together and said, "Twins?" He was so struck with the big fellow, he spoke of it two or three times. Bert isn't clumsy big, either, but he is a bright splendid boy.

Did I tell you that the check I sent in my last letter was not my savings? Mine would not amount to that in a long time, but Doctor did not need a couple of hundred he had here, and as there are no banks here, he told me I had better send it with mine to the bank at home. And did I tell you he had insured his life for another 5,000 dollars, in the New York Mutual this time? It sort of frightens me, his making such a point of it, for fear he may think that he is not strong. But I know it is the right thing to do for the babies' sake, though I hope and pray he may pay the interest on it many years.

I must write another fur chapter. Mrs. Campbell says she is so tired of hearing about furs, she doesn't want to have any or see any. Every time any furs arrive, the prices are different from what we expected. So if someone gets a handsome skin for so much and we make up our minds that we can afford to give that much, then the next skin that is offered is sure to be five or ten dollars higher!

Now for my fur chapter. A little schooner came in a few days ago with a few furs. It had been up to the Aleutian Islands and some men on board had invested in some sea otter. Doctor got one of them to let him (Dr.) bring them up to show me. I don't wonder they are thought handsome. Nothing can compare with it for softness and thick fur. The one I admired most had that beautiful silver gray appearance that is so handsome in the silver fox. The man had refused four hundred dollars for that skin. Another skin, which was nearly black, was said to be the most valuable. Then someone told Doctor that one of the men on the schooner had the best ermine that had been seen here for some time. Doctor saw them and wanted to get the whole lot — one hundred skins — but I induced him to think before he would be such an extravagant creature. What under the sun would we do with 100 ermine when we did not have fifty dollars in the house? I was glad to have a few to make something for Bess, so Doctor took 25 for 50 cents a skin. Then Mrs. Campbell took 25. They are No. 1 ermine and a little Russian tailor who is an authority on furs says what we paid is a fair price. They are not cheap but they are worth that. But he says, "In Russia for such skins you get anything you ask." Twenty-five skins will more than make a muff and cloak trimming.

July 4, 1875

Before I forget it, I want to ask you to save some of those pretty little wine glasses and decanters for me. You know it is almost a necessary part of military performances to have something of that kind about and I have seen two or three sets lately that were very much admired and that were not nearly so handsome as those of yours. What has put these things in my mind was a little lunch I had last night. The garrison spent the evening with me. We had a pleasant time and the babies were perfection. Mary behaved charmingly and everything was good but the coffee.

By this mail I am going to send Bep a pair of walrus ivory sleeve buttons. There is a pair for Sallie, too. I send them to Bep to give to her as I had gotten his pair ready to send first. Then Doctor got the second pair for me to send to Sallie. Tell Bep these are genuine walrus. The tusks are brought here by Indians that got them and these buttons are turned by an old man in Sitka. I don't think they are very pretty, but they will have come from Alaska. I will try to send canes home to Brainard and Uncle Essick. The canes from here are made of Alaskan crab with ivory tops and are right pretty. Don't some of you want a land otter skin? The fur is pretty. They are offered here much more frequently than the more expensive skins—sea otter, fox, etc.

Today is July 4th. Just a year ago on July 2nd we got to Portland. How time flies! Just think, if nothing happens, in less than a year from now we will be in Portland again. Then we won't seem nearly so far away.

If we are all well, what a nice little Christmas we can have this year. The babies will be at such a nice age to enjoy a little tree. Bess will be nearly three and Bert will be over one.

Sunday, July 11, 1875

This is such a lovely day. We are delighted with Sitka. Doctor has gone off on an expedition to some place north of this called the Redoubt. He won't be back until night. Mr. Quinan, a trader named Philipson, and Doctor went in a sailboat with the boat's crew. I did not want him to go because it was Sunday, but both he and Mr. Quinan thought they might not have another opportunity and were anxious to go before fall. Major Campbell expected to go but could not get off. They took their guns and fishing tackle, so they will make a pleasure excursion out of it.

We expected to celebrate the fourth of July by having an Indian war dance on the parade grounds, but it rained so hard they could not have it, much to our sorrow. They promise to go through the performance one evening soon. Mrs. Campbell had us all over there to spend the evening and we played poker and ate ice cream. See how civilized Sitka is! Mrs. Field is expecting to be sick daily, so she did not go.

A night or two ago Doctor and Mrs. Quinan insisted upon my going boating; you know that I hate it. There is a little boat here that belongs to the post and Doctor is out often. Mrs. Quinan is too, almost daily. I went, and indeed I enjoyed it more than I expected. The night was beautiful and I knew both my babies were fast asleep. We went around visiting some of the islands in the bay and found shells, flowers, etc. Our greatest fun was fishing. We took a trolling line with us and caught some enormous sea bass. We nearly ran into a shoal of porpoises, or rather, they nearly ran into us! I wish you could see them jump and tumble. Doctor tried to fire a shot into them, but they got out of reach before he could get his gun from the end of the boat. Fish of all sorts abound here. You can buy a salmon for a bit. I went on the beach the other day with the babies just as the salmon boats were coming. There were three and all were full. On one boat, I saw a pile with about four hundred fish.

We are very much in advance of you people. We actually have cremations up here. Yesterday Mr. Dyer called me to come to a place where we could see over the Indian stockade and I beheld one. The framework they build was all in a bright blaze and you could hear the crackling of the burning flesh. Mourners were sitting around and one individual was poking the fire while another piled on the fuel. Horrible idea, isn't it, to think of bodies we love being destroyed in that way? Doctor advocates it strongly, though, as a sanitary measure, and I suppose we who believe in the immortality of the soul should not have a horror of it.

I have some little pieces of pretty moss that are nearly two months old. When I found them the other day, they were dry. So I thought I would see if they would freshen up. I threw them into a basin of water for about five minutes and found they were actually nearly as pretty as ever, so I am going to try to send some for you to see. Just freshen it this way and then shake the water off the moss. If you put it in a shallow dish where the water can reach the lower part of the moss leaf and keep the dish full of water, it will keep fresh for ages. Let it lay in the water fully five or ten minutes before you shake it out and put it in a dish. If you think it is pretty, I will send some more when it grows larger. You can see by the brown leaves how it looks when it is full grown. Mrs. Field has pressed some and put it on little cardboard boxes, and it is lovely. I do hope when you wet it that this moss will show how pretty it is so you won't think I have exaggerated.

Later

Just as I had written about the moss, someone came in and announced that the steamer will be here in a few hours. I will finish this after reading my letters.

Monday Morning
July 12, 1875

Three letters arrived from you, one with the photograph and the two next to it. Thank you for the stockings, shoes, gelatine, and syringe. They all came in a nice condition. Your photograph is very good and I am so glad to have it. I wish you would tell me in your next letter what all the things you have sent in these bundles cost and what I owe you for the things that had been sent before. I would like to know if I only could, so I could guess how far that 40 dollars was going to go.

July 13, 1875

Em Alexander doesn't want Mary! I am sorry, but I did not feel at all certain that she would take her. I am going to begin over with her now, and she must obey or be punished.

Mrs. Field had a son yesterday morning. I will write more if I can, but if the steamer leaves this morning, I will mail this with lots of love from us all. John says, "Tell Mamma the photograph is lovely."

Your daughter,
Emily

P. S. Your photograph pleased Bess very much and she kissed it so violently she almost ruined it. I took it from her but she wept and I let her hold it again. Then she looked at it and said, "What old do think she is?" I said, "She is a little older than your Mamma, but 'what' old do you think she is?" She said, "I think two months."

July 14, 1875

I meant to look over my home letter and speak of several things you mention, but I have not had time. My Russian nurse left me the day the steamer came in. She and Mary had some fuss in the kitchen. I don't know what, but it has, of course, thrown Bertie onto my hands again.

Have you heard of the wreck of the *Saranac*? (It is a man of war.) It was on its way to Sitka and, in one of the narrow channels, struck the rocks and was entirely out of sight in an hour. It sank right down; the bottom was knocked entirely out of it. The officers turned it into the rocks on one side of the channel and got all the men on to them before she sunk. Four hundred souls! But they saved nothing — lost all the guns, ammunition, baggage, provisions, etc. It was a hundred miles north of any settlements and they were without food for two days.

P. S. Emily is busy for the moment and says for me to sign her name and say good bye again. With love to all, we hope that you are all well. Our babies are lovely.

J. A. F.

Sitka, July 25, 1875

Dear Mamma,

Two weeks ago today the steamer came in, and in two weeks more we can look for another. I told you the shoes had arrived. You sent me the sizes I asked for exactly. I want you to send me another dollie for Bessie, about as big as the one you sent her last winter. Poor Fannie has left us for good. Her head had caved in, but she was still admired until a week ago when she was lost in the grass. When found, Fannie was a mass of mildew.

August 1, 1875

It does seem to me my letter to you grows very slowly. Before I forget it, I want to tell you I think I will have to have little flannel tights for Bess for winter. She is so thin and we have so much chilly, damp weather, I think we will have to put them on her to keep her warm.

Isn't it too bad our lives have to be worried out of us about little money matters? I don't need or want for anything, but our income is limited and it takes nearly all of it every month to live on, so I constantly am planning and thinking what I can afford and what I cannot and all such things, which are annoying, to say the least. The grebe skins I invested in last winter are white elephants. I don't know what to do with them. They look too pretty to throw away and I am afraid they are not worth sending to the furrier.

The fate of the *Wright* has been unknown for so long. Various means have been used to see if anything could be found out about it, and now it has almost been proved beyond doubt that it struck some rocks near Prince of Wales Island and sunk in the night. Lots of the cargo she carried has been washed ashore in that region. Lately, other things have been found. The remains of Major Walker have been found, at least everybody has reason to think they are his. The remains of a man, that is the bones, were found on a sandy little island. A few brass buttons, a part of a military sleeve, and some cuff buttons prove them to have been his. The body had been tied to a spar. Nothing is so horrible to me as an account of a shipwreck. What I was going to tell was about the English squadron and the old admiral's prompt measures to aid the wrecked crew. After the crew of the *Saranac* took refuge on the rocks, two or three officers started off in a little boat to go down to Victoria (an English town on Vancouver Island) for help. They got there, after considerable suffering, and chartered the *Otter,* a little English coast steamer, which started at once to take off the crew. The English squadron was then lying at Victoria. The Admiral, an old man, Cockburn I think his name is, was breakfasting at his hotel and read of the wreck in the morning papers. He was quite indignant that the American naval officers had not applied immediately to him, but that did not interfere with his acting. He signaled to one of his ships to prepare for sea, and in an hour's time, she was off. Then he signaled to his own ship, an enormous vessel with a crew of eight hundred, and in a few hours was on it and on his way to the scene of disaster. Both of his ships got there within a few hours after the *Otter,* which had taken off the men, but that did not lessen the admiration we all feel for the Admiral for his haste to aid our people.

August 4, 1875

Doctor went off this morning for his tramp up the mountains. It is the first time in his life he has ever left me alone at home overnight without him. I am not afraid, but I feel anxious about him as it is such a wild, rough country, and he and the others are going where no white men have ever been, as far as is known. But it is just the sort of tramps that great, strong men like the Doctor, who have been accustomed since their boyhood to lots of exercise and moving about, delight in.

I have just washed and put away some salmon berries. Did you ever see any? They do look so nice and are the only fruit we see, but I am so afraid of them. The Indians pick them, and they are so filthy dirty. I got a few this morning and did not like to trust even my Russian cook to wash them. They are something like a raspberry and something like a blackberry, not being quite as sweet and good as either. This time last year we were just about leaving Portland and had the most delightful fruit. Here we don't see any.

August 7, 1875

I have been troubled for the last week with my eyes. Doctor says I have tried them by reading and sewing those long, light evenings we have had. He has put a stop to my doing anything! My writing up and finishing my letters is the only thing he excepted. And as we expect the boat within the next three days, I must write up. You never knew a child as young as Bess to have such an idea of dress as she has. Do you know she will almost break her heart to have on some particular dress she thinks is pretty, and she is just as particular about the way she wants her hair fixed as you and I are. I can get her to do anything I want if I promise her a new ribbon, or shoes, or some such thing. She won't let me decide which of the dresses is the prettiest to wear. Miss FitzGerald has her own ideas about it. I hated to put on that pretty blue wrapper you sent for fear the horrible washing here would ruin it, much to Bessie's disgust. She asked for it every time she saw it. At last I said she should have it when the sun shone brightly. A few days ago she said, "Please, Mamma, dress me. Put on my blue dress. The sun is shining. See, Mamma, see. I won't get it dirty. I be careful." She got it on because I could not say no. I want plenty of nice clothes for both babies when we go down to Portland next summer. We will see a great many people and I want the children to have lovely things.

August 11, 1875

Bertie has seven teeth and can say *Doctor*. He says it very plainly and is so pleased with himself about it. He stands straight up, holding by one hand. Don't you think that is smart for a baby his age? This is such a lovely day, one of the few bright ones. I do hope the steamer will come; it was due yesterday. I am always so anxious to get my mail; indeed, we all are. Mrs. Campbell says she has a Christmas every time the boat comes in. You can't imagine how we enjoy opening our bundles and packages, even if they are things we have sent for and know exactly what is coming out of them. I have not been writing as much in this letter as I wanted to on account of the trouble with my eyes. Doctor told me not to write long now, but I have the hardest kind of a time sitting around doing nothing.

August 14, 1875

Still no steamer! It has been so early in the month for the last three or four that we expected it to be early this month, too. This waiting for it is horrible. It spoils the days and makes everything disgusting. I will be so glad to leave Sitka.

The children have been so much trouble this last few days because it has rained and we have had to stay in the house. Bert will get into the slop bucket and the pot and will eat everything he can find — string — sticks, and dirt of all sorts. Bess will open all the drawers and put the contents on the floor. Now she has gotten a new wrinkle. She runs off and goes to some of the neighbor's houses. I have had to whip her for it two or three times. Poor little dear, she is only a baby and ought to be cared for and watched like a baby, but I have to let her amuse herself so much, though I always try to keep her in sight. If Miss Mary was only worth two cents, she might help me with the children, but as far as help about them is concerned, she might as well be in heaven or the other place! I even hate to send her to change Bessie's shoes or give her a drink. She is so ugly and cross and rough. Indeed, I would like to shake her. She gets provoked and angry at everything the children do and vents it on them in pushes and pulls and jerks, etc. She can work well, if she has a mind to, and keeps the house looking respectable, but it is sort of driving all the time. I would rather not have her about, if there was any possible way out of it. She is too big to whip. She is smart — I wish you could hear her talk — but she is such a fool!

We are all wondering why the boat doesn't come. Potatoes have given out and we have not had lard and two or three other things for a week. We want some money, too! How I wish I could look for some people on it as well as for my mail and bundles. Last night after the babies got off, I lay on the sofa waiting for Doctor to come in. I got nearly into a doze when Doctor came in. I told him I had sort of half dreamed and half imagined that someone woke me by kissing me and I had found you sitting by the fire and that the steamer had come in while I was sleeping and brought you. Doctor said he could kiss me, but he was sorry he could not bring the other part about.

My eyes still worry me. I have not done anything at all in the way of reading, sewing, or writing, and that is one reason that the steamer's not coming is so hard to bear. There is nothing alarming the matter with them, but John says I must rest them entirely.

August 20, 1875

The steamer has been in sight for an hour. Now that it has come, I am sort of afraid of the news it may bring. I have never been so anxious for one and am sure I will feel a great weight off my mind when I get my mail and see your writing on the envelopes. Bess has gone with her Papa to see the steamer arrive. This morning she came to me and said, "I want my grandmamma to send me a parasol on the boat." I don't know what put it into her head, but I believe she thinks everything she has, came from Grandmamma "on the boat." Poor child, she needs an umbrella more here, if she needs anything of the kind. I will make her a parasol out of paper that will answer all her purposes.

Later

Got our mail all right! I had four letters from you, all short ones, and in the last you tell me you received the check. I am glad it arrived, as I want my debts paid and want to feel I have a little in the bank. You have the receipts for the amount in the bank, I suppose. Tell me how you do yearly about the interest. I will feel very good when I have five hundred dollars in a bank. The checks are safe enough. No bank in the world would cash the check unless Doctor was known. You only get it done in Columbia because you are well known and they know he is your son-in-law, and if the check was lost (Doctor always keeps the number; so does the paymaster) after a certain length of time, he could get another one, and the risk is not much. You do not mention the 10 dollars for Mary's mother, Barbara. Be particular about it, please. Let me know what money was paid out for the gelatine, syringe, the stockings, etc. I never can understand how you get so much with so little money, but please tell me what everything costs.

You are awfully good about supplying my wants, but I wish you would keep a list of them and every time I write a new one, put it on the list. We count up how long it will take for anything we send for to come, and then if it doesn't come, we are disappointed, for our mails are our only excitement, you know.

Sunday
August 22, 1875

I was busy all day yesterday with company. Lots of people came up on the boat and I did not get to tell you about them when I wrote before. Mr. and Mrs. Boyle (army people we knew in Portland) spent yesterday with us. Major Cress from Vancouver lunched with us and tells us Em Alexander has a little girl at last and the Doctor is as proud as can be. Mr. and Mrs. Hammond were also on the boat. He is Reverend Edward Payson Hammond, the celebrated street preacher. The people who have come up with them on the boat say Mrs. Hammond is charming, a refined, lovely woman, but he is rough and noisy. Mrs. Hammond is always giving him little pulls and punches trying to restrain him, but after one of his queer performances, she said to Mrs. Boyle, "You might as well talk to the wind as to Edward." We at Sitka are doomed to have the queer Christians, but I do think Mr. Hammond is in earnest. First General Howard and Mr. Wilkinson, now Mr. Hammond. To say the least, Mr. Hammond has a very embarrassing way. He rushes at you in the midst of a crowd and says, "Do you love Jesus?" If you say, "No," you catch it. And if you say, "Yes," it is even worse! There is such a rejoicing made over you that you feel like sinking. It isn't very pleasant!

Major Boyle, Major Cress, Colonel Wood (the Adjutant-General of the Department), Colonel Bachelder (the Chief of Medical of the Department), and several other officers came on the boat. They are some sort of a board.

Bertie is almost sick with a cold. I have written this last page almost a line at a time. I don't want to let him on the floor today and have him shut up in his crib. Bess is playing about him and Mary has gone to hear Mr. Hammond preach. I wish he would move her!

Doctor has gone up Silver Bay to the gold mines with all the crowd of officers I mentioned. He would have stayed at home just because he knows I don't like him to make expeditions on Sunday, but they came up after him last night after eleven o'clock and talked at him for an hour about it. I do hope they will get home all right. They went in a horrid old boat.

I am the happy possessor of a box of apples. They are lovely early apples. Doctor found there were three boxes on the boat and had one sent up for me. He always thinks about little things of that kind and tries to satisfy all my wishes that he knows and can.

I am so afraid the stockings you will send Bertie will be too small for him. It is his fat foot that is the trouble. Mrs. Boyle had his moccasin and stocking off ever so many times yesterday to see his foot. She thinks it is the cutest thing she ever saw and says it breathes and looks as if it was something alive — not a foot. I must stop writing and go to Bertie. Lots of love to all.

Your loving daughter,
Emily FitzGerald

Sitka, August 27, 1875

Dear Mamma,

Both babies are playing on the floor and I will begin my letter. The boat left last Sunday. This is Friday. Bess and Bert have had such awful colds. Poor Bert thinks a handkerchief was made for his special torture. They are better now. I had my turn with them, but Bess, as usual, had the most alarming time.

Please get me some samples of flannel that would be pretty for a wrapper. All the ladies here are getting flannel wrappers and I want one, too. Get three or four samples that you think are pretty and send them with the price. Tell me how many yards it would take to make a wrapper with a Watteau back.

I want a flannel that will wash, but I want it to look nice for steamboat travel.

September 5, 1875

This is our first bright day for a long time. Major Boyle did not return on the steamer with his family but waited here on some business and, of course, can't get away until the boat comes again. He is the most disgusted man you ever saw and says, "I don't want any more Sitka." He is staying with Major Campbell, but he is here with Doctor every day and we tease him. He declared we Sitka people always said it was dreadful up here, but when the boat came and people came to see us, it was pleasant weather and we said it was an exception. But he has a dose of Sitka now. He said something last night about the first two or three weeks he was here. Then I showed him, to his horror, he had not been here two weeks yet.

Mrs. Quinan, my nearest neighbor, is going to have a baby. I guess I told you, but she is such a funny woman, I must speak of her again. She is about six weeks from her time and perfectly enormous. She is continually asking us if we think we would know it to see her. She expects the young men to be very much surprised when it arrives, for she is sure they don't know it. Doctor says he doesn't know what I would do if I hadn't Mrs. Quinan to amuse me. She really is a merry, pretty little woman, kindly disposed.

At this time next year, there will be an entirely new garrison here. We are all thinking about moving. I am looking forward to it. Do you remember the nubia or scarf you got at West Point? Mary has the greatest admiration for such things and, if you can, you might get me a white one for her. I still want two dark Calico dresses for her.

September 9, 1875

I have not written for a few days. It seems to me I have every moment occupied with the children. I am sure nobody ever had two such busy little scamps to look after. Bert is now worse than Bess. This morning he pulled up a poor flower I am trying to grow in a pot in the window. He pulled it up yesterday, too. He is perfectly charmed with the pot. Bess was, too. I suppose little "Annie," when she comes, will have the same fondness. It must run in the family.

I will be so glad to get their new clothes. I want to send you some money as soon as I hear about the winter clothes being off your mind. Can you have some spring dresses made for both of them? We will probably go to Portland in June. If not then, in July certainly, but we will only remain there a few days and then go to our post, but I want a few nice little things for both of them. One thing I want to ask about is cloaks for the children. I want little blue cloaks with capes and hoods lined with blue silk. They are for travelling. No matter where our post is, it will be nearly as isolated as this, and the cloaks will be nice enough for anything. It is not as if we were going to be in a city or even in a town.

Just think, Mamma, when we start from here, Bertie will be six months older than Bess was when we left Columbia. Tell me what you think of the cloaks. I don't want them until next spring and can send for them in January and get them in June. When I get to another post, I won't have to look so far ahead for things, and I won't have to write four months ahead for anything I want. Almost any other post in the Department will seem much nearer home, for I will be able to get a letter in two weeks and an answer to one I write in four weeks from the time I send it. Here you get my letter in about two weeks added to the time it takes the boat to go from here to Portland. Your letters to me are a whole month longer on the way, if they get to Portland after the boat starts up here.

September 14, 1875

Major Boyle and his son dined with us last night. (We have the pleasure of breakfasting and dining with lamps again after our long, light days.)

Mary has been so amiable for the last three weeks, I don't know what is going to happen. Doctor told her he did not believe that a girl who did so well as she had done for a few weeks could act as she had been doing before that. She could see now how much more we felt like making things pleasant for her, etc. It seemed to please her very much. Wouldn't it be funny if she became a treasure?

If you could see what "Mother Goose" has been to this family, you would feel repaid for sending it. I have just had to rush out to settle an altercation about it. Bert likes the pictures very much and gets it on all occasions. The back has long ago departed and so have a few pages on each side, but it still is valuable and fought over.

Saturday
September 18, 1875

The steamer came in and, of course, we are all in confusion. Besides our mail, it brought Dr. McKee of the Army on an inspection and, of course, he stays with us. He is very pleasant, but I hate unexpected company and I think we get our share. Doctor FitzGerald says it is time I got used to it, as I will have it all my life. The little shirts arrived and are very nice. That was the only bundle from you in this mail.

Three letters came from Columbia, one of them from Sallie. Her letter is dated April and I get it in September! She has seventy times as much time to write as I have. Doctor suggests (to give you an idea of how I get my writing done) that I put in everything I say to the babies and the times I jump up while I am writing a page. In the midst of almost every line, I have to speak to them.

September 19, 1875

Doctor is hurrying me to finish this and I can't write in a hurry. I will be thankful when the boat is off. Eveything is in such a rush, and company makes it so much harder (with my poor help and the two babies). This morning, for love or money, I could not get anything in the way of meat for dinner. I can't help worrying over such things, though Doctor says I am a goose, but the paymaster and his clerk will take dinner here besides Dr. McKee. Fortunately, I have one corned roast I can fall back on.

I hope you and Sallie got my last letters and have attended

to my wants. And, Mamma, I am glad you are going to Illinois: Tell me if I shall direct my next letter to Freeport, Illinois.

Your loving daughter;
Emily FitzGerald

Sitka, Alaska
October 3, 1875

Dear Mamma,

Bert was only eleven months old the day before yesterday and he walks all about, toddling around in his moccasins. I had his foot measured by a shoemaker in one of the companies and the measures have been sent to Portland to a shoemaker there. So Bert will have some shoes at last, I hope.

I have written you before about a black cashmere dress I want. I could have the dress made here, but I know it won't look stylish and I will have to plan it all by myself anyway. What would you do about it? Please tell me what the women are wearing now. Are there any new ways of trimming that are used more than ruffles or folds? Are polonaise worn as much as ever? Are they putting much trimming on polonaise and basques?

I have not written anything about furs for a long time. Major Rucker, who was up on the last boat, told me that Mrs. General Sheridan (his niece, you know) told Mrs. Rucker that in New York silver fox trimming two inches wide was selling for 60 dollars a yard. I know it sold for 15 and 20 dollars, but 60 dollars is rather too much to believe. One skin like mine would make five or six yards easily.

General Sheridan and his bride have been visiting Portland, and the army people and town people there have made it very gay for them. I pumped Mr. Dunn, a young fellow who is a cousin of Mrs. Major Rucker and is also the Major's clerk, to know what everybody said and did, and how the General behaved with his youthful bride. (She is twenty-four.) Mr. Dunn says the General is awfully devoted and that Mrs. Sheridan was waltzing with him (Mr. Dunn) at one of the receptions and the General came up to her with a most beaming smile and said, "Just give me a little of this. Just a little." Then he said to Mr. Dunn, as he waltzed off with his bride, "I will bring her back to you in a few moments."

On his way up here, Major Rucker bought two silver foxes at Wrangell and gave 60 dollars a piece for them. They are almost black.

October 10, 1875

I have had such a distressing week that I can scarcely yet bring myself to write about it. I can't get over the awful possibility that was presented to me of having lost my husband, and though I am thankful to God that he is safe at home again, I still feel as if something dreadful had happened and feel as if I could not bear to have him out of my sight.

Doctor, Major Campbell, one of the young officers, and half a dozen men have been off on an expedition to Mount Edgecumbe, the volcano I have spoken of. They were to go by water to the island, which is about 20 miles out in the open sea. They went in a little boat and did not come home when they were certainly expected, and a storm raged for several days. Of course there was a great deal to hope for, but there was no possible way of knowing whether they were safe or not. And though I tried to hope and fight against the horror, I could not help but dread the worst. Mrs. Campbell, too, was almost afraid to hope. I can't tell you how I suffered. I have never felt the distance from you so much before, and I felt if I could only send right off for you to come to me while I was in this suspense, it would be easier to bear. Then I could not help but think that if the worst should happen, how I should ever get to you over all these long miles with my two little babies? How helpless I should be without him, for he is so thoughtful for me and such a dear dependence always, and if I must exist without him, how could I bear it alone, without you or a single friend near? I positively feel as if I had lived fifty years.

The party left here early Monday morning and expected to

get back Wednesday evening, but they did not come. Wednesday afternoon the storm came up and we feared they had started back. All day Thursday we looked for them, and all day it blew and the rain poured down. Friday morning the little steamer that belongs to a man here started for Edgecumbe to look for them, and all that day it poured and blew. I was afraid to have the steamer come back, fearing the news it might bring, but late at night it came back and brought them all, alive and well, but worn out and soaked with rain. They had not started and were beach bound. They could not get their boat off the beach, as the wind was dead against them. I felt as if a horrible mountain had been taken off my mind, but I could not get my spirits up again for some time and felt like receiving Doctor with a shower of tears. He says I looked as if I had had a spell of sickness. He will never willingly leave me again in this wild country. Major Campbell, too, has declared he won't leave Sitka again until he leaves with his family.

October 16, 1875

Such a lovely steamer as came in last night. We never got so many bundles and things in our lives. I had two letters from you and one from Aunt Annie. I must tell you what came in the bundles; then you will know what has arrived. The wrappers (they all fit nicely), shoes, my slippers and corsets, little flannel drawers (Bess has a pair on now), aprons (I am in need of them — this just comes at the right time), two dollies which are fully appreciated, Doctor's knife, Bessie's scissors (which she is delighted with), and the buttons. I got two pieces of muslin from Portland. Major Boyle bought them for me at cost.

The steamer, as usual, brought visitors. Dr. McCarty took dinner with us yesterday and Major Egan is here. He came up with some new troops.

Mrs. Quinan is expecting hourly to be sick. Poor child, I wish she was over it. Take some soft yarn and your needles for little shirts to the West with you, so if I call upon you for number *three,* you will have them ready.

Mary worries me to death. I began last night to put by 6 dollars a month as her money. I shan't give her one cent of it at present, but I will buy everything for her and keep an account so she will have a little money to show, as well as her clothes, when I am happy enough to get rid of her. She is so impudent and is so cross with the children. But where there were no children and she could be kept busy, she would be a very useful girl.

Doctor got a whole case of Blood's Stout for me by this boat. I have not been feeling well for the last month. I feel pulled down. I believe this is the only letter I have sent off for ages without a list in it, but I think I asked for some things even in this one.

My babies are well, though Herbert has had an awful cold. We certainly expected croup two nights ago, but he has nearly gotten over it. They have so many colds up here. The continued rains and the damp, I suppose, affect them. And there are so many draughts in the house!

I am very much obliged for all the things you have sent me. Mamma, knowing you were going West and would not be in Columbia to superintend the making of a dress for me, I will write to the woman at West Point to see if she will make me what I want. I think she will and I will send her the cashmere.

I hope you will have a lovely visit. Give our love to all the home folks and tell Sallie to try to write to me every month while you are away.

Your loving daughter,
Emily FitzGerald

Sitka, October 28, 1875

Dear Mamma,

Day after tomorrow Bertie will be a year old! He is such a funny little fellow and runs around after Bess playing bear and saying, "Boo-boo-boo." Bessie has a shade over her eye; the light hurts her very much. I am afraid she is going to have weak eyes. She has complained of the light hurting them ever since she was a little baby. She looks so nice in her new wrappers, so I gave a Russian woman two more to make for her this morning. The cost up here will be much more than the home ones and the wrappers won't look as well. She will charge me about a dollar a piece for making them. The calico for one costs 75 cents.

The little schooner did depart at last and I hope you will get your letter. What a confused time my neighbors next door, the Quinans, are having!

November 10, 1875

Our steamer will come before I have a letter ready. Such a horrid month as we have had! I have been worried about Bess's eyes, I have been sick myself, and a hundred disagreeable things have happened.

I see I was discussing Mrs. Quinan when I finished the last writing. I believe I was only going to add that Major Campbell remarked to Doctor that they had "a devil of a circus in there," rather rough, but very expressive. Mrs. Quinan was confined yesterday, poor child. She had an awful time, and confusion is no word for the condition that family is in now. She has a boy, a great, big fellow, I believe bigger than Bertie was. Isn't it funny we should all have boys? Mrs. Quinan is comforting herself after her pains and trouble yesterday by telling us all what a young, charming looking mother her boy will have. Poor child, her troubles are just beginning.

I am sorry to say we can't get any moss for Aunt Annie. On the first of November it began snowing and we have the biggest snow we have ever seen up here — about three feet on a level. The drifts are awful. You should look out my window! Anything more Arctic I never want to see. The mountains of all heights that are on the three sides of us are perfectly white and, as all the buildings about here are low, they look (with the high piles of snow around them) as if they were nearly covered. Mrs. Field says she is positively afraid we will all be covered up. Indeed, the same idea struck me the night the snow fell. I went to the window before I started to bed, and the desolate loneliness of the scene startled me. We are so cut off from all communication with everything and every place. But the force of men could soon dig us out, even if it did happen.

I got a beaver skin last week and trimmed a cloth coat with it. The beaver here is darker than that of the plains and costs a little more. I got my skin tanned and plucked for four dollars and twenty-five cents (in coin). One skin will make the trimming for a sack and a muff. I am so pleased with the fur on my sack that I am sorry I did not have handsomer cloth, for the fur is worth it. Talking of furs, you know I have ermine for Bess and I have enough to make her a full set when she is older than now. I think it would be foolish to have them made up for her until we are going East. Out here no one will see her and she will outgrow them.

November 14, 1875

The steamer is looked for tomorrow. I hope it will come. I want Bertie's shoes and stockings so much. He has gotten a cute way for the last few days of peeping around the sides of the doors saying, "Mamma. Mamma." I have had to stop nursing him. I was not well for a few weeks. That was about a month ago. I was so weak, Doctor was afraid to have me go on with the nursing. I was sorry to stop, but Bertie takes to feeding nicely.

Bess has heard so much talk for the last few days about the steamer coming that she plays steamer arrival. Last night she came walking in to us with one of her blocks rolled up in dollie's afghan and said, "Mamma, see what the steamer brought you." I expressed so much delight over the package that after a while she brought in a whole diaper full of things and said the steamer had brought them to all of us. Then she distributed them around in quite a respectable manner. She is a funny child. She always says her prayers at night, has been doing so for months, but though she is corrected every night, she will say, "For gresus Christ's sake," and she can not get,

"Amen." She always says, "Any men," put her right as much as you will.

November 18, 1875

The steamer is not in sight yet, I want it dreadfully this month. Bess is too provoking! I have been so sorry that we cut her hair and have been taking great pains to get it to grow out again so I could tie it back with a ribbon. The front locks have been an awful trouble and I have fixed them fifty times a day to keep them out of her eyes. Within the last few weeks, for the first time, the hair has been manageable and stayed back where I put it. Last night she came walking in to me with a great lock in her hand and said, "won't you please send this to Grandmother." The little heathen had cut off, close to her scalp, all one side of the front hair, just cleared an inch square.

I don't know what put it into her head unless it was a few days ago when Doctor was shortening some of Bertie's locks. I said, "Save me a long piece. I want to send it to his Grandma to show her how dark it is."

I have such a trouble keeping the children's feet warm. Our floors are awfully cold and I am sure that is the way they get their colds. I wish the steamer would come. If shoes and stockings for Bert are not on it, I will be distracted.

November 23, 1875

Six weeks since we had a boat! We have almost given it up for this month and it is so disappointing and horrid. I expect so much on this boat, too. It will spoil our Christmas again, for we all intend sending to Portland for things in the November boat so they can come up on the December one. But now, even if the boat comes, we won't have another before Christmas. I made the children such pretty zephyr balls last week. I used up all the old scraps of zephyr yarn I had. The balls are such lovely looking things that after I had finished them, I concluded to keep them for Christmas, as we would not be able to get much here for them and Bess, at least, is old enough to know what is going on.

Mrs. Quinan and her son are getting along nicely. Bessie's eye is entirely well. We were very much worried about it.

Mary has been doing the cooking again for the last six weeks. I don't know what to do with her. I am a great deal more comfortable when she is in the kitchen, for I hate to have her about with the children. She is so horrible and she doesn't manage things nicely, and though she can cook nicely enough if she wants, she is such a silly goose that she spends half her time cutting up with the men or other servants and is no dependence. She is not a slim little child any more but a big, stout-looking girl or woman, and she worries the life out of me. She runs off, I don't know where, day or night, whenever she thinks she will not be missed. She is so ugly to Bess, but fortunately, Bess has not much to do with her. Jennie, a Russian nurse I have had since I was sick, is the nicest woman I have ever had with the children. Both Bess and Bertie like her very much, and I know she is kind to them. I do hope she won't depart from this house as long as this family is in it.

November 30, 1875

We had entirely given up the steamer, but it came in yesterday after we had been seven weeks without one. Thank you so much for all the things. Your bundles always do come nicely. You do them up very securely. The wax headed dollie for Bess got a mash, but it doesn't matter to Bess. She is nearly wild over it. Bert looks so cute in the cap. As soon as it was on him, he waved his plump, little hand and said, "Bye. Bye." To my great distress, no shoes came for Bertie. They could not be made in Portland and Major Boyle sent the measure on to San Francisco, but by the time the shoes do come, they will be too small for him, as the measure was taken four months ago. I don't know what the poor child will do.

The little testaments are very nice ones, much nicer than the one I got from Uncle Essick and paid 30 cents for, but did you think I was going to open a Sunday school? I didn't need so many. I want one for myself and one for Mary, but I will find use for them all. I am sorry those ivory buttons I sent Sallie and Bep did not arrive. They were real pretty, and I can't get any more now. The dollie Aunt Annie sent Bess is lovely, but it is too delicate entirely. Bess much prefers it on account of its hair, but it will be scalped in three seconds if Bertie gets his hands on it. It was too funny to see him following her around yesterday and reaching for it when I let her hold it for a while.

I meant to send for some more fixings this month but haven't any money and will wait until next. Doctor pays 169 dollars on his second insurance policy this month, and that just "skins" us for this month and next month, too. I don't believe I think it is the best plan, after all, to put nearly all you can save into insurance policies.

I have not been feeling well for a month. I know I look badly and I know Doctor has been a little concerned, for he has put me on cod liver oil, and iron and quinine, and all those lovely things. I did not think I would tell you until I saw you, but I will now. I had a miscarriage about five or six weeks ago, but I lost a great deal of blood and all my strength. I nursed Bertie until about a week after it, and then I had to stop. I have not gotten over it yet. I guess the climate has a good deal to do with it, but I don't get strong as fast as I would like or Doctor hoped. I am thankful now that I did have it, as another Sitka baby would have been my fate. Now we know there won't be anything of that sort to fear, but Sallie need not trouble herself to have any. I can supply the family. I don't believe there is a safe day in the month for me. Indeed, I know there isn't — 15th — 16th — 17th — or any other. Mrs. Campbell, Mrs. Field, and I have meetings of horror over the subject, as we all have gone through so much together here and we all seem to be awfully prolific.

I can't afford to spend much on pretty little fixings for the children for the present, much as I like them. I will dress them warm and comfortable and cute, but they must be dressed according to our means, which don't seem to be very much at the end of every month, I am sorry to say. What with changing our greenbacks into coin, then paying 40 dollars for servants, and more for other things, we feel awfully poor. Mrs. Field and I are continually devising means to save, but they don't "pan out."

I am glad you got the little blocks, and I will give them and the trumpet to Bertie, and the little dishes and pans to Bess. I will direct this to Leavenworth, as you tell me in your last letter. I did not know you meant to go to Leavenworth. I thought you meant to spend your winter in Illinois.

December 1, 1875

We will probably be six weeks on our way to our next post. It will be next summer and how I hate to be travelling for such a long time. But we go part of the way by steamer, and then by stage the rest, so it will be slow work. The studs that Sallie got me for Doctor are very pretty and they look very handsome in the shirt, but it is a funny ornamentation — the cross and crown. Doctor said that he will tell whoever notices it that he got them because he was serving under General Howard, but it is rather a queer device for shirt studs.

Mamma, you most likely have heard of the loss of the *Pacific*. We hear by this boat of a steamer being lost on the Atlantic, too, with no one left to tell the story. The steamer and a sailing vessel struck in the night, and the steamer went down with over three hundred passengers. It went down with all those lives in less than fifteen minutes after it struck. Of the entire shipload of passengers and crew, only three were saved. There were nearly two hundred miners on board who were going down to San Francisco with their earnings to join their wives and children. The rest of the passengers were whole families — women and children by the dozen. Major Canby says the whole city of Victoria is in mourning. The steamer was on the line from Victoria to San Francisco. I believe there was an attempt made to get out the lifeboats and save the passengers, but they were swamped in the commotion made by the sinking ship. The sailing vessel was very much injured but got ashore with its crew. They say the fault lies with the captain of the ship (not the steamer) who steered for the light of the steamer thinking it was a lighthouse. The *Pacific* was an old, unseaworthy boat and its lifeboats, even at the best, could not have saved but a small portion of those it carried. Isn't it horrible! When will these things make some people that have the power legislate something about this matter and make it against the law for companies to run rotten unseaworthy vessels, and to carry more passengers than their boats might save in case of accident. I shall be thankful when I and my precious ones are safe on the mainland again.

Doctor joins me in love to all. Write soon.

Your loving daughter,
Emily FitzGerald

Sitka
December 5, 1875

Dear Mamma,

The steamer has not left yet. You will wonder what has become of your letter. It was mailed four days ago when we heard the boat was to leave in an hour, but the captain was taken sick, and the boat still waits. I will add this to the mail and you will get thém together.

We are all well and are trying to plan so our little people will have a nice Christmas. Bess and Bert both have colds. We have so much snow around us; now it is piled up much higher than the fences. Major Canby came up on the steamer and he has been waiting to go back with it. We have been entertaining him with whist parties. They played here one evening and at the Campbells two evenings.

I have contrived quite a number of little things out of scraps for my Christmas gifts here. I am beginning to think I am an undeveloped genius. I got some of the loveliest cretonne patterns. They made me want some money awfully. I want curtains for our next quarters, but I won't send for them until February. I sent for cashmeres, but, Mamma, the ones I like all cost more than a dollar a yard and I don't feel able to give more than a dollar as I want twenty yards.

All join in love,
Emily FitzGerald

(Mrs. McCorkle wrote that she and Uncle Owen were planning to be married. The section of the letter in which Emily told her mother she approved of the marriage is missing.)

December 15, 1875

Dear Sallie,

I am so sorry the ivory sleeve buttons are lost. I found a set of mats that seemed right smooth and neat, so I got them and will send them to you by this mail. I hope they won't share the fate of the buttons.

I know Mamma will be happy at Chestnut Hill. I think Uncle Owen is good and is a man respected by everyone. I think she and Uncle Owen will be very happy together. They have always known, respected, and liked each other, and, indeed, I think it is a suitable match every way.

We have had two or three feet of snow on the ground since October. Only six more months of Sitka life. I hope and pray we may all live to go down from here to some civilized post. One of Bessie's gentlemen friends sent her a package of candy by the last boat. If it was not for that, I don't know what I would do for Christmas, for our November boat came too late to send to Portland for anything to reach us before Christmas. Mrs. Campbell is going to have a Christmas tree and I am going to have a little one. I wish now I had sent for some more things. Next year I will, so hold yourself in readiness to invest for me. Do write often. With lots of love to all at home, I am,

Yours lovingly,
Emily F.G.

Sitka
December 15, 1875

Dear Mamma,

Much to my horror, I have been in bed again since the last boat left. I had sort of a hemorrhage from the womb without any apparent cause, though its following on my miscarriage made Doctor think it was connected with that. Anyway, he sent me to bed and kept me there nearly a week. Mrs. Campbell is not well this winter, and Mrs. Field looks like a ghost. So we compare notes and we all know that this winter is rather hard on us. The little variety in the food we get, the little exercise we can get, and our all having babies can account for it. How near Christmas is!

December 19, 1875

Sallie was twenty-three yesterday; I wish I could see her. I have been busy for the last three or four days getting ready for Christmas. There is not a dollie in town. Everybody has been out looking for them. Bess is short of dollies. Did I tell you the sad fate of the one Aunt Annie sent? Bess was nearly crazy over it. (It is funny that children will play with dollies so much more than anything else without getting tired of them.) She took the dollie to bed and to the table with her for two days. The hair was the fascinating part. One afternoon she came in and said, "I fixed dollie's hair lovely." She had gotten the brush and comb at the wash basin and had combed poor dollie's locks straight down her back. After it got dry, it did not look so awful at first, but the same afternoon she put it up on the table to keep Bertie from getting it. While she went out, Bertie, who had been on the watch to find it unprotected ever since it came into Bess's possession, got it by the foot and pulled in onto the floor, breaking its head into a thousand pieces. Poor Bess was awfully distressed, but what was real good in her was that she never reproached Bert with it. I notice, too, that when he hurts her, which he does very often, she never thinks of retaliating. I have never known her to strike him back.

Mrs. Field and Mrs. Smith both had been looking for dollies to give Bess and had not found any. So I got the trunks of two of the dollies that had China hands and legs, and I made rag legs and arms for them and mended up two broken heads. I am going to dress them up brightly and have a little table set with the little dishes and dollies taking breakfast at it on Christmas morning. I mean to light my tree up on the afternoon before Christmas. Then Mrs. Field will light hers up on Christmas morning. You must always keep in mind it is dark here until nearly ten in the morning and before three in the afternoon. I have some little matters for all the children, at least I will have, if the little rubber toys come in this boat.

We are again disappointed about the steamer which ought to be here. I hope it will come before Christmas. Doctor hopes our next post will be Lapwai.

December 26, 1875

Christmas is over and the steamer that was to have taken this letter has not yet arrived. It is too mean we had to have our Christmas without it. Major Campbell is awfully angry about the boats. The company that owns the *California* is celebrated for looking after its own interests. Major declares the reasons they gave last year and will most probably give this year for not sending the boat up one of these winter months are only excuses to keep people from seeing the truth. They know that it is a good thing for them not to send a boat this month when there is no travel and little freight, and then send two boats in one month in the spring when the miners and other passengers are crowding up to Wrangell and the Stikiac mines. The contract with the Government calls for twelve a year, and the Government pays the company 36,000 dollars a year. The contract intends that there be one boat a month, and Major Campbell says the company is playing off. It is very hard for the poor garrison here, and I hope Major's statement of the case to the Postmaster General will bring about good results.

Our Christmas passed off very pleasantly. We lighted up our

tree, as we intended, on the afternoon before, and we had all the babies here together. Indeed, the whole garrison was here, but my tree was particularly the babies' tree. Doctor is so nice about such things. He took such pains with the tree and such an interest in it on the children's account. I had pretty little presents for them all, at least all except the little babies, as the rubber toys for them have not arrived. You would be surprised to see how many little things we got up out of nothing — little bits of ribbon and bright cardboard and little pictures, etc. Then Doctor made me some of the cutest rustic frames with his saw, and I framed some little gem chromos. I had two or three neckties I found I could spare and, as we were short of Christmas gifts, I made use of those. You can't imagine how pretty they look on a tree, tucked up in loops and just drawn under a round, scalloped paper. They look like bouquets; a pink one looks like a great big rose. It was my own idea, and I am quite delighted with it, as everyone admired it. Indeed I am feeling quite accomplished in getting up things. I made some lovely big stars to ornament my tree by cutting the stars out of cardboard and covering both sides with sheet lead, then pinching it down at the edges to make it hold. Doctor made candlesticks and got just the loveliest tree in the neighborhood. It stood on the floor and the first limbs came out just over Bessie's head. The trunk was wrapped with green and Bess's little dishes were set out on a little table under it. That pleased the children awfully, and they had a tea party under the tree while we big folks ate cake and talked. Bertie ate the spout off the tea pot! The tree, when lighted up, did look pretty, and I always mean to have one.

Then on Christmas night (last night) Mrs. Campbell had all the big folks over there and her tree was ever so pretty, too. She had almost as much contrivance as I had, but her sister had sent her a whole big box of decorations — all sorts of bright things and the prettiest little banners I ever saw made out of some transparent stuff with "Merry Christmas" on them. We had a real merry evening. Mrs. Campbell had sent long ago for costume bon bons. They are all sorts of garments made out of paper and put in these bon bons. Mrs. Campbell had sent for caps, in particular, and we were each to wear the cap our bon bon contained all evening. They were real funny. Doctor drew a jockey's cap. Since he brought an Indian pony up from Portland so he could draw his forage, and as it is the only horse in the Territory, they all thought it was a good joke. There were bishop's hats, Normandy hats, night caps, etc. I mean to have some next year, if I can get them. In talking of decorating the trees, I forgot to say rock candy is so pretty. Get it in long, thin sticks. It looks and sparkles like icicles.

January 2, 1876

This is your birthday, and I wish you could spend it with me. This letter that I thought would follow the other so soon will be a long month after it. We have had no December boat and are not pleased at all. Both babies have such awful colds and Mary gives me so much trouble, I have been distracted. I still have my Russian nurse, Jennie. She is the nicest woman I have ever had with the children and though she can't talk to them much, as she knows but little English, she is so kind to them and they both like her ever so much. It is so different in the nursery now from the time when I had Miss Mary with the babies.

Mary is past my understanding. She is perfectly horrible. I don't think she ever obeys; certainly every day she directly disobeys. She runs off daily and nightly. I am never sure she is in the house. She has no idea of duty or anything else. Doctor has whipped her half a dozen times, but it does no good. The evening after, I will go out to tell her to fix a fire, and I will find her sewing and lamp there, but Miss Mary is gone. She probably won't appear for an hour or two and then she walks in with an independent air.

She is a perfect fool besides. She is so silly about her clothes — is entirely too stuckup to wear patches. She tears a little hole in a dress and puts her hand in and tears it bigger, "just for fun," and to make the people standing by laugh. She sits on the stove hearth and burns the back of her dress, then laughs and sits down again to see if it will catch again. (I have been tempted to wish she would burn up!) She lifts the pots and pans off the stove with her clean dress or apron, whichever her hands get first. These things she does hourly. Tell her not to do so and so, and an hour after she will do it again, right under your nose. She positively treats me with no respect at all. She has often spoken to me in a manner that I would never dare to use to a servant. She deliberately disobeys. She doesn't do things just because she thinks we won't find out. She doesn't care if we do! I have told her as she started out to the baker for bread to come home immediately, and I have sat at the window waiting and have seen her go deliberately past the path that leads to the house and not come back for an hour. Then the most aggravating part of it is that when she does come in, she walks in as if she had done nothing and with an air as much as to say, "No one has any right to question my movements." At least a dozen times lately, when I have gone out to hurry up dinner or something I wanted done, she has deliberately sat down in a chair, put her hands behind her head, and did not move. When I said, "Mary, get up," she sat still until she was ready to get up. I can't fight her. I would have turned her out of my house a thousand times if I could. I don't dare to appeal to Doctor every hour to whip her. She is too big to be whipped and it doesn't do her any good. She is so horrible with the children and so dirty about the kitchen work that, indeed, she will set me wild. I can't afford to keep her and have her do nothing, and I must have her either cook or nurse. Nurse she can't, and I must do the best I can with her in the kitchen until I can get rid of her. I have been in the kitchen with her nearly all the time for two weeks, trying to inspire her with a desire to do things nicely and with some system, but it is discouraging. She could do so nicely if she tried. She is real bright and can cook well, but she gets everything into the most awful mess and is dirty. I have been so particular in telling her how to prepare birds and such things for dinner, and only the day before yesterday I went out to fix dessert and found her wiping the cleaned grouse with a questionable cloth. I said, "Mary, is that a clean tea cloth?" She said, "No." I said, "You mustn't use that. Have you been using it first to wipe the dishes?" Miss Mary said, "No. It is the one I use for the pots and the stove door," and she held up this filthy thing and giggled and laughed as if it was the funniest thing in the world.

She had been so ugly for the few weeks before Christmas that I was about tempted not to give her anything. But Christmas is Christmas, and I felt sorry for her, so she, as well as Jennie, had a stocking full of things to eat, as well as their presents. I gave Mary her nubia and earrings, a ruffle and a bow, a bottle of perfumery, and the little testament. She got up and got her stocking and called "Merry Christmas" in to Bess who was awake. I said, "Mary, let your things be now and fix your two fires first. Then you will have plenty of time for your stocking." More than half an hour after I got up with Bess, Mary had not yet moved from her things, and the fires were not touched. She is a trial! In the afternoon I let her go out but told her I wanted her to be home at half past six. Mrs. Campbell wanted us to come over there by seven, and I could not go until I knew Mary was in the house. She exclaimed, "I am only going out for a few minutes. I will be back long before six." I knew what a few minutes to her were, so I said, "Don't talk foolishly about it. Go out, but be home by half past six." Miss Mary never appeared until half past seven. Then she informed me she knew what time it was but she hadn't been ready to come home.

This is enough of Mary now. I have told you this much so I could tell you what I am going to do. Doctor declares he won't take her to our next post, if he has to "send her to the Devil." (That is his expression, not mine.) I can't send her home. It would cost at least three hundred dollars and I can't afford it. Even if I could, she could not get home alone, and she has declared ever so many times that nothing should ever make her go home again. She is not a child now, but a great, strong young woman. When we go East I will take her with us, but in the meantime, I can not and will not keep her in my house. I am going to leave her in Portland. She can stay with me the few days I will be there and find a place. You know girls are in great demand, and Mary, if she will try to do right, can get good wages. I will keep track of her and take her East with me when I go. It will do Mary good to rough it a little. She has had a "soft thing" with me and does just exactly as she pleases. She has talked all around about how she wishes she could get away from us and how well she could get along some place else. So I mean to give her a chance to try. She goes down to these storekeepers here and tells them she wants to see certain things and promises to buy so and so. Then when I refuse to give her money to buy with, she tells these men all sorts of things about us and talks in a very ugly manner. The little fool had ten dollars some time ago and wanted to buy a six dollar hat. I would not let her and she was perfectly furious. She told old Whitford that we treated her like a dog and that she was going off on the next boat. So I will put a stop to this thing, or else it will be the death of me. I don't know that I have known such a constant worry as this has been. I am going to write Barbara by the next steamer and tell her what I am going to do. I will let Barbara decide what I shall do with Mary's money which I have and which probably, by that time, will be thirty or forty dollars.

Doctor is laid up with a sprained knee. He went to the hospital day before yesterday on crutches. Did I tell you some time ago of the hospital's steward's using up the hospital's wines, brandy, whiskey, etc.? He was under arrest, and a court that was to try him is coming up on this boat. The poor man committed suicide a night or two ago — shot himself through the head. Such a horrible thing! He was quite a young man, but rather foolish and his constantly being under the influence of something had most probably affected what little brain he had.

Bessie and Bert are getting over their colds. Bess claims the little blue locket Aunt Pace gave me, and I promise her she shall have it when she is a big girl. A while ago Doctor was on the sofa with his lame knee, and he picked Bertie up and threw him up in the air a couple of times. Bess said, "Now, Papa, me." I said, "Bess, you are too big, dear, for Papa to throw up that way while he is lying down. Bertie is a baby, you know, but you are a great big girl." Bess said instantly, looking very much pleased, "Then give me my blue locket." Then she reached up on her tip toes to see how high she could reach and said, "Now I am a big girl, Mamma. Give me the locket now." I shan't give it to her, though, until next summer.

I am concerned for fear I won't get the children nicely fixed before we leave here. I particularly want to have them ready before we start on our travels, as at Portland they will see so many more people than where we will finally settle down.

Mrs. Field and I are thinking of sending for cretonne and cottage drapery for curtains to prepare our fixings here before we go to our next post. Our windows won't vary much, and curtains three yards long will suit any windows. I am perfectly crazy about cretonnes, but the sample Doctor has selected rather staggers me. It is a very handsome piece, but I am afraid too gorgeous. You can know what a good piece it is by the price — a dollar and ten cents a yard. Judging from the sample, it looks like some old-fashioned elegant stuff, a dark red covered with water lilies and morning glories. Doctor declares I must get this and not a piece I modestly selected costing eighty cents. Mrs. Field and I are going to get enough to make lambrequins, cover a lounge and two chairs, and trim our mantel pieces. The rest of the furnishings of my room will be folding chairs and a pretty table cover which I am going to send East for as soon as I can afford it. I wish I had a hundred dollars to spend on house fixings, but money seems to depart more rapidly now than it ever did before.

January 18, 1876

The steamer came in last night. I heard from you from Freeport and from Leavenworth. The little package with the book, the stockings, the gloves, and the cute little dogs arrived safely. The other package sent by Sallie with the two little plaid dresses also came.

Uncle Owen wrote to me by this boat. I was glad to hear from him. He speaks very lovingly and kindly of you and of us all. I believe I am very much pleased with him in particular, because I think he will bring you to us at our next post.

How would you like us to send you a silver gray fox muff and trimming for a cloak? The fur would be lovely for you with your soft grey hair and your black and gray clothes. I think it would be prettier than marten.

I am going to measure Bess in every direction and send the measures to you every three months. Then when I send for anything, you can go by the last measure. Where you are in doubt, always get it too big.

Doctor joins me in love to all. He doesn't believe you "wade" through all these sheets that I send you monthly. Lots of love, your daughter,

Emily FitzGerald

February 22, 1876

Dear Mamma,

I have been so busy that my mail has been neglected. And then the boat came with lots of people. Thank you for the papers and pattern books. I do hope we won't be sent down to Portland in one of these cold spring months. I will be better pleased if we could wait until it gets warmer and I get some of my things I have sent East for. I am not nearly ready. Every now and then I think, "What will I do?" if we are ordered to Portland in the course of a month.

I wanted to write something about furs. I do think sable will be nicer for you than anything else, and for myself too. There have not been a half dozen real dark sable here since we came, and the prices are awful, too—8, 10, and 12 dollars a skin. You saw those skins at West Point, didn't you, that were worth 3,000 dollars? They came from Fort Colville, and the skins there can all be gotten for six dollars a skin. They are much darker but not quite as long fur as those very handsome ones that I have seen here. As soon as Doctor gets to his next post, he is going to write to the Doctor at Colville and then send to him for what I want. And I want sable so much more than silver fox. My silver fox skins now have cost about 75 dollars in greenbacks, without being made up. The old grebe that Doctor still makes so much fun of, I still have. He says it is not worth making up. And now goodbye until next month. Love to all,

Lovingly,
Em

I sent 20 dollars in another letter by this mail. Let me know whether you get it.

Sitka, March 13, 1876

Dear Mamma,

For the last week our weather has been delightful, but there is a foot of snow on the ground yet, and we would rather see the rain than the sun for a few days so the snow would depart. Everybody expects the steamer next week.

Did you ever eat clam chowder? I made some the other day from a recipe in the little printed book that came in one of your packages. Doctor was delighted with it, but there was rather too much of a mixture for me. When the tide is out, the beach is covered with Indians and Russians getting clams. They poke around in the soft, wet sand with a stick, and every now and then a little stream of water spouts up like a whale blowing (on a small scale), and they know a clam is there. They dig him up and put him in their baskets. Doctor says it is the instinct of the clam that causes him to shut up his shell when he feels something strange (the stick) near him, and that causes the spout of water. The clams only do this at certain times of the day, though, the times that they are getting their food or nourishment or whatever it is from the water. After they get that, they spout up this water and shut up their shells to wait for their next meal. You can often see the little holes in the sand by the spouts of water. We all time our walks so we can go when the tide is out and we can walk on the beach. The snow has made the roads almost impossible. Doctor and I were out the other afternoon when the tide was very low and, walking down near the water edge, we found the sand just perforated with clam holes. Doctor got some sticks and we went to work for fun and soon had a mess of nice, big fellows. I was so delighted with clam digging as something to vary our life here, that we are going again in a few days with a basket. It is ever so much more fun to dig them yourself than to buy them, though you can get a whole lot for a bit.

March 14, 1876

This is another lovely day. Mrs. Campbell stopped for me to go walking yesterday, and we trudged for about a mile along the road the water cart makes through the snow. You can't imagine how we look for and long for spring. We have all had trouble about help, both in the kitchen and with the babies, and we have had such a little variety in our food and such long waits for our steamers. The Collins family (did I tell you he was the new preacher at Sitka) come in to see us quite frequently. Doctor remarked to me the other day, "Look here, I think the parson is getting too intimate." Mrs. Collins is a very pleasant old lady. Mr. Collins came in the other day while I was writing and saw a letter directed to Uncle Owen. He said he knew General Owen very well. Mr. Collins is a gay old parson, I can tell you. He hunts and fishes and plays whist and makes funny speeches.

Sunday Afternoon
March 19, 1876

This afternoon is one of the occasions when I feel I must have some female to take a particular interest in my affairs and help me make plans, and you would be the best of all. The boat came in yesterday and brought Dr. Baker to relieve Dr. Smith (he is our guest and a pleasant fellow) and brought us some news we were not expecting. Doctor FitzGerald is ordered to Portland and we go in the next boat. So goodbye Sitka! Just think of it. We are going back to civilization. I dread the journey in this cold weather very much for the babies, but I guess I can make them comfortable. The best news is that Dr. Bailey sends Doctor word that he can have Fort Vancouver. That is where Em Alexander is, you know. It is a big four company post only a half hour's ride from Portland, and there are two or three boats back and forwards a day. Now you can come to see us. Uncle Alex and Aunt Pace will be very mean if they don't take their next trip up in this direction. Two days by steamer brings you to Portland, and the fare is only 20 dollars. Then Doctor will meet you in Portland and in less than an hour you will be with me and the babies. Now come! Why I get all excited thinking about it.

The boat brought us three letters from you. Bess almost goes wild when the boat comes in. She dances around and says, "Open the bundles. Open the bundles." The two packages from you came. One was those cute little calico aprons and though they are a little small for Bess, she could wear them nicely. But they look so nice on Bert, I am going to give them to him, for they are just what he wants to travel in. I will have to get him a thick dress. I think I can get some soft grey flannel here and I will make him a pair of drawers to match. They will look funny but will be necessary on the steamer. The aprons look nicely on him and will make him look quite respectable. The other package from you was the little brown wrappers. They look too cute for anything. I am awfully concerned to know how to make my children look respectable in Portland. I had it all planned out for June, but this move takes us all without our best clothes ready. Aunt Annie sent me some real pretty black earrings, just what I want, as I have not a thing to wear in the mornings. She also sent me a very pretty collar and cuffs.

This steamer brought news to the people here that they would go down in June and where they would go. It has been rather funny, for some of them go where they don't want to. The Fields, who are society people in the fullest sense of the term and who have, while here, been just waiting to get below San Francisco, are ordered to Fort Canby at the mouth of the river, a one company isolated post, and they are awfully indignant. The Campbells go to Presidio; the Quinans, of course, go with Captain Fields.

My cretonne for my best lambrequins came, but I am disappointed. It is too gay. Doctor likes it and it is handsome — so heavy and rich looking — but instead of only being covered with water lilies and morning glories, as I judged from the pattern, it is literally covered with everything — lilies, morning glories, tulips, pansies — all more than full size! But each flower in itself is perfect and bears inspection. But with lounge and mantel piece and lambrequins, my room will look like a flower garden!

I must tell you about Mary. I almost forgot in my own news and the steamer. She has shortened my life, I am sure. She is an "imp of Satan," as Doctor calls her. She has been getting out at nights and going with these men. How do you suppose I felt the other day when Doctor told me his steward told him Mary had a *bad disease!* One of the men said he had not been with anybody else for six weeks and had gotten it from her. Doctor said it was a form of that disease with a discharge. If it should get into the children's eyes, even in a dry state, from clothing, it would give them almost incurable sore eyes. I wonder if you could imagine how I felt. This — added to the rest of her conduct — seemed almost too much. I declared that I did not believe it, and Doctor said her clothing would prove it. He went up to her bed and the sheets and nightgowns were a mass of sticky yellow and red streaks and spots. I almost shed tears.

After some time, Doctor called her in and talked to her. She denied having anything the matter with her and said she never had been with any men. At last, she said she had been with one man, but had had this yellow discharge all her life. Doctor gave her the benefit of the doubt, as an old leucorrhoea would very much resemble the other discharge and might also have the same effect on a man. The little fool said what did it matter if she had been with a man. It wouldn't be any worse for her to have a baby than so and so. She positively did not seem to care for anything but that we had found it out. Doctor gave her some washes and things to syringe with. Goodness, but he was mad! If she had seemed the least disturbed or sorry, we would both have felt so differently, but she continued her impudence.

Indeed, just to justify myself in what I have been writing you, I wish you could hear the way she talks to Bess. Well, do you think it any wonder, putting everything together, that when about six weeks ago she came to me and told me she wanted to go down to a place in Portland that she had heard about from some of her friends there and how big wages she could get, etc., do you wonder that I said, "Go and prosper." Well, I did, and she goes on this boat! I wrote to Barbara and I do think Mary will do better for a stranger, and I will take her East when I go. She says she wouldn't go home for anything, and she says she would drown herself before she would go home. Now don't tell me I have done wrong, for, under the circumstances, I did not feel that it was my duty to force her to stay. All the ladies and the officers here who have seen her performances wonder at our bearing it so long, and they all speak of how good I have been to her.

Now for something much more pleasant to me. You have heard me speak (or write) of Jennie, a Russian woman who has been with me nine months now. Bertie is devoted to her, and, indeed, she is so faithful and kind to them both, they go to her as willingly as to me, and Bert loves her dearly. Well, much to my delight, she tells me she would like to go away with me. Doctor says take her, by all means. She is older than I am and has no relations. She talks very little English, but the children understand her and she them, and she seems to love Bert very much and does all the housework nicely. I sort of feel as if the kind overruling Providence was going to let me have a very good time. I have had the two babies so close together that I sort of got into the habit of being uncomfortable and confined to home. But now, not to be either in the family way or nursing a little one, and to have Jennie with the babies, and Vancouver for a post — I shall grow young again!

Direct all you send me to Doctor, Care of Medical Director, Headquarters Department of the Columbia, Portland, Oregon. Dr. Baker says Dr. Alexander does not want to go East. It is probable Dr. Bailey will go East on a leave and Dr. Alexander will be Medical Director until his return. Lots of love to all. I will enclose five dollars. Let me know if I must send more.

Your loving daughter,
Emily FitzGerald

Monday Morning
March 20, 1876

Mamma, dear, the steamer leaves this afternoon. Just think! The next one we will go in! I am awfully afraid of the water but suppose there are no more dangers there than on land. One thing I must speak of. Doctor has two insurance policies on his life made out in my name, five thousand in the Mutual and five in the Equitable. It seems a horrible thing to think about, but it struck me that no one knows of them and if we should all go down under the water going to Portland, the policies would go with us. So someone should know of their existence. Doctor says there are a million chances to one of our getting down safely, but if we should be lost, Doctor's mother ought to have the ten thousand. Now I don't dream of anything so dreadful, but someone ought to know. I will write to you as soon as we get to Portland, and I will direct it to Columbia.

In this letter I put in some white feathers of an Alaskan owl that Doctor shot on Edgecumbe Mountain. You can see the provision of nature for this cold climate. I also send a foot and leg furred to the toes. The white things you can cut up into pretty little bunches of feathers.

We join in love to all.

Your loving daughter,
Emily FitzGerald

Sitka, April 9, 1876

Dear Mamma,

This is probably the last letter I will write you from here. I want to have one ready for the boat, though, and after this I will write weekly, as you do. We expect the steamer by next Sunday. I can scarcely believe we have but one week more in Sitka. I have been very happy up here and found it much more pleasant than I expected. Indeed, we all did, and if it was only a little nearer to any place, it might be a very good post. Doc-is glad to think of getting away, and I don't wonder. We have had such an awful winter — six solid months of snow and cold has been our experience, while your winter has been almost like spring.

I have not time to write to Sallie this mail, but tell her I have a very nice beaver skin for her. It is quite a large one, and if I don't hear from her while I am in Portland telling me to do differently, I will have the whole skin made into one inch trimming. I would rather have gotten Sallie an otter, but there have been none offered for months, and they cost three times as much as the beaver. It will only cost a few dollars to have it made into trimming. That Sallie can pay, but the Doctor sends her the skin. I can have it plucked and dressed and just send her the skin entire, if she likes. I hope she will write and tell me before I do anything with it.

Bertie has had an awful cold again. I do hope he is over it now and won't have any more, and I hope we will get safely out of this horrible climate. I am so happy without Mary. We have had such a smooth month.

Sunday, April 16, 1876

We looked for the steamer by this time. All month we have

been packing up and are now about done except those last things that we can't pack until the day we leave — beds, a few dishes, etc. I have had the house cleaned, and the carpets are all sewed up in their covering, and all Doctor's chests and boxes are screwed up and weighed, so I feel delightful!

I just came home from church and found the children mashing Easter eggs. My two Russian women had brought them seven or eight and, of course, the children spread them all over the floor. To the Russian Church, this, I believe, is their greatest holiday. We all went to the church Friday afternoon to see their performance of the burial of Christ, and last night at midnight they had Resurrection. The body and halls of the church were strewed with cedar branches on Friday, and the church candles were all burning. There are no seats in the church (except a bench for us); the worshippers all stand. There was a continual crossing of themselves by touching the forehead and breast and shoulders; and they (particularly the old women) kissed the floor over and over again. After a little while, some doors opened from the inner rooms of the church and a gorgeously gotten up boy advanced down the center of the church with a big banner. He was followed by the two priests in full robes carrying an image (nearly life size) of the body of Christ. The church bells set up a ferocious ringing, and the church choir followed the body chanting the most doleful music. This procession went out the front door of the church followed by every Russian man, woman, and child, and marched clear around the church building and in again. Then the body was laid in state and they all went up front — the priests first, and then the men and boys, and last the women, and kissed it. First they kneeled and kissed the floor, then the drapery on which the image lay, and then the hands and feet of the image. The mothers lifted their babies to kiss it. All together, it was solemn. I forgot to say that just as the big gilt doors opened and the body was carried into the church, all the worshippers lighted candles and held them in their hands.

Last night, I believe, the image was resurrected and carried around the church in the same way and in an upright position. I know both my Russians are nearly dead this morning for lack of sleep.

Just think! We are hourly expecting the steamer that will take us to Portland. This time next week we will be on our way. I will mail this letter up here and write another as soon as we are in Portland and know where we are going. I should be very glad to go to Vancouver, and it would be real pleasant to be there with Em Alexander. How I shall enjoy fruit and the good things of this life when I get below!

April 17, 1876

We found the steamer at the wharf when we got up this morning and we leave tomorrow night. I dread the seasickness for all of us. I only have time for a line or two. I had only one letter from you and some bundles. That percale dress is beautifully made. Aunt Annie sent me such a nice box of handkerchiefs. They are just in time.

I am not pleased at our news. We are to be detained in Portland four or five months. Doctor will be on duty there, for Doctor Bailey has gone East. The idea of boarding all that time with a nurse and two children is horrible. Then we probably won't get to Vancouver at all. Doctor Alexander is Acting Medical Director, but Doctor FitzGerald will have the duties in Portland, and Dr. Alexander's family will remain in Vancouver. He is to be relieved in November, and I should not wonder if we were kept in Portland all that time. Portland is a lovely city, but I would so much rather be at a post and at housekeeping.

I will write soon again. I sent 20 dollars to you in February and five last month. Let me know if you got it. You had not received it when you wrote the last letter. Love to all and we all join in it.

Your loving daughter,
Emily FitzGerald

On the *California*
April 23, 1876

Dear Sallie,

I have nothing to write on but this piece of an account book, but I want to mail a letter to you as soon as I get to Portland, so I will use this paper. I wrote to Mamma telling her some things to tell you, but the boat brought me a letter from Mamma telling me she was still in Leavenworth. I told Mamma I had a beaver skin for you, a very nice one, darker and larger than the one I had. If I don't hear from you in Portland telling me what you want me to do with it, I will take it with my other fixings to the furrier and have it made into trimming for you and send it at once.

We left Sitka Wednesday afternoon and have had a very smooth passage so far. In spite of the unusually good trip, Doctor, Bess, and I have all been a little seasick. This is a wonderful trip. The whole way we go through narrow channels between mountainous islands. Some of the mountains are thousands of feet high, and the channels we steam through are so narrow that sometimes we could almost throw stones to both sides. The water is of an awful depth. Captain Hayes was telling us of being caught in a fog in these narrow channels, and sounding with the lead line to keep from running into the land. He says they sounded, thinking, of course, that the water would grow shallow near the shore, but at eight feet from the shore, the water was hundreds of feet deep and the line could not reach the bottom. The sides of the islands seem to go perfectly straight down. This is what is called the Inside Passage. Every now and then we come to a sound when it is open to the sea; then we get a shake up and go to bed seasick. But in these narrow passages, the water is most always still.

It is wonderful to look at these hills. There is something awful in thinking that for thousands and thousands of miles this country is not only uninhabited but unexplored. We pass some of the most beautiful waterfalls, and just now they are very full. They come pouring down from the mountains and look like great white streaks until we get nearer and see and hear the rush of the water as they plunge into the channel we are steaming over. A little while ago we went through some rapids. I went on deck in an awful rain to see the place where the *Saranac* went down. It struck on a rock in these rapids.

I am going to mail this as soon as I get to Portland. I guess I have left Sitka forever. I am sorry I have not a few more little Alaska trifles for my friends, but I wouldn't go back there for anything. I have three baskets for myself and a wooden carving that Doctor declares he is going to send to some gentleman friend (it is for tobacco) but I am going to hold on to it. And I have a set of mats, too. Those with my fox skins and Bess's ermine are all I have of Sitka produce. Write soon and often. With lots of love to all, I am, as ever,

Your loving sister,
Emily FitzGerald

Portland, May 1, 1876

Dear Mamma,

It is time I was writing and telling you of our safe arrival here. We got here last Friday morning (this is Monday). I wrote a note to Sallie and mailed it in the morning I got here and meant to write to you, but I have been so rushed. We had some shopping to do for the Sitka people and the steamer was to go back today. Then we have had a great many callers. We are at the hotel but are very anxious to get to a post. I don't think we will be detained here as long as we expected, but we are not to go to Vancouver. We don't know where we go until General Howard gets back this week. We were able to stop our mail here, and I got out our bundles directed to Sitka. I got the one from you with the little white dress and some others. Among the bundles I got yesterday was my black cashmere dress. It is so nicely made — awfully fussy for me, but real rich looking. It is all trimmed with black silk and has black silk sleeves.

We took our furs to the furrier this morning. He says they are all first-class skins. He will charge about three dollars for trimming, plucking, and making into trimming the beaver for Sallie. It will be three or four times as handsome as the beaver I had fixed in Sitka.

Em Alexander came over to see me Saturday. I was so glad to see her. She looks well and her boys are lovely. She says the girl is, too. She has lovely furs. She says she never expects to be anywhere again where she can get them, so she has gotten all she wanted and can give one set to one of the sisters when she goes home.

I should not wonder if we go to Lapwai, and I want to very much since we can't get to Vancouver. Doctor could go to Vancouver, but it would only be temporary and we would both rather go to a less delightful post and be able to stay longer. Lapwai is a very healthy post and easy to get to. I think General Howard will be disgusting if he doesn't let Doctor have it after we have had Sitka.

Mamma, don't rush that sewing for the children, for we are going to some post where they will not need to be dressed up very often, and they can wear their little wrappers all day. I will send you some photographs in the next letter, I think.

Your loving daughter,
Emily FitzGerald

Portland, May 6, 1876

Dear Mamma,

These babies' photos are not as pretty as I wanted them to be, but Doctor says they are good. I send you one of each, and one of each for Sallie. We are still boarding here in a very uncomfortable manner. It costs us between 40 and 60 dollars in coin every week besides Jennie's wages and other little extras. Isn't it lovely? We are both disgusted with hotel life, and the children are six times as much trouble here as they were at home. We have a little shopping to do yet — some few dishes and kitchen fixings. After that, I will be ready to move on at a moment's notice. You don't know how little a hundred miles or so seems to me now.

I do so wish I had that old China with me. I mean the old blue cups and saucers that I fell heir to. Do pack them up in some way securely for me. There are four or five or six white plates among them with Chinese figures on them. They are what I want particularly. They would be so lovely for fruit or for bread plates. I have seen some displayed lately at some nice little lunches that were made a great fuss over by ladies, and I wanted mine, as they are handsomer and older than the ones they displayed. You know, army people are great on nice tables. No matter how plainly they furnish their houses, you almost always find their tables stylish and well provided for.

The bundle of little white dresses came in a splendid condition and they look nicely on the babies. My only trouble now is I have such lovely clothes for them and will have to hide both babies and clothes in some far away post where no one will see them.

Sunday, May 7, 1876

I will mail this tomorrow. I wonder if you are in Columbia. Sallie writes to me by fits and starts, and Bep never but once wrote me a line, and I am sure they both have much more time than I have. You and I must be the writers of the family! At least we keep up a much more desperate correspondence than any other members of it. Tell me if you don't think from these photos that mine are nice looking babies. I will try them both again soon, if I can afford it, and get prettier positions. Photographs, like all else out here, are costly — 5 dollars a dozen in coin. I got a dozen of each of these but want more, as there are some of my old friends I want to send them to. I won't get any more of these but will try again if this moving about doesn't break us up entirely. Doctor was fishing with some friends all day yesterday and is just awfully tired today.

I must tell you about Mary. She has not been near me, though she knows I am here. A day or two after I got here, one of the ladies told me Mary lived with a Mrs. Somebody, and they were delighted with her, only she had too much company.

Do write to me often. Our Portland friends all seem very kind, but how I would like to see someone from home! Em Alexander is the nearest I have come to it since I left Pennsylvania, and it did me good to see her.

Your loving daughter,
Emily FitzGerald

Portland, May 12, 1876

Dear Mamma,

I expect in your moving home just about this time you will not hear from me and will think I have not written, but this will be the third letter that will be waiting for you in Columbia. I will enclose 20 dollars in this. Let me know how much I owe you. I want to pay up square right off!

We start Monday morning for Fort Lapwai, in Idaho Territory, where you can direct your next letter in Doctor's care. The trip up the river is said to be delightful this time of the year. You must time your visit so as to reach Portland in the early spring, and then you can come to Lapwai and back again by the river boat. You can do this from about April till August. After that the river is too low for big boats and the trip is disagreeable, as you have three hundred miles to stage.

We have been rushed here. So many people have invited us to dinner and lunches, and we had lots of business to attend to. I was at a real pleasant ladies' lunch party yesterday. Half a dozen ladies and no gentlemen — we had a real merry time. The gentlemen returned it by having a big whist party in the evening.

I forgot to say the debage dress came three days ago and it fits me so nicely. I think with you that it is much nicer than an alpaca. I have worn the dress several times and am delighted with it. Please pay for the making with the money enclosed, and know that I am just ever so much obliged to you for your trouble. I am very nicely fixed for clothes now, and will have our house fixings at Lapwai very cozy, too. The children will do nicely for a year with one or two new dresses in the fall. I am very thankful, for we must not spend much money and must lay by a little for the babies. We are particularly poor these last few months, as this moving is awfully expensive. Doctor's mother has lost a considerable portion of her property and John has been helping her pay a debt that was distressing her very much. He is the best son and best husband alive!

I was so glad my debage dress came now, as I just wanted such a thing to travel up the river in. There are quite a party of military people going up for different purposes. I think I told you some time ago that, as you were so soon going away from Columbia, I would rather you would send me whatever it is you have in the way of a bankbook or certificates of deposit for the money I have in the Columbia bank, and I can, after this, send what I want to add to it right to the bank.

Sunday, May 14, 1876

Tomorrow at five o'clock we depart for Lapwai. We will go on the boat tonight, as it would be too early a start for the children.

I must tell you about Mary. She called on me the other day. I do wish you could have seen her. Such clothes! Much finer than any of us! A new light spring suit, new shoes, a fine new hat, a silk parasol that must have cost at least four dollars, light doeskin gloves with long gauntlets, and such an air with it all. I asked her a few questions about her place, but she gave me to understand she was doing much better than ever with me, and that nobody interfered with her. She thinks she will go East to the Centennial and will dispatch to her mother to meet her. I tried to give her a little advice about trying to keep a good place, etc. (for I know, not from her, though, that she has had three) but she tossed her head and said she could take care of herself. She said it in such a manner that Doctor wanted to tell her to march out of this place. I told her she had forgotten a roll of plaid like her dress, which was enough to fix the dress nicely, and I had brought it down to her. She said, "Oh, it doesn't matter. I do not want it as I have a black silk overdress for the plaid." Now she has not been down here more than two months and has not had a place all that time, and she only gets ten dollars a month. She told me, too, that she had ten dollars ready to send her mother. Where did all these fine clothes come from?

Write us at once at Lapwai. Doctor FitzGerald relieves Dr. Douglas. Then, you know, Doctor D. is to go to Fort Klamath. Mrs. Douglas and the children are going East, I believe at once, for a visit.

This is a scrawl! Lots of love to all.

Your loving daughter,
Emily.

PART III

THE WILD WEST

Fort Lapwai and the Nez Percé Wars — 1876-77

Emily's letters describing the journey from Portland to Lapwai are missing. Army records show that Dr. FitzGerald arrived at Fort Lapwai for duty as Post Surgeon May 19, 1876.

Fort Lapwai
May 26, 1876

Dear Mamma,

We got here safely a week ago and are pleased ever so much with the country we are going to spend the next two years in. Dr. Douglas is sorry to leave and, as they are not quite ready, Doctor F. has not taken their quarters yet, and we are getting along in another set. We will be very comfortably fixed when we do get into our quarters, and though they are small, I like them very much. Mrs. Douglas is going East. She is very pleasant and I wish we were going to be at the same post. Her children are such pretty, sweet little girls. Mrs. Douglas is a pretty woman herself.

We are living in a sort of confused style. This morning, much to my disgust, I found Bess has the mumps. I do hope she won't have a hard time of it and that Bert may escape, but they are in for it, I am afraid.

Doctor is delighted with this climate and country. After his first ride out to the fort from town he said, "Your Mamma must see this country. She will be charmed." Indeed the ride is through a lovely region, rich prairie land with such pretty wild flowers and such herds of fat sheep and cows as it would do you good to see. We are going to live in one half of a double house. The other side is occupied by the Commanding Officer, Colonel Perry. We have mail here three times a week, and this letter will depart to you in a few hours. I wonder how long it will take you to get it. Doctor says to tell you to direct your letters as I told you, but to add via Portland, Oregon.

This is a beautiful, green sunny place — such a lovely place for the children to play. I expect they will grow fat and sunburnt. Those lovely white dresses are not going to be the most useful things in the world here. They are too pretty to spoil, and I just wish you could see the condition Bess and Bert are in when I undress them at night. I never saw such dirty clothes. It will be too bad to not let them play, as it is just what they need. Bess is so delighted with the wild flowers. She brings me in such an amount, I can't find room for all of them. I have been writing this letter on my lap and I am afraid you can't read it, but I have not another sheet of paper. Our boxes and trunks have not been opened yet. I will take such pains with the next letter, you won't think I don't know how to write. I will write every week. Doctor sends much love to all. Give my love to all at home.

Your daughter,
Emily FitzGerald

Fort Lapwai
June 2, 1876

Mamma Dear,

I do want to write once a week, but this week has been such a confused one, I have almost missed it. Our third and last mail for this week goes out tonight. We got into our house Wednesday (this is Friday). Dr. Douglas left about noon on that day, and as we had to move in, unpack, and clean house all at the same time, you can imagine that we have not been able to see the "beginning of the end" until this morning. I have two carpets down, and Jennie is washing the last windows, and the house generally is clean. But I am afraid we won't get fixed up by Sunday as we hoped.

There is a good, old Presbyterian minister here on the reservation. He is old Mr. Monteith, the father of the Indian Agent (you know, we are in the Nez Percé Indian Reservation). I don't know whether to have him baptise Bert or to wait for Uncle Owen's visit next spring. That reminds me. One of our neighbors is a Captain Henry Smith who said, the other night, when in some manner I mentioned Chestnut Hill, "Do you know the Owens out there?" Capt. Smith's father is professor in the Washington or Jefferson or one of those western Pennsylvania colleges where some of the Owen family were at school.

Mrs. Perry is going to make an afghan and, as I told her the wool in mine came from Columbia, she wants to send for hers. Will you please order for her six ounces of the brightest red you can find? Just have whoever you get it from do it up and send it by mail to her. Tell them to send it with their address, too, for she wants to send on for the rest of the wool as she needs it and she will just write to the store without troubling anyone else. I send $1.25 for her in this letter. If there is more than enough to pay for the wool and the postage, let them send the change back in the package.

Such writing as these last two letters! But, indeed, I have no place to write and no place to sit down yet. I will improve as I get my possessions to rights. Love to all.

Your daughter,
Emily F.

Fort Lapwai
June 11, 1876

Dear Mamma,

We have been here nearly three weeks, and yesterday was the first time I heard from you. It was your letter written May 22nd. You had just gotten the babies' photographs. Do let me hear from some of you once a week.

We are nicely fixed in our quarters now and are real comfortable. Doctor likes Lapwai ever so much. Bertie, poor little man, has his turn of mumps now. He points to his little ears and says, "Hurtie, Mamma, hurtie." Doctor says he wishes Bethel could come out to us. You can get a fine Indian pony for thirty dollars, and Bep could ride all over the country to his heart's content.

As for my money in the bank, which Doctor calls my fortune, don't under any circumstances take it out of the bank for any investment, no matter how good. I would rather have it grow much more slowly and be safe in the old Columbia Bank than be invested in any other way where I could not get it any minute I wanted it. When you leave Columbia, send me the certificate of deposit. Don't send it now, for I want to send a little more this month or next and will have that added to the four hundred and fifty before you send it.

I have received, I think, all the packages you sent from Leavenworth. The last with the receipt book came nicely, and I was so glad to get the book and particularly glad of the band for Bertie. He is getting his big teeth and the weather is getting hotter and hotter, so I want to keep bands on him all summer. He talks a great deal now and is so good. Bess cries six times to his once. He gets all sorts of bumps and tumbles, and he picks himself up and rubs the hurt like a little man.

None of the three ladies here has any children. It does seem too funny to me. I and my whole set of intimate friends have been engaged in wondering how to prevent any more babies coming. Now I get among these people who would give their heads to have a baby and are just as busily engaged trying all sorts of means so as to have one.

I hope you have received the money (20 dollars) I sent just before I left Portland. Let me know how far short the money falls of paying all. How money goes! I think every month that we will begin to be rich, but the end of every month, we are just where we were before. I put one of the new little white dresses on Bess last Sunday. She wore it out at play on the parade ground, and of course, got awfully dirty. I expected that, but the juice of some of the flowers she played with stained the dress and it came from the wash last week with a hundred spots as big as a penny on it. I have been foolish to get either of them white dresses. It is torture to the children and to yourself to always be chiding them and not letting them touch or play with this or that when they are dressed, and my babies are too little to teach. All this summer long my babies won't have one occasion when they need be dressed up. I can keep them dressed much nicer in the winter when they will stay in the house, but then it is so selfish for me to wish it. They are so rosy looking and tumble about on the grass so delighted just to be out of doors in the sunshine after Sitka.

Afternoon

I did not finish this morning, so will say goodbye now. Poor little Bert seems real sick and uncomfortable this afternoon. Write soon.

Your loving daughter,
Emily FitzGerald

Fort Lapwai
Sunday Morning
June 25, 1876

Dear Mamma,

The second letter from you came last night. I am glad you are getting ready nicely. We are all pretty well and very comfortably fixed now. But I have had the most disgusting time — with mumps! Just think of great, big me having them—awfully, too. They made me real sick for three or four days, actually so sick I could not stay out of bed. I am much better now, but I thought I never should get over them. Did I ever have them before?

What do you think of what I told you about Mary in my last letter from Portland? Have you seen Barbara, and what does she say? I am sorry for Mary. She may be on her way

East now, as she was going to the Centennial. I only wish I had a cook as good as Jennie is a nurse. I would be just fixed right. Mary could do nicely if she tried, but the little goose was only good about one third of the time.

I wish so often I could bring my babies home to show you all they are such cute specimens. But I don't want any more. These two are just as much as I can look after and clothe respectably. Little Annie need not put in an appearance for some time.

We will come East when we leave Lapwai. When I think how the last two years have flown, I feel that the next two will be very short and we will soon be moving again. Doctor is certain he will be ordered before the Medical Board in New York at the end of his time here. Then, too, he will be entitled to three or four months' leave, and I will make straight for Columbia.

I have a great notion to sell my fox skins. I have been offered a hundred dollars for them, and indeed, I don't want such expensive furs. In the next six years, I will be, perhaps, only six weeks where I could want to wear them, and I can get nice furs for 50 dollars that will be as handsome for me. Doctor says I had better not, but I am thinking seriously about selling them. Write soon.

Lovingly your daughter,
Emily

Fort Lapwai
July 2, 1876

Mamma Dear,

Your letter written June 16th came yesterday. I hope none of your letters to me get lost, as I want them all. This is a warm Sunday here. Doctor has gone into town with Mr. Bomus (one of the officers) to hunt for some Chinamen for cooks. I am sure he won't get a good cook on Sunday, but Mr. Bomus thinks they will get two. I have been doing my own cooking. I had a soldier, but he was not nice, and Doctor sent him off. I don't think I am very fond of kitchen work. I don't wonder at the cooks asking 30 and 35 dollars a month. I am quite willing to give it, too. Jennie doesn't know anything about cooking. Anyway, I believe I would rather do it than run after the children. I have gotten along much better than I expected this week. My practical knowledge of cooking is mighty slim, though I know about how everything should be cooked. I feel encouraged, though, by this week's experience. I have had such good breakfasts and dinners for John that I began to think he wouldn't want to hunt another cook at all.

Bess and Bertie are brown as berries. You never saw two such sunburnt little scamps in your life. They get so dirty that the bath tub is brought in and we scrub them every night.

Lapwai is a pleasant post, as far-away posts go, but it is very quiet and lonely here. I am sorry if you give up your idea of making us a visit. I wish we could come East, but nothing would induce me to go East with the children and then to come right back again. Travelling isn't fun! Doctor thinks we will be East of the mountains before 1879. I won't go home until he does. It would be dreadful to be home with him out here, but I do want awfully to show off the babies.

Nothing goes on here to tell about. We see the people from the Agency every few days. The Indians are passing by the post continually, but Indians are no novelty to us now. We are all very much interested in the news from the Black Hills and Sioux War as we all have friends with the troops, and as we are surrounded by Indians here, we are all the more anxious that victory doesn't crown the Plain Warriors. You know, two-thirds of the Nez Percés are Non-Treaty Indians, and they are intimate with the Sioux and other tribes on the warpath. The men of the cavalry company here are wondering and fearing that their regiment will be called on to join General Brok's expedition. The largest body of Indians that has ever been on the warpath is on it this summer. They should be shown no quarter!

Write to me often. Love to all.

Yours lovingly,
Emily F.

Fort Lapwai
July 9, 1876

Dear Mamma,

I have a Chinaman in my kitchen today. I held out a long time, though. I would much rather get any kind of a woman, but after doing all the cooking for two weeks, I felt thankful to see Mr. Sing, and I will cheerfully pay him his thirty dollars in gold a month, though it does seem awful. Doctor said my experience of Pacific coast life would not be perfect unless I tried a Chinaman. All the other officers here, except Colonel Perry, have Chinese help, and some of them pay forty dollars. Sing moves around the house like a mouse in his soft shoes. Bert calls him a "lady." His long hair and gown confuse Mr. Bert. Just think of paying 35 dollars in greenbacks to a man who does not do nearly as much as a woman in the East does for 14.

Mrs. Perry's wool came yesterday. It is beautiful and soft. How much it has improved even since I used any. She is very much obliged to you for attending to it, and she will send to the store for the rest. Doctor and Colonel Perry went out yesterday for prairie chickens and got three or four apiece. They are very nice.

I made Bess a new set of garters yesterday out of some rubber Aunt Annie sent me. She is so delighted with the bright gum, she pulls up her clothes to show them to everybody. I never saw anyone so devoted to flowers. She gathers every one she passes and plays with them for hours. I can bribe her to do most anything with a flower. Even Bert has now gotten to bringing us flowers. We often have flowers on the dinner table, and the other morning I was frying Saratoga potatoes and heard Bess at the table. I called, "Bess, don't touch the table." In a minute she came out and with the utmost satisfaction said, "Mamma, just come and see your table." I went in and found that she had gotten a glass and put a great handful of grass and white and yellow flowers (wild things) in it and set it just in the middle of the table.

Everything with Bertie now is a horse! He insists upon you singing about a horse when you put him to sleep, and everything he gets he sticks between his legs and says, "Get up, horsie." Last night John was going out and took Bert up in front for a few minutes. The horse started into a gallop, and Bert laughed out loud, perfectly delighted. Bess delights in dollies, and, much to my delight, Bertie does, too. Doctor has an idea boys won't play with girls' things.

Doctor came home last night from his hunt perfectly delighted with the country he had seen. He says it is the loveliest his eyes have ever looked upon, and he is quite anxious for money to invest in a Ranch and to go into stock raising. He says a man could make a fortune in ten years, but Doctor (fortunately, I tell him) has not means to invest.

My Chinaman, I hope, is going to prove a success. He made delightful muffins for breakfast and is now making a cake for dinner. I am going to have a baked stuffed salmon for dinner, and I am awfully hungry. It is such a comfort to go out and sit down to a nice, full table and not have to fuss over things beforehand.

I will write soon. Love to all,

Your loving daughter,
Emily FitzGerald

Fort Lapwai
July 16, 1876

Dear Mamma,

I heard from you this week and got the Centennial pictures from Aunt Annie. Thank her very much. The little book particularly is such a nice thing to keep to remember the event.

Did I write you from Sitka and speak of Bert being vaccinated? He had two awfully sore arms and has two good marks. We thought one arm was not going to take and had the other vaccinated. And both took!

We are all well. My brown babies are the picture of health, but such solid, round, little brown toads you never saw.

Did you ever hear anything more terrible than the massacre of poor Custer and his command? This whole part of the country is excited about it, as indeed, judging from the papers, is the entire country. We wait for the news here most anxiously and hope the Indians will be shown no quarter. War is dreadful anyway, but an Indian war is worst of all. They respect no code of warfare, flags of truce, wounded — nothing is respected! It is like fighting to exterminate wild animals, horrible beasts. I hope and pray this is the last Indian war. Don't let anybody talk of peace until the Indians are taught a lessen and, if not exterminated, so weakened they will never molest and butcher again. These Sioux Indians will give trouble as long as they exist, no matter how we treat them, "for 'tis their nature to." They will never stay on their reservations and the lives of settlers in this entire western country are not safe as long as the Indian question is unsettled. This is all we talk about out here, but I won't write any more. Love to all from all of us.

Your loving daughter,
Emily F.

Fort Lapwai
September 9, 1876

My Dear Mamma,

This is probably the last letter that will reach you in Columbia, but I will continue to write and direct as usual until I hear from you not to.

I have been all this week sewing, getting our winter underclothes into a wearing condition. Doctor went into town this morning and means to bring me out some peaches. I do hope he will be able to get them. How is the fruit at home? Mamma dear, I hope you will be very happy in your new home, and I think you will. I hope you won't have any more troubles to worry about in your life, and your mind can be at rest from now on. Won't it be nice to see you fixed in your own home when we come East again? Columbia will seem very lonely without you, though, and you will have to meet us there in the old home. I want my children to know the old place.

Later

Jennie and I have just been giving the children their Saturday afternoon baths. They look so clean. If anything should happen to me, I look for you to take some sort of care of my babies until they would be old enough to live with John and a nurse. I don't mean that I am expecting to die soon, or anything of that sort, but I just happened to think of this. Doctor would send lots of love when he gets back from town, but I won't wait for it. I will go and take my scrub. As always,

Your loving daughter,
Emily F.

Fort Lapwai
September 16, 1876

Dear Sallie,

You owe me a letter and so does Aunt Annie. I am going to write to you this week and not to Mamma, as I expect she will be away from Columbia when this reaches you.

I have been the only female at the post for the last two weeks. Mrs. Perry is in Walla Walla. Colonel Perry took Mr. Fletcher and the cavalry company out to the mountains. And that reminds me that I have not told you of our Indian troubles. We are waiting tonight's news anxiously enough. Dispatches arrived here, after Colonel Perry had started on his trip, to the effect that "Joseph's Band" was driving the settlers from that valley they claim, Wallowa Valley. One company from Walla Walla had already been sent out to try and prevent bloodshed, and Colonel Perry's company was ordered to be in readiness to move at a short notice. Two soldiers were sent out immediately to follow the cavalry company's trail and give these dispatches to Colonel Perry, but they came in last night and said they had not found him. In the meantime, other dispatches have arrived saying the trouble threatens to be much more serious than usual and the cavalry here shall be fully equipped for starting. So an Indian from the Agency was sent out to find Colonel Perry's company. He took three horses, meant to use them all, ride day and night, and find the cavalry tonight.

Then we have other news through the papers and the officers (who are already in the Wallowa Valley) that makes us all feel worried and anxious. The Indians have forced the settlers to leave, and the settlers, about seventy or eighty, have joined together and are armed. The Indians are determined that they shall not settle in the Valley, and they are determined that they will, and, of course, have the right and must be supported by the troops. Everybody wants to prevent bloodshed, for this lot of settlers in the Wallowa are an awful set of men and have made all the trouble for themselves.

I am in terror for fear Doctor will have to go out with Colonel Perry. My only hope is a real sick man in the hospital, and there is a medical officer, I suppose, from Walla Walla out now. But, of course, the ladies are all anxious, and everybody is waiting to see what is going to happen. I hope it will all blow over as it did last summer, but the gentlemen seem to think it means business this time. We are between sixty and seventy miles from the Wallowa.

I heard last night from my friend, Mrs. Collins, in Sitka. They leave there on the next boat, and then the last of our old Sitka garrison has departed. The 4th Artillery people just got down to San Francisco when they were ordered onto the plains, that is, the companies were ordered to Cheyenne to guard the railroad. Major Campbell had to rush off and just leave his poor family to help themselves.

How do you wear your hair, and why don't you have any babies? I am gathering together a nice little outfit for number three, hoping *that* will keep her away for a little while. I believe I have everything ready for her but the flannels and the diapers. We are just being devoured here by moths. They eat everything — our best clothes hanging in the closets, our blankets on the beds, and coats and hats on the rack!

Do write to me oftener and write good, long letters.

Your loving sister,
Emily FitzGerald

Fort Lapwai
September 30, 1876

Dear Aunt Annie,

What a good time you people are having all together at home this week. I have thought about you so often and wished I could see you all.

We are still living along here in a quiet manner. Our Indian trouble ended in a sort of compromise, and five Indian Commissioners will be here next month to treat with these dissatisfied Nez Percés who made the trouble. I wish they would kill them all (the Indians — not the Commissioners).

This fall weather is lovely, and we are enjoying being out-of-doors so much. We have two or three pretty walks, but we are surrounded on all sides with high hills, not covered as our lovely old hills at home are with big trees, but with prairie grass. There is not a tree or bush from one end of them to the other. Our post, though, is right on a little stream, the Lapwai, and its banks have some nice, big trees (mostly cottonwoods) on both sides, so we don't have to pine for something green.

Last night's mail brought me the two little bundles from home and those nice little presents from you. It is so kind of you, Aunt Annie, to think of me when you see nice little things, and, indeed, if you knew the pleasure they give me, you would know that I am much obliged. The little box of cotton is such a lovely, neat little thing to keep from the Centennial, and the sleeve buttons are just as pretty as they can be. They look as if they were enameled. But I have not had any letters from any of you for ages. It doesn't seem that I am any nearer home than I was in Alaska. I hope you will write me a long letter soon.

Your niece,
Emily FitzGerald

Fort Lapwai
October 8, 1876

Dear Mamma,

I believe I am really beginning to think I am neglected. I have your last letter dated August 28th. You tell me in it that I must be satisfied for the present with few letters and that Sallie and Aunt Annie are writing. They may be writing, yet, for all I know, and I think I have had to be satisfied with few. I am comforted by thinking that there must be two or three on the way for me by this time.

I am going to be "chief cook and bottle washer" for a while. Mr. Sing departs tomorrow for the mines. I believe I am glad he is going. The clothes from the wash have such a horrible smell and I can't help imagining it is his horrible old teeth (you know how they sprinkle clothes), and I am almost certain I saw him spit into the dish pan the other day while he was washing dishes. But he is a good, old fellow and I wish he would stay over this week, as Mrs. McFarland is coming up to spend it with me and I would rather not have to think about the kitchen. Sing has been with me four months, and I have given him one hundred and twenty-three dollars in gold. Just think of it!

We are beginning to think about Christmas since the cold weather is upon us. Mrs. Perry is planning for a tree with some little trifles on it for the laundress's children. I will have to have a little tree for my babies, but I am going to have a very inexpensive Christmas. I think some little things I have been keeping from your packages, with some other things I can make, will do for the children. Doctor and I will give each other mutual admiration, etc. I will send to Sallie for some candles and candlesticks and such little things, and then I will be ready. I did want to get John some nice handkerchiefs, but I will wait now for his birthday, as by that time, I hope we will be over the effect of that eight hundred dollars!

(Emily's letters to her mother for the latter part of July and all of August are missing. Apparently she explained in one of those letters why eight hundred dollars was being withheld from Dr. FitzGerald's salary.)

This is a real pleasant little post, you know, and it takes so little to make children happy and a tree look pretty. I expect we will have a very nice Christmas. I do hope the shoes for the babies come soon, as their little feet look badly, and their stockings get so dirty through the torn shoes.

I have your photo in our bedroom. You should hear Bess and Bert discussing whose Grand Mamma it is. Bess says it is her grandmother; Bert says, "No. Me Grand Mamma." I have to convince them daily that you belong to both of them. They imagine their grandmother to be something between Red Riding Hood's ancestor and a beneficent being who gives them all their possessions, and to whom they only have to say, "Send me so and so," and they have it.

The mail is waiting. I did not know it was so late. Do write often and long. I have more to say, but this is the last time the mail goes in for some days. Doctor joins in lots of love.

Your daughter,
Emily FitzGerald

Fort Lapwai
Monday
October 16, 1876

Mamma Dear,

Last night's mail brought me the *Spy* with your marriage notice in it. That is the first certain knowledge I have that you are Mamma Owen. Doctor and I talk and talk about you a great deal lately and think how nice it would be for us if we were with all of you at Columbia. By the time this reaches you, you will be fixed in your new home and receiving calls from all the Chestnut Hill people. Tell me all about your wedding presents when you write and make a list for me. John and I both felt very sorry that we could not send you something pretty, not because it would have been any more of an indication that we think a great deal of you, but just because we would have liked to send you something from us now. But we weren't able to do what we wanted, and you must just believe we think as much of you as anybody else. I am still in hopes we will be able to secure some nice furs for you this winter, but the prospect is not sure, for this country's day as a fur country is passed. I told you I had thought of parting with my fox skins. Mrs. Field writes me from San Francisco, "Don't on any account part with them. Hold on to them. We will never again get anything so handsome," and says hers have been so much admired. She says that since she went down there and saw how much all furs are prized — otter, beaver, and everything — she regrets she was not able to bring more with her from Sitka for her friends. Just a little money would have gone a great way. We have made a great many inquiries about marten for you, but the skins are scarce, and I feel disappointed that you have not had furs from us before now.

Sing, our Chinaman, has departed. I have Jennie in the kitchen, and the children for my own care, and am trying to see how it works. I rather like to take care of them myself, but I am never still ten minutes.

I sent for shoes for the children more than seven weeks ago, and then calculated the shoes they were wearing would hold together just about till the new shoes came, which I thought would be in about four weeks. Well, they have not, and I must tell you the consequence. Miss Bessie's toes came clear out of her shoes and then the bare toes came out of the stockings. Yesterday morning I was in despair when Mrs. Perry happened to think of a pair of shoes that grew too tight for Mrs. Douglas's little girl, and Mrs. Douglas gave them to Mrs. Perry for some poor child. Mrs. Perry brought them down to the porch, and although they were about nines, Bess was delighted and almost wept tears of joy over them. Mrs. Perry says they do protect her toes and stockings, at any rate.

I told you, didn't I, of Doctor's having to refund some money? Not refund it, either, for he can't do that, but it has been stopped from his pay — eight hundred dollars. It is horrible and will make us poor all winter, but Doctor has hopes of getting it back eventually. Through his friend's, Doctor Billing's, advice, he appeals to Congress in its next session and has a precedent in the case of another medical officer who, in a like case, had his bill put through without any trouble, but it was a long time coming. We have had a great deal of quiet amusement over our troubles, though I don't know whether you would appreciate it, as you won't allow any of us to say we are poor. But the army people at a little post like this all know ever so much of each other's affairs, and we talk them over like family matters. When we found we were not going to have any pay for more than four months our friends here offered us all sorts of funny donations to keep the "wolf from the door" until the pay begins to come again. All sorts of suggestions were made as to what we might do to get along (they were awfully laughable), and many more suggestions were made as to what we might do in the way of a "splurge" when Doctor gets his bill through Congress. Mr. Fletcher remarks there is sort of an importance attached to people that have a bill before Congress that common people don't have, and we may get very much stuck up. All this is on the principle that

"It is better to laugh than be sighing," for it really is a very awkward thing for us and very, very inconvenient.

You will have to make up, Mamma Dear, for all the time you have lost in writing to me, or rather in not writing to me, now that you are settled. Now I must stop, as the mail goes out tomorrow. Ever so much love to yourself, Mamma, and to everybody else. We are all very well but Bertie, and he has his old, bad cold. Hoping to hear now often, I am, as ever,

Your loving daughter,
Emily FitzGerald

Fort Lapwai
October 22, 1876

Dear Mamma,

Two days ago your letter that you mailed in Albany arrived. I am glad your journey was so pleasant and don't wonder you had such a good time seeing so many pretty places and things. You mention a matter in your letter that I never thought of before — that is my calling Uncle Owen "Father." I haven't the slightest objections to such a thing, but I thought I should go on calling him Uncle Owen. But if you and he preferred it, I expect it would soon come to be a matter of course. Unfortunately for me, I shan't be able to call either of you anything for some years to come. I have talked to Bess and Bert quite a good deal lately about their Grandpa in connection with you, and they talk about you both considerably.

I am beginning to be concerned for fear Bertie will grow up before I have him baptized. I think I will have him baptized by the first minister I come across. I wish I could make Doctor feel differently about such things, but nothing in the surroundings we have, or the life we lead, tends to help me. John is so good and thoughtful for me and the children, and he is so sensible about everything but that. But it seems to me, of late years, that everything and everybody is getting loose about religious matters. Everything I pick up—journals, papers, standard periodicals — that people consider good authority, speak in a matter of course way as if it was settled about beliefs being done away with that I have been brought up to think sacred, and of liberal views that, if they are carried out, don't leave me anything to believe. I have read so much about Adam not being the first man, and of that story being told to illustrate something else. Indeed, I don't see how he could have been the first man or, at least, the only man. I have also read so many attempts of good men, clergymen mostly, to reconcile the Bible's account of the creation with what the most intelligent men of the age have discovered for us. They are all liberal in a certain sense, and yet they give way on some points and say we must not take so and so literally. All this confuses things for me still more and makes we wonder less at the Doctor's way of reasoning, though it does not make me feel any more comfortable about it.

I am sending you "The Gospel of St. Matthew" in Nez Percés, thinking you might like to have it as a curiosity. See the length of some of the words.

Your loving daughter,
Emily FitzGerald

Fort Lapwai
October 30, 1876

Dear Mamma,

This is Monday morning and Bertie's birthday. I gave both babies books I had kept out of a lot you, or someone at home, sent them last winter. They have been in their high chairs at the dining room table looking at pictures and have been real good for an hour. But now Bert has gotten tired of his book and is pulling me and saying, "Don't write, Mamma. No, no."

The paymaster is expected this week, and the Indian Commissioners are, too. We all want to go to the Council, if squaws are admitted. There was an Indian funeral in sight the other day, and the brave was tied onto his horse and taken that way to the burying ground, his arms, head, and legs hanging over the sides of his horse. He was a young chief, only about 20 years old. That does not come up to Mrs. McFarland's story, though. During church, a few Sundays before Mr. Monteith died, an Indian came in, and as he came up to his seat, he stood something, tied in a pillow case, up in a corner. Mrs. McF. says she thought he had brought a present of a ham to the Agent, but after church he produced a little dead baby out of the pillow case and wanted it buried.

Sometimes I wish most earnestly you could be with us a few weeks, just to see what we see of the Indians. A little of it would be very interesting. On Sunday mornings we see dozens and dozens of the Treaty Indians, dressed in the brightest combinations of colors, going down to church. The women nearly all have babies strapped on their backs in those funny things, one of which I sent you.

I hope the Commissioners will be able to settle matters so we will have no Indian scares next spring. Doctor had a long letter from Major Campbell in the last mail. We live so quietly here, we almost thought the Indian war was over, but Major's letter takes us right into the midst of it again. He is near the Cheyenne agency with his command of four or five companies, building one of the new forts and hurrying matters up before the cold weather is upon them. Major says that they all see the necessity of a winter campaign. If we wait again until spring when the Indians have grass for their ponies, we will only have a repetition of this summer's hunt for the Indians. In the winter, the ponies can't live out of the cottonwood bottoms, and as the Indians can't get about without their ponies, you know where to find them. That is our advantage. In the summer, the advantage is on the other side.

Within a few miles of the Cheyenne Agency (and the Spotted Tail), there are from 12 to 15 thousand friendly (so called) Indians, but Major said he "doesn't go a cent on them," and that it makes his blood boil every Tuesday to see them get their rations, for the hostiles are all around them in small bands to the number of several thousand, and they get a big share of everything that is going. General McKenzie had an interview, just before the Major wrote, at the Cheyenne Agency with the hostile chiefs. One of Sitting Bull's chiefs broke it up in a very summary manner and Major says that for a few minutes everyone thought there would be another Canby massacre. I expect we will hear dreadful things yet. These beasts of savages, driven as they will be this winter to extremities, will be desperate, but I don't believe in commissions or treaties at this stage of the game. They must be thoroughly whipped, but the cost, I am afraid, will be awful.

I am so sorry for Mrs. Campbell. She has had so much to worry her, and then just to get back from Alaska and to be left alone as she is! Major had only 30 hours when he got his orders to break up and abandon the post, equip his company for the march, make out all his papers and things for leaving, have supplies shipped, and get himself into travelling order and arrange his little family to be left behind. But that is the fate of army people.

Our cold weather is upon us, and I expect the winter will almost be the death of us. It will be so much colder than we are accustomed to in Sitka. I just stopped for a little while to wash and fix some mushrooms to serve on toast for dinner. We do enjoy them so much and every now and then someone finds a lot.

I had a nice long letter from Sallie last week, and the mail after, a little bundle of things I ordered for Jennie. Poor Jennie, it doesn't seem as if she ever would be civilized. She is a perfect child in everything. That reminds me that I want a book for her. She is learning to read and can get along pretty well in the little words like, "The dog has the pig by the ear," etc. I think she would be very much pleased if I could get her a book, even some sort of a primer that she could read herself. It must have some pictures, though. She is as bad as Bess in that. I wish you would look for something for me. If we could get some words of good advice in such little sentences illustrating pictures, it would be killing two birds with one stone.

Right now Bess and Bert have the chairs in a row. Each is sitting on one, Bert in front with a strap through the high chair, which is the horse. Each of them has a cigar box for a trunk, and Bess has a dollie. Bert says it is the Cambalance (ambulance).

I have come to the conclusion that some of the people who live way out here and never did any shopping East in their lives are just about as well off as other people. There are some people at the Agency who, some way or other, come across advertisements in New York, and the cheap things they get just astonishes me. One of the girls does a good deal of fancy work and gives eleven cents an ounce for all her zephyr. It is nice zephyr, too, as nice as I ever gave 25 cents for. Then one of the girls got a heavy beaver cloth cloak the other day trimmed with silk folds, handsome buttons and pockets, for — what do you think? Seven dollars! I know of an army lady who sent five dollars and wanted a wrapper, and they sent her a dark red wrapper, nicely made, and sleeves, pocket, and collar with silk beautifully quilted, etc., and sent ten cents change. The wrapper had been $4.50 and the postage 40 cents. Can you do any better than that shopping? I give up. I see in Altman's Catalogue calico wrappers trimmed with a dark band, pockets and all fixings — for one dollar! What is the use of sewing any more?

I must stop writing and say goodbye. Bess, when she is playing, always says, "Goodbye. I hope I will have a good time," in the same tone we would wish someone a pleasant journey. All join in much love.

Your loving daughter,
Emily FitzGerald

Fort Lapwai
November 10, 1876

Dear Mamma,

By this time, I suppose you are settled quietly at Chestnut

Hill. It will be nice for you to settle down after all your journeying about.

The shoes and some books arrived yesterday. You should have seen how delighted Bess and Bertie were over the new shoes. They rushed about like wild people. Bess wore hers a little while and then said, "Mamma, ask Grandma to send me some more — not tight ones. The thumb of my foot hurts in this one."

Well, the Commissioners arrived on Tuesday. General Howard and Colonel Wood are here at the post, and the rest are at the Agency. The business will probably keep them ten days. We have had to turn our sitting rooms into sleeping rooms for our guests and sit in our dining rooms. My dining room is the brightest and coziest little room in the house, so it was not very hard.

The Indians are gathering in by thousands to see the Commissioners and all are in their "good clothes." Mrs. Perry is confident the Indians won't come to terms and we will have an Indian war in the spring.

I had a nice long letter from Mrs. Campbell last week. She says Major Campbell is building a post near the Red Cloud Agency. Mrs. Campbell is a lovely little woman. She is ever so much better and more cheerful over her troubles than I would be, though it is dreadful to her to be alone with her babies and have no hopes of seeing Major before spring, if then.

We are thinking about Christmas and getting ready on a small scale. I am dressing up a dollie for Bess, the one Sallie sent. Bert is to have Katie. She is that iron-hoofed, jointed dollie sent to Bess long ago. Katie is having a moustache painted on her face and is going to be dressed as a Zouave. John says if Bertie will play with a dollie, he must have a boy. Sallie wrote me she liked her fur. I am so glad she did, and I think it will wear well.

There is nothing new at this post, only it is getting colder and colder. We had our first pumpkin pies this week. I was very much pleased with them, as I tried to make them rich and nice, but Doctor said they were pretty good, only not like his mother used to make (a remark which I have punished him for a great many times). I told him I wouldn't make them any more, but I was comforted by Colonel Perry telling me to send him a whole pie the next time I made them, and that I beat his wife at pumpkin pies. Mrs. Perry is about the best cook I have come across. Her dinners are celebrated among army people all over this region. She has such a way of dressing things with fancy sauces. Oysters, drawn butter, and such things are scattered about in a delicious manner, and she seasons things to a degree that would give you the dyspepsia, but it is awfully good. I know I have improved in my chicken stuffings and mushroom cooking since I have had my kitchen next door to hers. But how I hate kitchen work. I can do anything with a better grace than wash pots, kettles, and pans. Happily, I never do it, but I am always in constant terror for fear sometime my domestics will suddenly depart and leave me alone in my glory for a short time.

I forgot to thank you very much for the little books with those scripture illustrations. I have felt the need of something special to interest the children on Sunday, to have the day a little different from other days, at least. but there is so little you can do with such little children. Still, I know it would be so much easier for them to keep the Sabbath as it ought to be kept when they are older if they got into the habit of it now.

Later

Colonel Wood, Mr. Fletcher, and Doctor came in and I did not get my letter finished. It is now eleven o'clock, and as Doctor must take this when he goes to sick call in the morning, if I want it to go this mail, I will just say goodbye. Write to me as often as you can.

Your loving daughter,
Emily FitzGerald

Fort Lapwai; X marks the FitzGerald home, 1876.

Some Nez Percé Indians who attended the Council at Fort Lapwai—Chief Joseph standing in the center.

Fort Lapwai
November 15, 1876

Dear Mamma,

It is raining hard outside today, and such days always make me want some of my home people to drop in. We are just about as usual out here. I write so often, I never have any news to tell you.

The Indian Commissioners arrived since I wrote last. They are all such good, pleasant men. One of them, a Mr. Stickney from Washington, reminds me of Uncle Essick. Then there is a lovely, old Mr. Barstow from Providence, Rhode Island, who, when he spoke to my babies, said he had seventeen grand-children between the ages of 10 years and two weeks, who were all waiting for him to spend Thanksgiving with them. Then there is a Mr. Jerome who is an exceedingly good-looking gentleman. He is President of the Commission. They are all fine looking men, and men of means.

I went down to the Council yesterday as the wild Indians were coming in. The Commissioners wanted to see the Chiefs, particularly Chief Joseph, who has made the trouble in the Wallowa Valley. I wanted to see them arrive in their best clothes, but all the way down, I kept thinking of the horrible Indians and my two little babies left up at the Fort with Jen-nie. I supposed, for my own comfort (?), all sorts of things, such as the Indians murdering the Commissioners and the officers (who were all going down to the Council), and having a sort of Canby Massacre. Then I wondered if Doctor and I were both killed and the children spared, if anybody around here would know what to do with them or know where any of my relations were. Delightful sort of thoughts to leave home with, but I did want to see the Indians come in. I didn't think of going into the Council, but when I got down, Mrs. Monteith said she did want to hear what Joseph said and whether we were to have trouble again next summer. The gentlemen were all going over, so we went, too.

The Council was held in the church. When we got there,

Joseph's band had arrived and were all in one side of the church, most of them sitting on the floor, horrible, dirty looking things all rolled up in blankets and robes. On the other side of the building were a lot of Treaty Indians who came in to hear how their wild brothers were treated. You noticed at once a difference in the appearance of the two parties. The Treaty Indians nearly all wore shirts, pants, and coats or jackets. Only here and there was there an old fellow in a blanket among them. They nearly all had their hair short, that is, short for Indians, cut off about their necks. A good many of them looked like colored people. Very few of them were painted, too. But the other people were very Indian looking, indeed. Such ferocious looking headdresses you never saw. They took their head fixings off when their heads got tired (I suppose) holding them. One old fellow, sitting on the floor, had an enormous fur of some sort gotten up into a headdress. It looked like a whole beaver skin. By and by, he took this thing off and began scratching or rubbing his head, which was not braided as they usually do it, but the long hair was all hanging around and was evidently powdered white with flour. He rubbed so hard, the flour looked like a cloud of smoke around his head. Some two or three of them had all the front hair cut off but about six or eight inches, which they combed straight up and stiffened with something so it stood straight up from their heads like a comb, and the long, back hair was hanging down their backs in a braid with some kind of an ornament at the end. Some of them had all their hair stiffened, and it stood out all around their heads.

One old fellow, not of Joseph's band, sat down (rolled in his blanket) on the floor close by where we were sitting. He seemed very much amused by a little black dotted veil Mrs. Perry had over her face. By and by, he took off his headgear, which was stupendous and was made out of a whole collection of things, and took out of it an old black cotton net which he fixed over his face, like Mrs. Perry's veil, and then nodded to us, as much as to ask us what we thought of it. He evidently was pleased with its effect, for he wore it nearly all afternoon.

None of the squaws but us were inside, but they were all gathered around outside in their best, brightest clothes, with lots of babies on the mothers' backs. They wore such bright colors — yellow skirts and blue scarfs, red dresses with green aprons, and all sorts of combinations. Some of them had very handsome robes. I saw one squaw with a robe tanned almost as white as muslin (they always wear them with the fur turned in) with a band of heavy, bright bead work, six or eight inches wide, all around it. Joseph's brother, who is called young Joseph, a wretched looking Indian with his hair and forehead and eyes painted a bright red, had on a robe very elaborately painted with hieroglyphics.

Well, the Council was not very satisfactory. Doctor and I left soon. We did not stay more than an hour. The Indian smell was awful, and I wanted to get home to the children. We heard, after the gentlemen came up, that Joseph will make no terms or acknowledge any authority. I hope they can arrive at a more comforting settlement than they hope for today. This Joseph will admit no boundary to his lands but those he chooses to make himself. I wish somebody would kill him before he kills any of us. The Agent leaned over in the Council room yesterday and asked me if my hair felt on tight. It doesn't feel very tightly on when I think of these horrible devils around us. This is enough of Indians.

General Howard had a little service in the Infantry Barracks Sunday night — nothing more than a little temperance talk to the men — but the whole thing was very pleasant. Mr. Stickney led the singing, and all of the men sing well.

Yesterday when I got all ready to go off in the ambulance and got all my things on and a veil over my face (you can see how seldom I leave the children), Bertie did not know me and would not kiss me goodbye. He ran to Bess and put his head on her shoulder, buried his face, and said, "No, no." Doctor took him and brought him to me, but he wasn't satisfied at all and only kissed me because his Papa told him to. But today he kisses me or offers to every time I tell him about it. He has been sitting on my lap ever since I got onto this page, so excuse the scratching on that account. Bess and he get along nicely together. We all send lots of love. I just asked Bertie if he knew who Mamma was writing to, and he says, "Yes. Tell her please give me kiss."

Your loving daughter,
Emily FitzGerald

Fort Lapwai
November 19, 1876

My dear Mamma,

I wrote you a note after your last letter had arrived and told you, I think, how glad I was to hear from you again. It doesn't seem to me that we are one bit nearer together than when I was in Sitka.

The Indian Commissioners departed on Wednesday without Joseph coming to any terms. They all got indignant at him at last and threatened him. They told him of the Modocs, who had tried to stand out against the government and their fate, and of the Seminoles and the Sioux, who have lately been over-powered and had their arms and ponies taken from them. He said he was ready for them. General Howard was telling me of it the evening after the last Council and said the Indians were just unwilling to admit the government's authority or any authority but their own, and he believed if the Commissioners had said to Joseph that he should have Wallowa Valley, he would not have accepted it from them or admitted their right to give it to him. General Howard says Joseph has taken the course to make him lose all sympathy for him, and next summer, if the trouble in the Wallowa is brought up again, he will send out two men to Joseph's one — no matter how many he raises — and whip him to submission. Delightful prospect for us whose husbands will probably be in the fight, isn't it?

But I have heard so much of Joseph, and our officers here all think, if brought to the point of a fight with annihilation staring him in the face, Joseph will give up. The Indians, too, about here say he is a coward, so I am not as anxious as I otherwise would be. Mrs. Perry is worried, though, and says she feels that we will have trouble. But then there is one thing, rather pleasant, I forgot to mention. Colonel Wood felt all the while that Joseph would come to terms so soon as he knew they were in earnest, and the last evening here, after the Council was all over and the gentlemen were going to leave early in the morning, Colonel Wood said a dozen times in the course of the evening, "I am expecting to hear from Joseph every minute. I am certain he will come to terms, knowing this is his last chance and that we leave in the morning." Joseph did not come or send word, and the party started off for town at six in the morning. About nine o'clock, in the rain, four most gorgeously gotten up Indians rode up to our back gates and asked for General Howard. (They seem to think he is the most important big chief.) I wish you could have seen them. You never saw such style. I happened to be in the back of the house and went to the gate and called John. Mrs. Perry soon came to her gate, then the Colonel, then two or three officers joined us, and we all stood in the rain, as we hadn't seen such a gorgeous array before. One of them who did the most talking had a headpiece for his horse that covered his horse's whole head. It was just covered with beads. There were holes for the eyes, and it really was very showy. His own costume was of some kind of skin trimmed with ermine. A fringe of ermine shins (whole skins) was around the jacket, and about the knees, and down the seams of the sleeves from shoulder to wrist, and around his cap. Their faces were all painted, and all had bows, and quivers of arrows swung at their backs. The quivers were all highly ornamented with beads. A ferocious looking old medicine man was with them (an old, old man). The other three were quite young chiefs. One was Joseph, himself, who is a splendid looking Indian. As far as we could understand, they had come in to make terms of some sort with General Howard. They all were very smiling and pleasant and seemed very sorry about not finding him. We don't know whether this is the beginning of a settlement, but we hope it is.

How I wish you could have seen them, Mamma. I said to Doctor, as we came in, "What a nice little bit of Indian life that would be to show some of our home people." But doctor said you would not be interested, although I know you would. He has seen so much of it himself, it is an old thing. You must be tired of hearing about it, though, and I will stop talking Indian.

Senator Mitchell of Oregon is going to introduce Doctor's bill in the Congress. I do hope it will go through all right. We won't be any richer if it does, but will be eight hundred dollars poorer if it doesn't, which is a small fortune. I feel so happy, though, to think that even if it comes to the worst and we do lose it, that by economy we can live on a little money Doctor has in the house, just as we are, until he gets his pay again without having to borrow or go in debt. I don't believe six army families out of every twelve I know could do that.

Tell me why Bessie's stockings always wear out at the heels. I can account for the thin places on the knees, for she crawls about. But the big holes in the heels rather amaze me.

I will write again next week. We all join in love. You speak in your last letter of sending me another book, for which I am very much obliged It has not come yet, but I am looking for it. We see so little in the way of books out here. With ever so much love to all, I am

Your daughter,
E. L. F.

P.S. Mamma, Jennie is in trouble about her shoes and wants me to send for some like I wear. They do bring awful shoes to the stores out here. Jennie came in to show me hers and said, "No good. All same nothing." I told her I gave a whole lot of money for mine — five dollars and a half. She said, "Me give, too." Will you get Jennie a good pair of buttoned boots of the same sort, number 5? I will be much obliged to you for her. The poor girl has worn out three pairs of these store shoes since we came here, and I don't wonder she is disgusted. She has had a great admiration for my boots all along.

Monday Evening

I am just going to bed and will say goodbye. Doctor and I are going in to town in the morning to get some shoes for Bess and to attend to some of Doctor's business. It is a long ride of 12 miles. I hate it, and the town is simply awful. May Town and Little Washington are enormous cities compared to it. We will take this in with us and have it mailed there, as our mail does not leave until Wednesday. With much love, I am,

Your affectionate daughter,
Emily FitzGerald

Fort Lapwai
November 26, 1876

Dear Mamma,

This week the three packages arrived safely, and I am very much obliged for all. I felt so glad you were sending me a book, but it seems, at these isolated places, as if we never were allowed to have more than one new book at a time. Just the evening before your package arrived, Mr. Fletcher told me he had a new book that Old Mr. Barstow had left with Mrs. Monteith. He had told her to let the post ladies read it. It was "Helen's Babies," and when I opened my bundle, I could not help smiling, for the same thing happens so many times Last winter when I was in Sitka and wanting something to read awfully, I got two copies of "Mrs. Mainwaring's Journal." Thank you ever so much, though; I read my own copy and did laugh over it. Those children were the most wonderful I ever heard of.

Nothing ever happens at this post. We live along from week to week without seeing a strange face or hearing anything new. Our gentlemen are all exercised about the election and are wondering whether they will know before the 4th of March who is elected. Some of them have driven into town almost every mail to get the dispatches, not able to wait until the mail matter was brought out here.

Only four weeks until Christmas, and what a nice time you will all have together. We have decided to light up the children's tree on Saturday night, as we (the big folks) are all going to spend Monday evening with Mrs. Perry, and it would be awfully hard to keep the children's things from them over Sunday. We shan't give them much, but you know how little things will delight a child. Doctor could not get a gun of any kind for Bertie. He wanted one of those that shoot a cork, and the cork is tied to the gun with a string, so he has concluded to make his own, and also to make a dollie trunk for Bess. He worked at the trunk last night after the babies were off. You should see it. Sallie and I would have gone crazy over it when we were young. It has a little tray and two top trays and is to be all nicely lined. It is a very good thing to have such a husband when you can't possibly buy things for the babies. I have the dollie nearly dressed. It is to have a cloak, cap, and nightgown. We will have quite enough to set Bess nearly crazy, but I am not so well satisfied about poor Bertie's presents. He does want a dollie, too, and I told you that we meant to fix Katie as a Zouave, but poor Katie has disappeared. I am afraid the Indians have carried it off. The children had it about the back door.

Mamma, I meant to ask you (and forgot) in my last letter whether you would like to have beaver trimming like Sallie's? You know I have another lot just like Sallie's which I intended for Bertie, but it is too long a fur for a child, and anyway, he won't want such a thing for years. I see in the magazines that beaver, plucked and unplucked, is much worn for common trimming, and as it is so dark, I happened to think you might want such a thing to wear in and out in the cars. You are perfectly welcome to it; indeed, I will be very glad to send it to you. I think there is over six yards in the piece I have, and if you will wear it, I will send it to you as soon as I hear.

Tuesday
November 28, 1876

The mail will leave in a little while and this letter is not finished. A mail came in a few hours ago and brought such a nice pair of woolen stockings directed in your writing.

Doctor just heard from Washington about his pay being stopped. Instead of stopping all for four months, they will stop part for a longer time, so I think I will be able to make that 450 dollars in the bank 500 before the year is out. Did you give Uncle Essick whatever papers you have connected with that money? If so, I will just send to him, if I can get what I want to add to it. Doctor joins me in very much love. I hope you will have a lovely Thanksgiving; indeed, I know you will, all there together. John and I will spend a quiet one alone. Love to all.

Your affectionate daughter,
Emily

Fort Lapwai
December 21, 1876

Dear Sallie,

I heard from Mamma last night and got three nice bundles from Columbia and one came the mail before. I will write soon to Aunt Annie. In the meantime, thank her ever so much for me. I am very much obliged to you all for the nice bundles. The one with the animals in it got mashed dreadfully, but Doctor has fixed up all the toys except the animals, so they are all right. One lion came out whole and Bert was more delighted with it than with anything else, much to our amusement. The box with the dollies in it came nicely, also the dishes and a box with candles and candle sticks directed in your writing. Indeed, you are all so kind that I don't know what to say to thank you. I am writing this in a hurry as a mail goes out tonight and I want to get off a note to some of you telling you the bundles had arrived. The children will be crazy, I am afraid, when they get all their toys.

Someone called in that the Christmas trees had come. I must go and see about them. Everybody at the post has something for the children, and I don't suppose I will have any peace for a month. Too much is worse than too little, as Bert is to have a horse, a drum, two guns, and a trumpet, besides his other toys. I don't see our future as very delightful. Lots of love.

Your affectionate sister,
Emily FitzGerald

Fort Lapwai
December 28, 1876

Dear Aunt Annie,

Your letter and all the bundles arrived this week. Indeed, you just sent us lots. I don't think you are to be depended upon to make out lists, though, for there were about three times as many things came as you had on the list. Bertie's admiration for his dollie that he calls "My boy" is real funny. It was so nice to get all those bundles Our mails were delightful for weeks before Christmas.

We are awfully cold out here. I wonder how you all keep warm in Columbia. I don't like cold weather a bit and will rejoice to go where there is perpetual summer.

I am going to have the people of the garrison (seven) all here tomorrow evening, the gentlemen to play whist. After this holiday week is over, I suppose we will settle down and be quiet until next Christmas. We took our Christmas dinner at the Agency. I wish you could have seen the winter costumes of some of the Indians we met who were going to dine with the chief. It was an awfully cold day, and we went down in a sleigh, but the favorite costume of most of the Indians we met seemed to be linen coats and straw hats. (These are Treaty Indians.)

You send me so many nice things, Aunt Annie, I don't know how I shall ever make it up to you.

Your niece,
Emily FitzGerald

Fort Lapwai
December 28, 1876

Dear Mamma,

On Christmas Eve, the two packages arrived (the pictures) and I knew what they were before I had them undone any farther than the box. I was so glad to get them. It is just what I wanted most and I think it is such a lovely Christmas gift. Indeed, Mamma, if you had thought about it for a year you could not have sent me anything I would like better than these photos. We have had a busy week, or I would have written before. The children's tree was real pretty. Everybody came to see it and the babies were delighted with their things.

Mrs. Perry had a tree for the laundresses' children and had it lighted up, and she had all the garrison in on Monday evening. She gave us a delightful cold supper, and we had a merry time. This evening we were all invited to the Agency. I did not go, as I want the garrison all here tomorrow evening, and I knew if I was to stay out late tonight I would not feel like getting my own little lunch ready tomorrow for the evening. I can stand anything better than loss of rest at night. That just takes all the strength right out of me.

December 30, 1876

I must finish my letter, as the mailman will call tonight. Such a day as I had yesterday! I told you that Doctor was going to have a little whist party and I invited the rest of the garrison to drop in. Well, the night before, Jennie concluded to go on a bust. Are you too respectable to know what a "bust" is? Poor Jennie likes a little whiskey. She has only been a little tight once or twice since she lived with us, and I hoped, really thought, she had gotten entirely over it, though I scarcely ever left her alone with the babies more than an hour or two at a time. Her failing in that direction was one thing that influenced me in having her in the kitchen and being nurse myself. But this time she was worse than I ever saw her and she kept it up yesterday until John had to send her to bed. I had gotten all ready for my lunch the day before, but I had the house to get in order, and the dinner dishes and kitchen to get cleaned up, and the children to look after, etc. The children deliberately put in disorder everything I fixed, and I had a raging sick headache from my worry and disgust at Jennie. She put all the coffee I had in the house (about 3 pounds) in the stove and burnt it black. Then she upset a boiler of greasy water over the kitchen floor and sat down and cried. Then John sent her to bed about four o'clock (we had had dinner early) and I felt too sick to do the dishes. So I washed the forks and glasses that I wanted for the evening, fixed up the sitting and dining room, set my table, and then found I could not stand it any longer. My head was splitting, so I told John I had to give up — he must run the party himself. He said some very bad things about women in general and about me in particular for having such headaches, and then he came around beautifully and was an angel. So I turned in, just a few moments before the first people came in. Wasn't it disgusting?

John did beautifully. I have seen Mrs. Theller and Colonel and Mrs. Perry this morning and they say they had a lovely time. Doctor made them the best coffee they ever had, and they drank four cups around. I had a nice little lunch, and the table did look very pretty when I went to bed — baked ham, cold roasted chickens, chicken salad, buttered biscuit, and three kinds of cake. We were all invited to spend Monday evening at Mrs. Theller's, and that ends our Christmas festivities.

Jennie is all right this morning, and it may not happen again for a year. I am sure I hope it won't. Now I know you will say I ought to talk to her and reform her, etc., but I would just like to know how you would go about it. If you could have heard my conversation with her this morning (in what

Mr. Fletcher calls my Russian) you might imagine how difficult it was. John talked to her first, a little fiercely. Then I took her in hand, something after this fashion, "Jennie, you give me plenty trouble yesterday. You all same bad woman up in Sitka. Doctor your friend; me your friend; Bess, Bertie like you, but we no like you yesterday," etc. Now tell me how to reform a woman that you have to converse with in that style? This reminds me of Bess and Bertie. They both talk as Jennie does a great deal. Bess will say, "Bertie, you no good boy. Me no love you," etc. And yesterday Bert came to me to tie a handkerchief over his head, and after I tied it, he said with great satisfaction, "All same Grand Ma." (Some grandmothers in their picture books have caps on.)

Mamma, thank you so much for the little magazines. I have always meant to resubscribe for myself but forgot it. A little tract which you sent me some time ago, "The Little Captain," has been wept over by us all and by General Howard, too. Mrs. Perry and I are going to start a little Sunday school with Bessie and the laundresses' children on the first Sunday in the new year, and we mean to invite the men in to help us sing; and leave "The Little Captain" and such books of the sort about for them to entertain themselves with. I feel sure it will benefit me, if it doesn't the children, to have something going on to mark Sunday. We have some little catechisms and will get some kind of hymn books, and I hope, we will be able to interest the children.

Write to us often. I have not been able to get off the beaver trimming, but will certainly by Tuesday's mail. That will be your birthday! I must stop, so with lots of love,

Your daughter,
Emily FitzGerald

Fort Lapwai
January 7, 1877

Mamma Dear,

We began our little Sunday school this afternoon and have

ten real nice children, most of them infants about Bessie's age. There are three little girls and a boy about nine or ten, and the other five, who are my lot, are all between four and six. They are real nice little things and seem glad to come. I will be thankful to you for any hints as to how to be of use to my little people. I am going to ask Uncle Essick for a primer, such as they used to use in the infant school at home, and I am going to send him a dollar or so and ask him to get me some of those little packs of verses of scriptures and pictures he uses in the Sunday school for little people. I hope we can do the children some little good, and I feel so thankful on my own account that we can do something to mark the Sunday. I take Bess with me, and John promises to devote every Sunday afternoon to Bertie and, when it is pleasant, bring him over to meet us. Mrs. Perry has a very sweet voice and will lead us in singing, though we must depend on the tunes we know, as neither of us sings by note.

Our last mail brought me the second bundle and stockings for Bess. They fit her beautifully and are lovely, but the price rather takes my breath. If I had any more children, they would certainly have to go barefooted.

I did not tell you about their Christmas stockings. I think they enjoyed them much more than the tree. They hung them up themselves, and before eight in the morning, they called to ask if Santa Claus had been there. I put the trumpet, the little china dollie, the bells which Aunt Annie sent, an apple, a little cake, and two or three pieces of candy (all their Papa would allow them to have) in the stockings, and they were the most delighted mortals you ever saw.

The mail came in about a half hour ago and brought me two more bundles, the tablecloth, stockings, and Jennie's things. I am so much pleased with this table linen. How I would love a closet full of towels, sheets, napkins, tablecloths, etc., but I want to try to make what I have do until I come home. I think you have gotten me a lovely lot of things and are a "first class" shopper. I am ever so much obliged to Uncle

Owen for settling you down in Philadelphia where you can get just everything I want for me.

Tell me what you would do with a little money that I have of the children's. They have six or seven dollars a piece, and Doctor thinks it absurd to do anything with such small sums, but I know if I don't do something with it, it won't be their money long. Some change will be wanted, and it will be taken by their Mamma or Pappa or someone, and I always thought it a good plan for children, as they grow up, to have a bank account of their own. Would you put it in a dime savings bank, or what?

I must finish my letter as our first mail for this week is gathered up tomorrow. With much love,

Your affectionate daughter,
Emily F.

Fort Lapwai
Sunday
January 14, 1877

Dear Mamma,

Our mail has just come but I am disappointed, as it did not bring anything for me, and I always look for more in our Sunday's mail than in any other.

There is a case of scarlet fever down at the Agency. I hope it won't spread. I know Doctor feels a little anxious about it every time he thinks of our children. He takes the utmost precautions, and if the children up here do get it, it won't be brought up by the Doctor. I have such a horror of scarlet fever that I feel like picking up the babies and flying. I know, too, that John would much rather have an epidemic of smallpox.

I wish you would tell me how Sallie and the other girls wear their hair. I don't think I shall change the fashion of mine, for I have such comfort in wearing nothing on my head but my own hair. I shan't feel like burdening my poor head with anything that doesn't grow there. Nevertheless, I would like to know how other people do fix themselves. I have not spent one day for two years without a little band of velvet around my head, and I miss it now more than my earrings. Isn't it funny how one becomes accustomed to those things?

Later

Doctor was down to the Agency this morning and there is a second case of scarlet fever, much worse than the first. He says we must hope our babies will escape, and if not, they are strong, well children and with the care we will give them, we have every reason to hope for the best, but it would be awfully hard to have them sick way out here. I hope the dear little scamps will not get it at all.

We all join in love. With only Jennie in the house, I don't get much time for writing. At the end of some days, I can't see what I have done all day. Yet I could swear I have not had an idle moment. I can only say the babies, the babies, the babies! They take up all my time. Doctor is waiting. That accounts for the rush of these last two pages. With much love,

Your daughter,
Emily F.

Fort Lapwai
February 9, 1877

Dear Mamma,

This morning's mail brought me the package of little books. I think I will propose to Mrs. Perry that we use them as a sort of little library in our Sunday School. It might encourage the children who can read if we let them take a little story home to read. Bess and Bertie set up a cry of objections and distresses when I opened the package of books and said I would not give any to them but would keep them for Sunday school. There is a particular attraction in a little book to my babies that nothing else seems to have.

I am glad that the fur trimming arrived. You must wear it yourself and not keep it for the children. And you are not depriving me of it. If you can make any possible use of it, I will be delighted. Put it on a petticoat, if you can't on anything else.

You make me quite envious telling me about pretty lockets, for that is the one article of jewelry I really do want. I have never gotten a locket for my chain, though John has often intended to, but I have suggested waiting, as I did not think just at the time that a locket was the most important thing wanted in the family, but tell me about them and what sort of prices, etc. I won't get one now, for I am going to save everything for the next few months to invest in a watch for John.

February 11, 1877

Bess and Bertie have both been so cute and lovely today. I have been awfully afraid something would happen to them, particularly as they both have awful colds. I got to thinking after I put them to bed how dreadful it would be if they should have croup and I should lose them. After they got in bed, Bess said her prayers and finished off with, "Please, God, take care of my Mamma and Pappa and all my friends." Bertie raised his head up from under the covers and said, "Bessie, please God take care my little buzzer." After she had taken his hint, the little darling laid himself down and said, "Please, God, take care my Bessie." This is really, though, an unusual occasion. He doesn't often get so surprisingly angelic. They do a thousand cute little things every day, but it must be awfully stupid to read about it, and, as John says, I am their mother and must make allowances for other people. Lots of love from both John and me.

Your affectionate daughter,
Emily FitzGerald

Fort Lapwai
February 26, 1877

Mamma Dear,

I have not heard from you since I wrote my last, but I know

you were up in Columbia and I suppose that was the reason. I have been anxiously watching the mails since your last letter, for in it you tell me you will send the stuff to darn the new stockings, and I know you will be as much disgusted as I am when I tell you they all need darning.

We are a little troubled about the Indians. Joseph himself was in yesterday to "talk," and things look as if there would be trouble, but, I hope, not attended wih any danger to our garrison. There are some renegade bands belonging to all these tribes around here that would probably join Joseph if he resisted being forced onto the Reservation. They even say there is a band of Sioux up north of us, but that is supposed to be a cock and bull story.

The children are well, but poor Bert always has his awful cold. They are playing out today. The weather is delightful and mild. You would think it was May. The prairie around the post is quite yellow with buttercups. Think of it — flowers in February!

I have written in an awful hurry, as the mail goes out tonight and I want to get this ready before I take a walk with John. He joins me in love.

Your affectionate daughter,
Emily FitzGerald

Fort Lapwai
March 9, 1877

Dear Mamma,

Your little note with the bundle came this morning — my birthday! I thought it would be disgusting, this of all mornings, if I did not get any mail, but I did and was made happy. Why did you spend the money which I sent to repay my debts to you for the children? You are too good, and I don't know how to settle with you. The mail yesterday brought me the nice little package of yarn. Thank you very much. I darned all the stockings and feel quite comforted about them.

I never saw such a winter, at least this part of it. For the last three weeks, it has been so much like spring we have all felt like putting away our winter things. One day we went for a walk, and I got so hot, John carried my shawl and I walked the whole afternoon with only my ordinary house dress. The prairie is yellow with buttercups. There are thousands of them, and Bess picked a bushel.

I am very much pleased with what you tell me about a watch. I told John about it, and if the watch you describe is a stem winder, it is just about what he wants. I like the works covered with crystal, but John is particular in wanting a stem winder. He has been looking over a catalogue of the American Walton watches and is much pleased with the best quality of that watch, but I want him to have a Swiss watch. Doctor says if he sends for the watch which you tell me about, he would like Uncle Owen to satisfy himself that the watch is what they represent it to be. We feel satisfied to leave the matter in Uncle Owen's hands.

Mamma, I want a locket awfully. About the time you get this letter and I get your answer to it, I will be ready to send for the watch, and I think I may be able to send for a locket and get them together. It is sort of fun to be extravagant sometimes. I do want a locket, and I am going to let John get it for me. I want something in that dead yellow gold, and something that does not have a little fussy bunch of something on the front of it to catch in neckties, etc. I would like something odd that would not cost more than 35 dollars. Now, Mrs. Mamma Owen, do you think you can find something that will fill all those requisitions? I am very much afraid you will tell me we can't get anything real nice for that price. If so, I will just do without it for the present.

After she said her prayers last night, Bess came back and said, "Mamma, may I say one little prayer all myself, and will God hear me?" I said, "Certainly," and she knelt down and said, "Please, God, give me my little sister Annie very soon." I am awfully afraid her prayer might be answered. It completely took me by surprise, for I had no idea that was in her mind.

Bert is continually quoting rhymes he has picked up. This morning he went to Bessie's dollie bed where her dollies were supposed to be sleeping, and said very impressively, "Under the hay stack fast asleep —." At the table John asks him, "Will you have some potatoes?" And he replies, "Yes, sir. Yes, sir. Three bags full."

We all join in lots of love to you all. Write soon.

E. L. FitzGerald

Fort Lapwai
March 20, 1877

Dear Mamma,

Last week I did not write. I let my usual time for getting off my letter pass and then I thought I would wait until now, particularly as John was doctoring my eyes. If this writing is beautiful, please attribute it to the fact that I am writing with smoked glasses on. My eyes gave me a little more trouble than usual a few weeks ago, and Doctor put me through a little course of treatment, just resting them and wearing smoked glasses anywhere there was any glare or too much light. I have not read, sewed, or written any for the last two weeks. Doctor talked quite seriously for a little while of sending me home with the babies for a visit so I could see that eye man in Philadelphia, I forget his name, but I have no trouble serious enough for that. I could scarcely get home with the children without John, unless it was absolutely necessary, and the expense would be rather more than we could meet conveniently unless, of course, it was necessary. I shall use my eyes very little until they are quite well. I miss my reading very much, for I find lots of comfort and entertainment in my books and papers at this lonely post.

Did I tell you all the quarters at Sitka had been destroyed by fire? The last link is broken since the house we lived in there is gone. We have just heard of the death in Washington of Mr. Goddard, one of the young officers who was with us in Sitka.

Your last letter made me feel very happy on the locket question. You say I can get a beautiful locket for 20 dollars. That is very comforting, as I do want one very much.

It is spring-like here. Since the first of the month, seven kinds of wild flowers have been blooming all around us, and they are the most fragrant wild flowers I ever knew. All are sweet, and a bunch of them in the house perfumes it like sweet violets. Bess is almost wild about them and brings bunch after bunch into the house and then cries because she can't find anything to put them in. The children live out of doors now. They are sunburnt and freckled, and their hands look like a stableman's, but they are so well, go off to sleep at night like logs, and eat like little pigs. We all join in lots of love to you. I hope you are all well.

With very much love,
I am,
Your loving daughter,
Emily FitzGerald

Fort Lapwai
March 27, 1877

Mamma Dear,

Your letter has just come — the one in which you tell me you think little pleated shirts and skirts would be nice for Bert. I think they would be just the thing. Doctor won't let me sew a bit until my eyes are better, so I can't think of making them myself. Doctor says he wants Bert dressed the way you suggest. He wants him to look like a boy.

My eyes are troublesome when I use them much, but my general health is very good. I am quite well in every other respect, and John thinks my eyes will be quite comfortable and that I can use them a little for everything, if I give them a good rest now. I must have strained them some way or other this winter. I read a great deal in the evenings and began to feel them after finishing a big book of very fine print. As I was nearsighted anyway, Doctor says it was a constant strain. I suppose I will have to use glasses for fine work all my life. Won't I look interesting with spectacles or eye glasses cocked over my nose? I have not written any letters but yours for some weeks. I was obliged to sew a little, or the family would be in rags.

Doctor is still undecided as to whether he wants an American or a Swiss watch. Mr. Monteith, the Indian Agent (a son of the old Presbyterian minister) has an American watch he has carried nine years, and it has never varied five minutes. His brother, Mr. Charles Monteith, has just gotten one of the same kind, which John likes very much. They sent right to the company that makes those Waltham watches. John has one of their catalogues and is very much pleased with one style of watch they advertise. I still want him to have a Swiss one, but some way or other, everybody at this post is crazy over American watches.

This letter is written awfully, but I am writing fast to get it done. I have an awful cold in my head which makes my eyes, in their sensitive condition, feel watery. I am quite attached to my smoked glasses.

In your letter you tell me you want a beaver muff and marten for muff and boa. Dr. will write to Colville at once. I know we can get the beaver, but Doctor says marten are very scarce and there are no good skins. I hope we can get real nice skins for you, though.

How I do want to see you! I feel as if I would be satisfied to go any place, if first I can just have one good visit at home. John is awfully good and the children are very precious, but I feel the need of some of my relatives every now and then. With lots of love, I am,

Your daughter,
Emily FitzGerald

Fort Lapwai
April 9, 1877

Mamma Dear,

Doctor says he will write to you this week, but I am sure he can't tell you about the children's clothes, although he insists he can. I will begin the letter and he will finish. The mail today brought the two pink dresses you have made for Bess and they fit her just as nicely as if you had her there to try them on a dozen times. She looks very sweet in them.

I won't want as many dresses for the children this summer as I thought I did at first. Bess will do with four more dresses, and I am glad you can buy me them all made up. For Bert I want stockings and gossamer flannel shirts. He won't need more than four suits, if I have the big aprons to put over them. I sent 10 dollars to you, and I will enclose five more today. I am feeling awfully poor, as nearly a hundred dollars was stopped from John's pay this month, and I am afraid I see my locket and John's watch some months farther off than I did hope to at first. So, I won't send for some more things I did want until I see what comes to pass.

(Doctor FitzGerald continues the letter.)

Dear Mamma,

As Emily's eyes are not strong, and as I am insisting on her resting them as much as possible, I will attempt to finish this letter for her. This weakness of her eyes has been brought on by several causes and is strictly local, i.e., does not depend on general ill health. I think a few months of rest will make them as good as ever.

Emily wishes me to ask if you have heard through Aunt Pace of the death of Mrs. Dr. McParlin at Santa Fe, New Mexico, a few weeks ago. This is the only item Em has given me and she tells me to finish by "telling you of the children," just as if you had not already been deluged with subject matter relating to them. We do wish, however, that you and the friends generally might see them, as we feel they would so well pass their closest criticism as to mental brightness, health, and possible good looks. They are as brown as berries with playing out in the sun these long, pleasant days. Bess is, however, only a little bit tanned, while Bertie is a fine nut color, and is developing quite a patch of freckles across his nose. The morning is the only time of day in which they are presentable. They spend the greater part of the day gathering wild flowers, which are now very abundant, even on the parade ground.

I think I never experienced so pleasant a spring nor one so early as this, and I am sure I have never seen wild flowers so early. I believe the climate cannot be excelled anywhere for salubrity, and in this belief, I am reconciled to a reasonably lengthy sojourn at Fort Lapwai. Emily is not as kindly disposed, however, to a long residence here as the undersigned, and she thinks she would like to bid it "goodbye forever" next year, although that event is extremely doubtful.

Em says to say that the three *Scribners* came by today's mail and we are very much obliged, as we have been enjoying the contents very much. Em says to tell you she has made two very interesting Sunday school lessons out of the story of Joseph and she illustrated them with pictures, much to the delight of the youngsters; and she wishes you would suggest some lessons she can draw from the various Bible stories that she could impress on the minds of the children. She says she can tell them all the Bible stories, but, to save her life, she can't find any points in most of them. Em says she is going to use the little books sent her as the beginning of a Sunday school library from which the children can take one every Sunday, and that Mrs. Martin sent six more books of about the same size and the biggest children seemed delighted with the idea.

This is all Emily has to say, and, for my part, I am sorry it is not more connected. I regret also that it is not better written. Please make allowances for this. We join in sending love to you all.

Very sincerely yours,
J. A. FitzGerald

Fort Lapwai
April 19, 1877

Dear Mamma,

Emily's eyes are much better than they were when I last wrote for her, but it is too soon for her to resume either writing or reading, and so it is again my duty as well as my pleasure to write you. I am much pleased at the idea of the dresses you speak of for Bertie, for he is now quite large, and I think he should begin to wear something distinctive of his gender, and Em thinks likewise. I shall be quite glad to see the change.

We hope you had a pleasant visit to Columbia. A letter received from Aunt Annie, since your last letter, spoke of your expected coming there, and we hope you found Bep in better health than he has been in. By the by, if practicable, we would be glad to have him visit us. There is no better climate in the U. S. We are enjoying perfectly delightful weather and have been for many weeks. It has been quite warm and summery for some days, in fact, more like June weather in the states than April.

Last Sunday we had a visit from Bishop Morris of Oregon and a Mr. Wells, Episcopal minister at Walla Walla. The bishop recollects Mr. Owens and will call to see you at Chestnut Hill. As they were preparing to leave last Sunday, their team of horses, in being brought up to the door, took fright and ran away, breaking the wagon to smash, but, fortunately, without injury to anyone.

By this mail we send you a few Sitka papers which we received a few days ago. They may contain matter of curious interest to you. Did we tell you that our old quarters at Sitka had been burned last February? The whole row was destroyed, comprising of 4 sets of quarters, and by the last papers I see that the Secretary of War has ordered the troops away from Sitka. We are disappointed that he did not think of it a little sooner so that we could have had the benefit of the shorter term of service there.

There is nothing of special local interest to tell you at this time. The children are just blooming with rosy cheeks and wholesomeness. Emily and I took them out a few days ago, picnicking and fishing over in the woods by the creek, and we enjoyed it so much that we determined to repeat the experience frequently this summer. Emily joins me in love to you. I think she may be able to write to you again in two weeks or so.

Very sincerely and
lovingly yours,
J. A. FitzGerald

Fort Lapwai
May 1, 1877

Dear Mamma,

Much to my delight, John says I can write a little. It is the most aggravating thing in the world to have him write my letters. He is always suggesing what he calls better words, when I give him a sentence to write, and doing all sorts of troublesome things. For instance, if I say *too,* he writes *also,* which spoils the effect and doesn't sound like me. I wanted to write by this evening's mail and tell you the two nice bundles had come. The things were all as nice as they could be, and, indeed, the stockings were too nice. Didn't I beg you to get me common ones? It is necessary for the children to dress here in common things, both on account of the way we all live and the way they conduct themselves, and, too, on account of our means. You see so many nice little children that you don't like the idea of your grandbabies not having as nice fixings as any of them, but, indeed, we don't want it, and it is foolish to wear nice things here on the frontier where there isn't an individual to see them ever but the Indians who go stark naked, or nearly so. I just want good, stout, plain little garments to cover the children, and one or two things just a little better for Sunday, and then I am satisfied. For myself, I don't need a thing this summer. We are dreadfully straightened with Doctor's pay being stopped. Fortunately, we don't need to spend much here, and we have no debts. I do want a watch for John and I will send you the check for the amount or P. O. orders about the middle of this month. I am sorry I have not been able to send for it before. Doctor would like the permission to exchange the watch if he is not pleased. I have forgotten what you said (exactly) the watch would cost. I know it was something under 130 dollars. I will send 125 or 130 dollars, and if there is anything left over, it can go to the bill you will have against me by that time.

My eyes are much better. The light doesn't hurt them at all, but I can't read any or sew or write, and they only hurt me when I try to look at anything — that is, when I try to concentrate my eyes on anything. You insist in your letters that my health must not be particularly good, but, indeed, Mamma, I am very well. Do you know my throat scarcely ever troubles me any more, and my headaches are few and far between? I am not particularly strong, that is, I get tired easily if I do anything out of my usual course. One thing I always notice is that I always get so tired if I stay up (at a little party or evening out some place) after my usual time for going to bed. If I keep regular hours and preserve the even tenor of my ways, I never have an ache or pain or ill feeling. I almost always have some tonic on hand. John takes the very best kind of care of me. I never knew him to be put out, no matter what I was doing, if I called him to help me with something that was heavy or high or tiresome for me, even churning. If I am churning, he takes it in hand, if he sees me, and makes me look on. But I am well. I weigh 116 pounds, as much as when I was married, but I am so anxious to get fat that John got me another case of stout which I am going to drink all up. I am afraid you won't let me into such a respectable family as yours when I come home with my failing for "Porter." Now, about having someone to help me with the children, I am obliged to get a Chinaman, as I can get no one else to do the washing. My trouble is to know what to do with Jennie. As it is, with my fixing my own room and looking after the babies,

I am often distracted to find something to occupy my time, particularly when I can't read and sew, and when I turn these duties over to Jennie, I will be the most doleful object you can imagine.

Poor Captain Smith died and was buried. His death makes changes here. Mr. Fletcher leaves by promotion, and Major Boyle comes to Captain Smith's company. That will give us another lady, Mrs. Boyle. I know her. She is very pleasant and I am glad she is coming. Then the Indians are to come onto the reservation at once, or be driven on. General Howard and has two aides are at the post and will be in this neighborhood until Joseph is on the reservation.

Next Friday there is to be a big Council here. How I wish the girls were here with me to see the performance. Joseph is to have his last day of grace. If he doesn't promise at this Council to come at once, General Howard departs for Portland the same evening to collect all the available troops and drive him on or kill him. We all think there will be no trouble, and that Joseph will come to terms when it comes to the point.

I must stop, as my eyes burn and John will scold like a ferocious man if he sees the length of this letter.

Your loving daughter,
Emily F.

Fort Lapwai
May 4, 1877

Mamma Dear,

I will write a note today as I am afraid I won't have time tomorrow. I am going to get a new Chinaman and also have the back rooms of our house white washed. Besides all that, there will be an Indian Council at the post.

There is a big tent pitched on the parade ground, about as far from our porches as from your front door across the street, and in and around it, squatted on the ground, are about a hundred Indians in the most gorgeous get-ups you can imagine. General Howard and his aides, the Indian Agent, and several of the officers of the post in full uniform are inside talking with Joseph. The outside line of Indians around the tent consists almost entirely of squaws and papooses. We go over every now and then, but I soon get tired, and the smell is strongly Indian.

I suppose the talk will continue for two or three days. We feel just a little afraid, just enough to keep it interesting. I feel like hunting up the children every few moments and asking, "Where is the Doctor?" No one really expects anything horrible, but I felt very glad of the precautions the General saw fit to take, not that he feared a surprise, but he says that he has made it a rule all his life to be prepared for one among hostiles of any kind. The guards were doubled this morning and both companies are armed in their quarters. Of course, all this is out of sight of the Indians, and none of the officers in the Council are armed. It is interesting, though, to see the bright picture before me — the tent and the bright blankets out on the parade.

The proceedings before this Council were weird and queer enough to remind me of our Bible stories of the early conquering of Canaan. The Indians rode out from the Canyon in single file. All were on ponies and in their gorgeous array and instead of turning into the post gates, they circled the post three times, cupping their mouths with their hands, making the sound of Wah-Wah-Wah. When they finally stopped at the gate, they stacked their arms before entering the post. At one time during the Council, Mrs. Perry and I were listening to the speeches when one young brave got very excited in his gestures. As he raised his arm in emphasis, a long, sharp knife fell on the ground. (They were to enter the Council unarmed!) Well, it did not make us feel any more comfortable, and we felt less so when we heard the command whispered among the officers to send word out to "double the guard."

We are all well. My eyes are better, but I don't use them much yet for sewing or reading. With lots of love, I am

Your loving daughter,
Emily FitzGerald

Fort Lapwai
May 5, 1877

Dear Mamma,

The Indian Council has not had the result we expected. Joseph won't answer yes or no, and so he must be made to answer. On Monday the Indian chiefs, Joseph, White Bird, and Ollikut, will again see the general and the Agent and unless they say unconditionally *yes* (which no one thinks they will) six or eight companies of troops will be on the move after them by Tuesday morning. Two-thirds of the troops from Lapwai are of the number that will be under marching orders. We are safe here, but if they would only leave the Doctor here, too, I should be happy, but he will go with the troops. Poor Mrs. Perry is almost crazy. Her husband was badly wounded in the Modoc War.

We can all see that General Howard is very anxious, but I don't think it is only about this, for Joseph's band is the only one under consideration now and the only roving band that belongs to this reservation, but the General expects to spend the summer in the field, as his orders are to have all the Non-Treaty Indians in this Department on reservations by fall. The Government had decided to put up with no more roving Indians, and the same policy that is being carried out on the plains is to be carried on here. There are ever so many bad Indians that belong to the Columbia River region, and I am afraid it will be a long campaign. You will probably soon see something about it in the papers. General Howard is very careful, though, and will not march out his troops unless he is sure of the number of the Indians and sure of having three to one. Of course, I shall feel lonely and anxious if the troops from here go, and, as Doctor said last night, "Now if only there were some of your friends that could stay with you." Think how nice it would be for me if some of you could be with me while John is away. My comfort is this — I don't think Joseph's band will make much resistance, and after they are on the reservation, the troops will have to be left here to keep them on the reservation.

It would seem sort of funny to you that the people here take things so quietly. I am continually wondering why no one (but Mrs. Perry) seems excited. Yesterday an Indian (a good one) was sent off with dispatches, taking with him spare horses and going to ride day and night so as to have certain companies of troops near here by Monday night, but we fuss over our dinners and clothes, etc., as if it was the most usual thing in the world to have trouble with the Indians. Oh, how I hate them. I wish they could be exterminated, but without bloodshed among our poor soldiers. General Howard is promenading the porch quoting scriptures. Indeed, I think he is real good, but he is awfully queer about it.

(Mrs. Hiestand (Bessie) said, "One of my early recollections is watching with awe General Howard marching up and down the porch which ran the width of the two houses. I remember the light falling through the hop vines covering the porch and General Howard, his empty sleeve tucked in his blouse (he lost an arm in the Civil War) quoting verse after verse of scripture.")

My China boy came yesterday and I have him on my mind, too. He has to be taught our ways. His name is Tome.

With much love to all, I am

Your loving daughter,
Emily F.

Fort Lapwai
May 11, 1877

Dear Mamma,

We have been quite gay at Lapwai for the last three weeks with our Indians and our strange officers at the post, and all this following on poor Captain Smith's death, and all connected with it. The Boyles will be here in another week, and that will be something to stir us up a little, too.

General Howard and Captain Wilkinson are still here, and next week an inspector and a paymaster will be here. We can't complain of any monotony in our lives for these spring months, at any rate. We all feel much more comfortable about the Indians. Joseph seems inclined to come in now. I guess he sees too many soldiers about. Major Trimbell's company is encamped just outside of the post, and Joseph's brother, Ollikut, who was on his way down towards the Wallowa to see about his stock, met Colonel Whipple with a couple of companies of cavalry on their way up here. He was rather alarmed, for he has sent word back to Joseph to make the best terms he can with General Howard. I guess Mr. Ollikut thinks the soldiers are too many for him. He has always given more trouble than Joseph and has kept his band from coming to terms. He is a splendidly horrible looking Indian, over six feet, and straight as an arrow.

Joseph has his camp about half a mile from here, and he comes down every few days and shakes hands all around. Indians must always shake hands whenever they see you. No matter how many of us should be sitting on the porch, when an Indian came up for anything, he would shake hands all around. I happened to go out this morning when General Howard was talking to a couple of them on the porch, and they all shook my hand fervently and looked straight into my eyes as they departed. One was "Looking Glass," one "White Bird," and the other, some unpronounceable Indian name with three h's in it. "Hush-Hush-soot" is quite a big man among these Non-Treaty Indians just now, and there are quite a number of other wonderful names that I can make an attempt at pronouncing, but can't spell. Our minds are relieved (mine is, at least) as there is no probability of Doctor's being obliged to leave home for the present, at least.

My eyes, to change the subject, are still improving. I don't use them much but can darn my stockings, etc., without any trouble. I have not heard from you for two weeks, but probably tomorrow's mail will bring me a letter.

There is a Mr. Thompson, a Presbyterian minister from Olympia, at the Agency this week. He came up the other day and I found him very pleasant indeed. He says he is sent up here by the Board of Home Missions. His title is "Presbyterian Missionary," and he is to establish churches, etc., where he thinks them needed and possible. I asked him to baptize Bert while he was in this neighborhood, and he will be up this week to do it.

General Howard is to preach at the Agency on Sunday. He doesn't like it called "preaching." He calls it "talking." He is quite an interesting talker. Captain Wilkinson, his aide and right hand man, does the singing. Our little Sunday school is flourishing. Some of the children seem to like to come very much. I hope we do them some good. I am sure the going does me good, at least, and I like to talk to the children, too.

We are feeling dreadfully poor, but I am still holding to my decision that the Doctor's watch is to be my first thought until he has it. The money or check will be mailed to you next week. Have you any idea what the express on such a package will be?

I told you about John's pay being stopped in part. Now, to make matters better (?), the funds for the payment of the army have "run out," and that last, mean, rebel Congress refused to make a new appropriation for it. So, after this month, there will be no more money for poor army people until the next Congress meets sometime in the fall and makes a new appropriation. We will pull through some way, but I am afraid that John will have to draw on the little sum I felt so comfortable about in the Columbia bank to meet the payment of his insurance policies. This is a pretty sort of a government. It is as bad as repudiating the national debt to refuse to pay the hired soldiers. If the government is worth anything at all, out of respect for itself, it should keep up a respectable army. We are all sort of disgusted with things at Washington.

With much love, I close. The children are very well, and we all talk of you often.

Your loving daughter,
Emily FitzGerald

Fort Lapwai
May 16, 1877

Mamma Dear,

The enclosed check is the best plan, Doctor thinks, to send the money I want in your hands for the watch. Get the watch, but if in the meantime you have written me about lockets, don't send it until I write to you about them. This check for 150 dollars will get both, won't it?

Major Fowler will mail this to you from Portland. I believe I will have you send the watch immediately. The rest of the money you can hold. The locket can be sent by mail, registered, any time. That will be the best plan, as I want the watch as soon as possible and don't want the locket until you tell me of the two or three I can choose.

Your loving daughter,
Emily FitzGerald

Fort Lapwai
May 18, 1877

My Dear Mamma,

I want my regular letter to go off tonight. I have not heard since I wrote last, but my letters from you almost always come on Sunday, and tomorrow's mail may bring one. I wrote you a hurried note to enclose a check for 150 dollars, the biggest investment I expect to make for a long time, but one that I want to make, as the pleasure of having what I will get for it will more than compensate, I hope. I only intended sending the price of the watch, which is something less than 120 dollars if

I remember right, but John declared if I wouldn't get a locket, he wouldn't carry a watch. I hope the check will get both watch and locket and leave a little over to pay part of what I will owe you. I will be so delighted to have John have a handsome watch. Don't you think you could get me some sort of a little chain, something neat looking? I expect you think I have lots to say about the small matter of investing in a watch, but in the first place, it is a big investment for us in the present state of our pockets. And in the second place, Doctor's having a good watch is a matter that for a long time has been very near my heart. I am so much obliged to you and Uncle Owen, and I am sorry I have given so much trouble.

I have had a Chinaman for two weeks. I got him because I could make no other arrangements about my washing, but I find now I can, and I am going back to the old arrangement. I have suffered these last weeks in not having a single thing to do to occupy me, as my eyes won't allow me to read or do more sewing than putting on buttons. I told the children this morning that Tome was going away, Jennie would cook, and Mamma would dress and undress them again and wash their faces. They went off into such an uproar of delight that I thought to myself, "Mrs. F., there is your work, and you ought to do it always as long as your health is so good and you are not rolling in money."

Well, Mamma dear, your grandson was baptized last night—William Herbert FitzGerald. I think I must have forgotten to tell you that we meant to add the William. What do you think of it? It was John's doings. I believe he thought it would please me. Bertie has called himself Willie boy or Billie boy all winter because of the red stockings you sent him and the picture in a Mother Goose book. ("Willie boy, Willie boy, where are you going?") Bess was very much distressed this morning. I said, "Come here, William Herbert FitzGerald." She said, "No, no Mamma. It is Bertie."

Mr. Thompson had a little service at the post last evening. He came up early and took tea with me. I like Mr. Thompson very much. He made the children perfectly happy by a romp with them. He made our tea table very merry by some funny stories, and he pleased John by discussing with him all sorts of questions that he (Doctor) is interested in. I was so glad to have John meet such a man as Mr. Thompson. Doctor, you know, insists that all ministers are always harping on the one subject, religion, and bringing it into all discussions and not willing to see anything else. So after Mr. Thompson left last night, I said, "John, don't you like him?" He said, "Yes, very much. He was an entertaining, interesting man." I said, "Well, was he all those bad things you say about ministers?" He said, "No. Mr. Thompson and Uncle Owen are exceptions." So, much delighted, I pulled his ears and told him to wait until we made our long visit home. I would show him that he would find a whole lot more exceptions among the people we were accustomed to. All such little matters encourage me very much.

John heard this week from Colville about the marten furs we have been trying to get for you. The furs this year are not good and are seven dollars a skin, which is a dollar a skin more than we expected to pay. I don't think you want to invest under the circumstances.

I have not told you the most important news of all. Doctor has to go to Portland next week as a witness for Major Campbell in some suit about those Alaska troubles. While Major Campbell was in command at Sitka, some men were arrested for introducing whiskey into the territory. They abused Major Campbell dreadfully in the papers, and ever so many brought suit against him in the civil courts. Major writes Doctor this will be a test case. John may be gone a month. I shall be lonely, but how much better I shall feel than if he was out after the Indians. John would like to take us with him, but we can't afford it. At any rate, what is the pleasure of going away from home to a hotel with two babies?

With lots of love, I am
E. L. FitzGerald

Fort Lapwai
May 27, 1877

Dear Mamma,

The *Spy* just came and I have been looking over the local news. It revives all my old interest in Columbia and makes me want to ask a thousand questions. I see name after name that I know, but I shall never get up the same kind of interest in any people again as far as neighborhoods and surroundings are concerned, for we never stay long enough at any place for me to feel at home. Of course, I always do in my own house, and I hurry up the fixing to get us all settled and home like, but beyond that, to save my life, I can't help feeling all the time as if we were just waiting (like our friend "Micawber") for something to turn up. And when I inquire into it, I find the something I am waiting for is to go East and be among my own people and old surroundings again.

John may have to go to Portland this week. I will miss him so much! Mamma, I forgot to say I am so much obliged for the bundle. Yesterday's mail brought the *Mother Goose* book from Sallie and there was great rejoicing over it. The children took it to bed with them last night. The package had some other nice little things in it for them. You are all so good to think of them so often. We enjoy the things you send them as much as they do.

Later

We have just come from a walk in the woods with the entire family. Bess would stop to pick every flower and kept calling after us, "Oh do wait. I am afraid you might loss your children." Doctor had a little whist party last night for the officers who are here with the extra company. I had a nice little lunch. I rather like him to play and enjoy whist as he does. There are so many other things that other people, we are often with, do that are so much worse and that he doesn't do, that I am glad he does enjoy his rubber of whist. I always enter into the sport of the thing by getting up a lunch for him whenever he wants it.

I hope the check for 150 dollars will reach you safely. I feel concerned about it until I shall hear you have gotten it. Now, Mamma, will you please get me sacks and a couple more garments for them each to wear for summer dresses, and then we will have a final settling up of money matters and I will send you at once what I will owe you.

I have had such a time getting them hats. I got Bess a little brown sundown and trimmed it with my pet necktie (a brown one) as I could not get any brown ribbon. I got her a smaller one, too, which I will trim for better. John will bring me a couple of sailor hats for Bert from Portland. The hats they bring to this town, 12 miles from us, are perfectly awful. We all join in much love to Uncle Owen and all of you.

Your loving daughter,
Emily F.

Fort Lapwai
May 29, 1877

Mamma Dear,

John does not go to Portland for another week. I have gotten now to wishing he would get off and back so I would have it over. He will not be gone quite three weeks. I was afraid it would be longer. Your letter came this morning and I was so glad to hear from you. It was written just before you left for Chicago. I hope some place in your travels you will find some sacks for the children. The evenings and mornings are all too cool for them to play without something, and their present wraps are positively shameful. I am ashamed of them myself. I wish I had something real common for their play and then something a little better for Sunday School and dress up occasions, but we are feeling awfully poor. Do you know the army will have no pay for practically six months? We heard from some army friends in Portland this morning and they say army people are very blue. It will be a great inconvenience to everybody. I am so glad, though, that John has sent for the watch, for if he had known this first, nothing would have induced him to let me get it. I won't be able to buy anything more until we begin to feel a little richer. I won't be able to get some things I wanted for the house, but, goodness gracious, after all, our happiness or comfort doesn't depend upon them, and I can just as well get on a little longer with my old table covers and old hall carpet as not.

May 30, 1877

I stopped writing yesterday and will finish this for tonight's mail. Nothing in this world has ever been so annoying as this trouble with my eyes. As John says, it is so hard to rest them entirely. I am continually forgetting and doing some little thing thoughtlessly that makes them hurt again. John goes to Portland on Wednesday. He will write soon himself.

Your loving daughter,
Emily F.

Fort Lapwai
June 13, 1877

Mamma Dear,

It seems a long time since I wrote to you, as I did not write all last week, but I suppose you will find so many of my letters waiting for you when you get home, you will think I spent all my time writing.

John is in Portland and I am awfully lonely without him. I do hope he won't make many trips of this sort away from us. I know, too, he wants to be back as much as we want him. He left a week ago today, and I hope he will be home a week from tomorrow, but Major Boyle and Mr. Monteith told me they don't think it possible for him to come so soon. I will be dolefully disappointed if he doesn't.

I hope the check for 150 dollars has reached Uncle Owen long before this and that the watch will soon be on the way. I am anxious to know what it costs and how much money there is over and how much I owe you, so I can make up my mind if I can comfortably invest in a locket or whether I had better hold on to the money. We are going to be very short of funds until after Congress meets in the fall, and we won't be very rich then.

Major Boyle's family arrived last week and they are nearly fixed. Mrs. Boyle is a very pretty woman and pleasant. They have children, for which I am very glad. They are much older than mine, but it is pleasant to see the young people about this quiet post. They have a pretty girl about twelve, a boy about ten, and a grown-up son.

Friday, June 15, 1877

Well, our Indian troubles, that we thought all over, have begun again, and this time the officers here seem to think it means business. General Howard is here again, and an Indian inspector from Washington is at the Agency. The thirty days that was given the Indians to come onto the Reservation expires today, and early this morning a party was started from the post to the upper part of the Reservation to see if they were keeping their promises. The party came back an hour ago, riding like mad people, and brought with them two friendly Indians that they met on the mountains and who were bound for the post and the Agency. The Indians had been riding all night and said other Indians, not friendly, were after them. These Indians bring word that the Indians have murdered four settlers up by the mountains, and that they are holding war dances, and that White Bird is riding round his tent on horseback and making circles on the ground, which is his way of declaring that they have taken up the hatchet, etc.

General Howard sent at once for four companies more to move up here and has sent off for hard bread and all such things that troops on a scout need. Things look exciting.

The story of the Indians is corroborated by a letter sent to the General from some settler up in the region asking for help and stating that the Indians were making trouble already and saying, "For God's sake, send plenty of troops. Don't handle them with gloves on." I have heard officers discussing it, and the general impression is that if the Indians have begun, the troops are in for a summer campaign. General Howard said, "I wish the Doctor was here, but I will dispatch at once for Dr. Alexander, who is at Wallula, and he can join us at once." My first thought was that I was glad John wasn't here, but I know he would feel that his place was with the troops from the post he belongs to. If there is trouble, he will have to go anyway, as soon as he gets back. So I expect that all my delight in getting him back will be spoiled by knowing he will have to leave me again at once. We here will feel perfectly safe. The post will not be left without a good garrison. Two companies of infantry, at least, will be left here. But how anxious we will be about the little party out after the Indians. It is all horrible!

Mrs. Boyle just ran down the back way for a minute to discuss the matter for a little. She says it makes her feel sick. It is dreadful to think what might happen, but I can't think these Indians, those we have seen so often, are going to fight the troops. General Howard, the inspector, the Agent, and Colonel Perry and the aides are all just now counciling together as to the country and best plan of action. I wish John was home, and I wish the Indians were in the bottom of the Red Sea. I don't feel as if any other matter deserved consideration this morning.

But I must tell you about the children's stockings. I wish you would get me two pairs more, not any better than those you paid 42 cents for. The children are very well and they miss their Papa very much indeed. He plays with them, or rather, entertains them so much. I do wish Doctor would come home. I feel as if the bottom was knocked out of everything.

Afternoon

Mamma, dear, I only have time to write a few lines, as the mailman will be here. Oh, Mamma, we have just heard such horrible news. The Indians have begun their devilish work. An Indian and a half-breed came in this afternoon with dispatches from Mount Idaho, a little settlement up on the mountains. The Indians have murdered seven more men on the road and also have attacked an emigrant train killing all. They broke one poor woman's legs, and she saw them kill her husband and brother. They say everybody is gathered into this little town. They want help, and arms, and ammunition immediately. They say in the most piteous manner, "Hurry, hurry, hurry. We are almost helpless and bands of Indians are all around us." They fear the settlers in the ranches around them are killed, as nothing is seen of them.

Our post is all in a commotion. The two companies of cavalry will leave in a few hours. They don't dare to wait even for more troops, though dispatches have already been sent everywhere to gather up the scattered troops in this Department. My dear old husband will have to follow Colonel Perry's command, as soon as he gets back here. These poor people from Mount Idaho say, "One thing is certain. An Indian war is upon us." You know these devils always begin on helpless outlying settlements. Mrs. Boyle and I have just been sitting looking at each other in horror. Poor Mrs. Theller is busy getting up a mess kit for her husband. Major Boyle remains in command of the post. The talk among the officers is that there will be a great deal of trouble.

Later

We have just watched the little party of two companies start off at dusk. General Howard remains here. If John had been here, he would have been out tonight marching with them. I can't help but feel glad that he is not, but I know he will feel he ought to have been here, and General Howard was so much concerned tonight about the command starting off without a medical officer.

It is ten o'clock and I am going to bed. We all feel so anxious. I will write soon again. I have only told you the news we have had that we know is true. Rumors of all sorts have been coming into the post all day. Everything centers here, and you can imagine how we all feel. I hope and pray it won't be another Modoc War. Love to all,

Your loving daughter,
Emily F.

Fort Lapwai
June 19, 1877

Dear Mamma,

We have lived through so much since I wrote last time that it seems months. It has all been so horrible, I should like to tell you about it and not write. Doctor has not come back yet, but probably will on Thursday. You know how I mourned over his having to go, and he did not want to go at all, and now I am so thankful, I don't know what to do. He, of course, would have left here with Colonel Perry's command, had he been home on Friday night, and that poor little band we will never see alive again. I can't write you how everything is going on here. I only hope, if we all live through it, sometime to tell you, but this Indian War is many times a more extensive affair than any one imagined.

The Non-Treaty Nez Percés, to a man, joined Joseph's forces, and he is being constantly reinforced by bands from other tribes that are encouraged by the success he has already met with. Colonel Perry went to Mount Idaho to reach those settlers. More than thirty had been murdered before he started, including quite a number of children and women. When Colonel Perry's troops (not a hundred men and two officers—all that could be possibly found in reach) got there, the Indians were gone and were supposed to be retreating towards the buffalo country by a certain pass. Colonel Perry hoped to catch them while they were crossing a river. They were supposed to be about eighty under Joseph and White Bird. On Sunday, by forced marches, they came up with what they thought was a detachment of Indians, and the fight began. It was such a hot day, and we waited here for the news with heartaches. It is only about fifty miles from us. Yesterday morning, at daybreak, the news came. More than half the command is dead and missing. Poor Mr. Theller is dead. The wounded were left on the field. Colonel Perry with twenty men had gotten back to Mount Idaho.

June 24, 1877

I have not been able to write or even to think for a week. Such a confusion as our quiet little Lapwai has been in. When I can, I will write the particulars. Since the battle, we have all had a great deal to occupy us. Mrs. Boyle and I have been with Mrs. Theller. The poor little laundress, who has also lost her husband, has been staying in our house ever since her husband left, as she was afraid in her own quarters outside the garrison. Then all week there have been troops passing through and we have entertained the officers. I had eight for lunch and seven for dinner, and I think Mrs. Boyle must have had a dozen today. The parade ground is full of horses, the porches are full of trunks and blankets, everybody is rushing about, and everything is in confusion. My brain is in as much confusion as anything else. The army is so reduced, and none of the companies are full, and all the troops that can possibly be gathered from all this region only amount to three hundred. Those are now in the field, and it is a little handful! Oh, the government, I hate it! Much it respects and cares for the soldier who, at a moment's notice, leaves his family and sacrifices his life for some mistaken Indian policy. It is well enough to have the army when troubles of this sort break out, but the moment the troubles are over, the cry is, "Cut it down. It is an aristocratic organization," etc. I wish we all were well out of it. The Nez Percé Indians are at war with the Whites. What a blow to the theories of Indian civilization. The whole tribe is wavering, and we don't know when it will all end.

This last week has been the most dreadful I have ever passed through. John came home, and I felt a little relieved of the horrors that hung over me when I heard he was not to go out with the first detachment. I heard General Howard say, when arranging his orders, that someone must, for the present, be left here to arrange supplies, medicines, etc., and Doctor had better be left here, as he belonged to the post. I had Dr. Alexander (Em's brother-in-law) with me the week before John came from Portland, and also Doctor Sternberg. You can't imagine how sad it all is here. Here are these nice fellows gathered around our table, all discussing the situation and all knowing they will never all come back. One leaves his watch and little fixings and says, "If one of those bullets gets me, send this to my wife." Another gave me his boy's photograph to keep for him, as he could not take it. He kept his wife's with him, and twice he came back to look at the boy's before he started off. One officer left a sick child, very ill; another left a wife to be confined next month. What thanks do they all get for it? No pay, and abuse from the country that they risk their lives to protect.

My poor little neglected children! If I could only send them to you until this is all over, for I could not leave John, and even when he goes to the front, I must stay here to be near him. The other day we had a fright, a false alarm of Indians attacking the post. I thought, "If my babies were only with their grandmother, how brave I would be." Doctor says we are in no danger here at the post. He says to tell you he wishes he could just pick us up and set us down with you for the next month out of all this hullabaloo. But, indeed, I would not go. I will write soon again and tell you of some packages I have received which I have not time to tell about now. Lots of love. I hope and pray my dear, old John will be spared to me and not sacrificed to those red devils for a country that isn't worth it.

Your loving daughter,
Emily F.

P. S. Can you imagine how terrible it is for us women at Lapwai with all this horrible Indian war around us, and with these two women, who have lost their husbands, constantly before our eyes, and we not knowing who will be the next sufferer. They are the first, but they will not be the last. It seems to me that it can't be possible I can love my husband this way, but I suppose they felt so, too. If John had been there, he would have gone with Colonel Perry and, in all probability, been killed. I am so thankful of that trip to Portland and hope and pray God will watch over him as wisely through all this horrible war. Even if he goes away from Lapwai, I shall be glad I am here, for we can hear from the troops in a few hours. We do hope this next fight will decide the matter forever.

Em.

Fort Lapwai
June 25, 1877

Dear Aunt Annie,

I intended writing a note to either you or Sallie this morning as I feared you would hear of the war in this Department and be anxious about us. Your nice letter came this morning and decided me to write to you.

You ask about the Indians. They are devils, and I will not feel easy again until we are safely out of the country they claim as theirs. Joseph's Non-Treaty band was given thirty days to come onto the reservation. On the last day of the thirty, when everbody was comfortably settled and never dreaming of trouble, they began to murder the settlers.

Doctor was away in Portland. He came hurrying home horrified. He had heard this post was burned and all sorts of alarming rumors. I felt all my calmness and bravery departing when he came home, as he only came in the morning and expected to move out with the troops in the evening, but the General found it necessary to leave someone to forward supplies and look after the troops that are passing through here and left Dr. F. for the present. Dr. Alexander (Em Houston's brother-in-law) is the chief medical officer in the field. He was with me here the week before John came home. Dr. Sternberg (Uncle Essick knows about him) was also with us last week and has moved on to the front. We have been busy entertaining the officers who are passing through, with our hearts aching, knowing they will never all come back, and fearing, too, all the time, an attack on the post.

We had one horrible false alarm of an Indian attack last

week. The long roll was sounded, the men were all under arms, and the women and children all gathered into one house around which there are breastworks. For a few moments, I think, we women with our helpless little children suffered as much as if the Indians had really come. We were very calm and brave, though, that is, Mrs. Boyle, and Mrs. Theller, and I wore ourselves out trying to quiet the excited laundresses.

(*According to Mrs. Hiestand, Mrs. Theller put on her dead husband's gun and cartridge belt and looked as if she were ready to avenge her husband.*)

We fear there will be a horrible battle within the next few days. Everybody here is busy day and night. My poor John! I have not had five minutes talk with him since he came home. We keep our tables set nearly all the time, and people rush in and take a cup of coffee and rush out. Poor, peaceful little Fort Lapwai is right in the midst of everything.

Doctor wanted to send us right home, but I can't leave him or leave here, even when he goes to join the troops that are in the front, as I can hear of him so often and so immediately here. If I should lose him (I hope and pray he will be spared to me) I would, of course, come right home to you all and expect you to take care of me, at least until I could think what I could do with my helpless little babies. Our officers here don't fear the Indians will take the post or anything of that kind, but there might be a band dash down through the post whooping and shooting as they rode, and that is why the women and children were put out of the road. Doctor says he thinks us safe here, or he would not let us stay. We are all well, only nearly worn out by the excitement and constant strain. I start at every unusual sound and feel the strength departing from my knees and elbows. John declares I have lost ten pounds. Everybody feels blue and anxious for the result. Another victory for Joseph would bring to his standard all the disaffected Indians in the Department, and the whole Nez Percés tribe is wavering.

After Lunch

The Nez Percés Agent lunched with us. He says he learns from friendly Indians that Joseph's command is not a large one, does not number much over a hundred, but that hundred is prepared to fight to the death. The Indians say they know they will be hung if taken, and they mean to kill as many soldiers as they can first and then die themselves. Our officers going through here think the campaign will be a short but severe one. I wish all the Indians in the country were at the bottom of the Red Sea. I suppose the country will have trouble until they are exterminated.

Thank you very much for the receipts and also for the pretty little pictures. With much love, I am,

Your affectionate niece,
Emily FitzGerald

Fort Lapwai
June 27, 1877

Dear Mamma,

I was very glad to get a little letter from you yesterday, as I had not heard from you since the one from Leavenworth.

I am so glad the check got there safely and that John's watch will soon be on the way. You say you have a notion to get the locket, too. I hope you won't, as I have been feeling that I had better wait until fall for it when there would be a little more money in this family. Half my pleasure in receiving the watch for John will be gone, I am afraid, because of the troubles we are now living through.

Our little post is quiet today, but more troops will be here on Saturday. Major Boyle, Mr. Bomus, and Doctor, along with twenty men, are our entire garrison just now. All the rest are in the front. General Howard sent in dispatches last night hurrying up the troops. He wants to make an attack, and we all feel today that there may be a fierce fight raging and many poor fellows suffering not fifty miles from us. The Indians are in a horseshoe of the Salmon River, a place with the most natural fortifications, equal to the lava beds of the Modocs, and we know them to be well provisioned. They have at least five hundred head of cattle in there, and quantities of camus root, which they use a great deal. We hear this place has only one trail leading into it. So you see the advantages they have. Oh, how I hope our commanders will be cautious and not risk anything. I suppose General Howard has out there now about four hundred men and some artillery, which I don't suppose he will be able to use at all. Those four hundred men are nearly the entire body of troops from this Department. The army is so small at best, and the various companies are so small, that it takes five or six companies to make a hundred men. None of the companies, not even the cavalry, is full.

How glad I should be if I could pick up John and the babies and get out of this region. I feel that nothing else will let me feel calm and settled. My brain seems in a whirl, constantly seeing the distress of these poor women who have lost their husbands, and constantly expecting and fearing to hear from our friends in the front, and also sort of half afraid for ourselves here. I wonder if poor little Lapwai will ever seem peaceful and calm to me again.

Do write soon. I will be glad of some common slips for the children (Bess particularly), but I have not written to you about them as I knew you would attend to them, and I have been so worried here, I almost forgot them. We all join in love, and I am glad you are safe home again.

Your loving daughter,
Emily F.

Fort Lapwai
June 29, 1877

My Dear Mamma,

Your letter came in this morning. I was ever so glad to hear from you. You tell me the watch and locket are on the way, and

I will look for them next week. I am very much obliged to both you and Uncle Owen for the trouble you have taken. When I first read your letter and found you had gotten me the locket, I felt rather worried, but Doctor says he had no idea I had thought of not getting it, and he is very much pleased that you have sent it with the watch, but I am not quite sure I will like it, as I think, from what you say, it is an oval locket, and I don't like them one bit.

Now about my eyes. Your plan for me to come home and be there with you almost makes me homesick. It would be just lovely, but there would be one thing to interfere with my perfect happiness — Doctor FitzGerald would not be there. I am afraid I should have so many blue days and be obliged to shed so many tears when I thought of the thousands of miles that were between us that I would counteract all the good anyone else could do me. Indeed, you think I am worse than I am in reality. Doctor knows just exactly what is wrong with my eyes and says they won't get any worse unless I abuse them. When we get home, (East), he will take me to someone who can tell just the sort of glasses I will need to use and, I suppose, after that I will have to flourish them all the rest of my life. Indeed, if it had been any reasonable distance between you and us, I think I would have arranged to go home for a visit this summer, but I got to thinking it over, thinking that the shortest time a letter has ever come to us from home has been seventeen days, and even dispatches take a week to reach us (they are brought part way by stage) and I concluded it was too long a distance to put between the Doctor and his children and wife, unless it was necessary. I would give the world and all to see you, but I guess we will have to wait until the Doctor takes us in. I hope and pray the time will pass quickly until our time here is over, and that we will all be spared to meet again.

This horrible Indian war hangs over me like a gun. I can't shake it off and am daily expecting the Doctor will be ordered to join the troops in the field. We are all very anxious here. The dispatches that came in last night told us the troops were in sight of the Indian stronghold. I shall hope and pray that I shan't have to come home to you, after all, without my dear husband. Poor Mrs. Theller is still waiting here. She won't leave until she can get her husband's body. This losing one's husband in this way seems too horrible to think about. I can't help feeling how awfully hard it would be to lose my dear John any way, but that way would be hardest of all.

Your loving daughter,
Emily F.

Fort Lapwai
July 9, 1877

I must send you a note this morning or you will be anxious about us. We are all alive and well, though all very anxious and in confusion. If you were not so far away, I would come home at once, but I can't bear to think of leaving John and going so far from him. I am thinking seriously of going down to Portland on the next boat and waiting there until things are settled. This post is in such confusion and excitement continually that I feel my strength departing, though I do so want to be a strong woman and able for whatever happens.

There have been so many alarms of Indian attacks, and so many horrible stories are continually being brought in that John says he wants to send us away. This matter may be settled in a few days, and I will not make up my mind what I will do until we hear further.

Our trouble is not enough troops. Another regiment is expected here in this Department at once, but what is a regiment these days? The companies are so small that it only means a hundred or so men after all. Joseph has had strong reinforcements and he has managed so wonderfully that he has been successful everywhere. Another fine young officer, such a nice fellow, has been killed, and we have lost about fifty men. It is time the tide turned!

Four days ago the little box came with the locket and watch.

Doctor should have written to you at once, and he meant to, but the commotion here interferes with everything. He is very much pleased with the watch and is also delighted with the locket. It is a lovely one, one of the handsomest I ever saw, but I have not quite made up my mind about it. Indeed, I have been so worried, I have scarcely had time to look at it. I will write a longer and more connected letter next mail. We are all right here. Don't be alarmed about us. It is only the worry and anxiety that Doctor wants to save me by sending me away. I don't think I will leave Lapwai, not unless the troubles increase. We all join in love.

Your loving daughter,
Emily F.

Fort Lapwai
July 11, 1877

Dear Mamma,

The last letter I sent off to you was written in such a hurry, I am afraid you weren't able to read the scrawl. There were a great many things I wanted to mention, things you have spoken of in your letters, but everything here has been in such confusion that I believe my mind is in the same condition. I can't tell you, or expect you to imagine, what a horrible time we have had and the unsettled state of everything for the last few weeks. I shall be so thankful when it is all over and we can go to sleep at night without imagining that we will be awakened by hearing Indian yells before morning.

You probably see by the papers what Mr. Joseph is doing. He is the smartest Indian I ever heard of, and does the most daring and impudent things. The command under General Howard in the field is so small that scarcely anything more can be done than to protect settlements. The country all about this region is so particularly adapted to Indian fighting that Joseph has every advantage and would have, even if the soldiers outnumbered him three to one. We know that Joseph's force numbers over two hundred, and we think it may be much more, as it is thought that there are a great many Indians who have joined him lately. No one has any doubt but that a few more successes for his band will bring to him all the Non-Treaty Indians in this Department, and there are hundreds and hundreds of them, different tribes all scattered along the Columbia River. Another regiment of infantry will be here within three weeks, but what Joseph and White Bird will do in those three weeks, no one knows. At first the idea was that Joseph (Indian like) was getting out of the road and making for the buffalo country. There was great fear that he would get off, but it was soon discovered that he had no idea of getting away, and that he was quietly doing all the mischief he could, and reinforcing his band, and preparing for a fight with the soldiers. He says he can whip them. I do hope there won't be a chance for him to try until more troops get here. Companies of volunteers are gathering from all around, and they will help to swell the number. Colonel Perry was here for three or four days last week. He came in to escort a packtrain for supplies. He stayed with us, and I wish I had time to tell you of so many little things that I know would be interesting to you.

One thing I must tell you. The two companies of cavalry that were in that first fight were, in the early dusk of morning, making their way into that canyon where they nearly all met their death. Just as Colonel Perry was passing some bush, a voice said, "Are you soldiers?" A woman carrying a baby dragged herself into view, with another little girl, three years old, holding on to her skirts. She had been hiding there since Thursday (this was Sunday morning). Her house had been burned, her husband and another child killed, and she, with these two little ones, had escaped to the brush.

Some of the stories of the poor people who have suffered so much make your blood run cold. There was something dreadfully touching to me in the defense that the Norton family made. They were among the first of the settlers molested. After the first four men had been killed, they sent a man from Mount Idaho down here for help. I think his name was Day, and he lived near White's house. (You can think how near this all seems to us — White's house is not twenty miles from the post. Doctor has gone up there to see a patient several times and was back in part of a day.) The man (Day) was shot. He turned and ran his horse back and was followed several miles and dangerously wounded, but he made his way to the Cotton Woods (the house and ranch belonging to the Norton's) and told his story. It was in the night, and they at once hitched up the wagon and put this man in it. There was Mrs. Norton, her young sister, a boy of ten, Mr. Norton, and two other men, besides the wounded one. They wanted to come to the fort but feared, as Day had been shot between them and here, that the Indians were there, so they started for Mount Idaho, the nearest settlement.

Just about daybreak, the Indians attacked them and fired volleys into the wagon. The men returned the fire, but both the horses were killed, Mrs. Norton was wounded in both legs, and Mr. Norton was also wounded. They got under the wagon and used the dead horses for breastworks. Norton found he was bleeding to death and told his wife's sister and his boy, who both knew the country, to take to the high grass of the prairie before daylight and try to make their way to Mount Idaho. (They were found afterwards on the prairie and saved.) At last these people had used up all their ammunition. They had not a cartridge left that fit any gun with them, but they knew that in Norton's pockets were some cartridges that fit another gun, and one of them crawled under the wagon where Norton's dead body was, and got them. Then this poor wounded woman and one of the men, who was so wounded as to be unable to use his gun, opened these cartridges and got out the powder, so the men could, at intervals of five and ten minutes, make a flash with it to make the Indians think they were still prepared for them and on the alert. Think of that poor, wounded woman, with her husband dead under the wagon and her only child escaping for his life on the prairie, opening those cartridges (there was a great risk of their exploding) and grinding the little grains of powder in the palm of her hand in the hopes that those few flashes might deceive the Indians until help could come. They were only a few miles from the town, and three mounted scouts got to them in the early morning, cut the harness from the dead horses, put it on the live horses, and were just lifting the wounded men into the wagon when the Indians attacked them on all sides. They did not stop for Norton's body. They whipped up the horses and ran for their lives followed by the Indians, but they got into the town.

We are uneasy today about a packtrain of arms and ammunition that left here yesterday with an escort of one company of cavalry (50 men) and about 20 Indian scouts. They feared an attack, as the Indians know of the train, and we heard they were going to jump it.

Thursday, July 12, 1877

Mamma, I wish I could talk to you this morning instead of writing. One of the things I meant to tell you yesterday was the active part the Indian squaws take in these fights our soldiers have had. They follow along after the men, holding fresh horses and bringing water right in the midst of all the commotion. Colonel Perry says that in that fight of White Bird Canyon, he saw one Indian (one buck, as they speak of them here) have as many as three changes of horses brought him by his squaw. See what an advantage that is to them. As soon as their horses are a little blown, they take a fresh one, and our poor soldiers have perhaps ridden their fifty or sixty miles before the fight begins. In their efforts to get at the Indians, they do their fighting on their tired animals. Then, in the fight, the soldiers fall scattered in all directions and the bucks can't stop to plunder in the midst of the fight. So, wherever a man falls, they set a squaw to watch him. I do hope their successes are at an end.

We are waiting anxiously for news from General Howard

who is about 50 miles away from Lapwai. A young man named Rains was killed last week. It was his first fight. He was a lovely boy. Mrs. Theller felt dreadfully about his death. He was the officer in charge of the party that found and buried Mr. Theller's body. Rains had so marked Theller's grave that he would have no difficulty in finding it again, and now we don't know that it can be found. Mrs. Theller is so anxious to have the body. Poor woman, I have felt so sorry for her. It was two weeks after the fight before they were able (from the small number of men and the large number of Indians) to go out to bury the men killed in that first fight, and Mrs. Theller used to say, "If he was only buried. Oh, my poor Ned, lying there with his face blackening in the sun."

John says I must stop writing on account of my eyes. I will have to keep lots to tell you when I get home. Last Sunday night, an Indian (friendly) came in and told that he had seen Joseph's men and they were coming to "clean out" the post that night. "Maybe in the night. Maybe in the morning," they said. "Only little bit of soldiers here. Is good time. Plenty muck-a-muck (food) and plenty gun." The Indian is a reliable one, as the good ones go, so every precaution was taken to guard against the surprise. Everybody at the post slept in one house, and the men slept in the breastworks. You can imagine the sort of commotion we are living in. They did not come, but we have had many such alarms, and though our officers don't seem to have any fear, they unsettle us.

I am not going away, though, unless something else than has happened comes to pass. I would rather stay here with John (the other ladies all stay as a matter of course) than leave, as long as he thinks it all right. The only reason he wanted me to go was on account of my health. We have lost so much rest at night and had so much to make us feel anxious that I am all shaken up, but if things get a little more settled here, which we look for soon, I can recuperate here better than in Portland alone. Home is too far off, or I would go there for a while.

An infantry regiment is on its way to this Department and

the talk is that when this war is over, the regiment now coming will remain in this Department, and the one now here, which has been here a long time, will go.

I did tell you that John was delighted with his watch, but he has been scolding at it several times. Three or four times the hands have caught and stopped the watch. He separated them with the fine point of a knife, and for the last four or five days, they have not caught and I hope the trouble is over. He is really much more pleased with it than he expected to be, and thinks it a very handsome watch, and hopes, and indeed expects, it will prove as good a one as it looks. I am so tired of all this excitement, but the children seem to thrive on it. They look neglected but happy as clams at high tide.

July 13, 1877

I find a mail will go out in a few minutes and I want this to go, though I am not done writing. We all join in love. There has been no news from the front since I began this. Everybody is anxiously expecting.

Your loving daughter,
Emily FitzGerald

Fort Lapwai
July 13, 1877

Dear Mamma,

I hurriedly finished up a letter this morning, as John came in and told me a mail would leave in five minutes. I did not say half I wanted to, and I will begin this and write a page a day.

Just after your letter went off this morning, the news we were all expecting from General Howard came. There had been a fight, a very severe one. Our loss was 11 killed and 26 wounded. Two of the officers, Captain Bancroft and Mr. Williams, are wounded. We know both of them well. The Indians must have lost heavily. They make desperate efforts to carry off their dead, and 13 dead Indians were left on the field. General Howard is at Mount Idaho and will push the Indians. This is our first good news and we all feel thankful. I hope the end of the war is near, but John and other officers think that after more troops come, the Indians will get out of the road, and there will have to be a winter campaign organized to finish them up. That is what Dr. F. is expecting, and he wants me to think about going to Columbia in the fall, if, as he thinks is possible, he will be sent with the troops in the field, and some older man or more feeble man left here. Two of the medical officers now in the field are not in good health, and I am dreading daily that they will give out and be sent back here to look after the hospital and supplies, and John will be sent out in their place. In case he should go, he would not like me to stay here, as his movements for the entire campaign would be uncertain. If it should be so, I will come and will stay, of course, until John is sent from this Department, which might not be for an entire year. And happy as I should be with you all, I don't know what I could do for a whole year without him, so I do hope something else will be arranged.

Before I forget it, the jack straws came. The children have had two or three nice plays with them. I meant to speak of these things long ago, but indeed I have forgotten everything I ought to remember for the last month.

July 15, 1877

This is such a bright Sunday morning. The children look so nicely in their best blue stockings and little brown linens, and they are playing on the porch. This is the first day this summer I have felt like fixing them up from top to toe. Even now I am afraid we will hear something horrible before the day is over and spoil all my pleasant feelings. The Indians (friendly ones) who were in that last fight say that one officer nad his leg cut off by the officers in the field, and they describe it so plainly, it must be so. Then from the fact that General Howard named the Camp "Williams," we fear poor Mr. Williams has lost his leg. He is only a young fellow and a very fine one. How unfortunate to lose such an important limb!

Dispatches came in from General Howard yesterday saying the Indians had recrossed the Clearwater River and were making for the mountains with the troops in pursuit. The trail over the mountains, which the Indians are supposed to be making for, leads over into Montana into what they talk about here as the buffalo country, but from a great many things, nearly everybody thinks Joseph doesn't want to get out of the country around here, but is only withdrawing in that direction to prepare for another fight. You never heard of such daring Indians in your life. In this last fight, they charged to within ten feet of the soldiers, and charged up to the artillery, and tried to take the guns from the men. General Howard was heard to say he never had seen such desperate fighting in his life.

There are lots of things I want to speak about connected with the children and things you mention in your letters, but to save my life, I can't think of them when I sit down to write. My head is full of Indians. It was very warm yesterday, and I baked a cake and churned my butter on a table on my back porch, and I kept one eye and one ear up the ravine watching for Indians all the time. It is a horrible feeling, this constantly expecting sounds that you dread to hear. I don't wonder I am getting thin. I suppose John would laugh at my fear of the ravine even in daytime, but I notice other people watch, and pickets are out in that direction, as well as others, from dusk till daybreak.

Everybody here seems to feel a little more cheerful since the last fight. The men from the Agency talk of taking their wives and children back there in a few days. The fruit and everything there is going to ruin. But I think it is too soon. It is like the old cry of "Wolf! Wolf!" and when we don't look for it, the wolf comes.

We all join in love and hope to hear soon.

Your affectionate daughter,
Emily FitzGerald

Fort Lapwai
July 16, 1877

Mamma Dear,

I just mailed you a long letter this morning, but I guess you won't object to another note. This morning I got a letter from you written and mailed April 9th. Where it has been all this time, I don't know. I had a good laugh after I read it. You tell me of a wrapper sent me to make overalls for the children, but I must tell you of that wrapper's reception.

John brought in the bundle, and I opened it and said, "Somebody has sent me a calico wrapper." John picked it up and said it was better looking than any he has seen yet. Just then Mrs. Perry came to the window and said, "What a lovely wrapper. I hope it will be too small for you and then I will take it right off your hands." Well, I was very much pleased with my wrapper and lengthened it a little, made the cuffs a little smaller, and flourished it. I went up to the Boyle's one morning with it on, and Mrs. Boyle said, "What a pretty wrapper. Did you buy that made up?" *Now* you tell me it was intended for overalls for the babies.

I took a good look at my locket. I don't like the square thing and the pearl in the center, but John thinks it is lovely, and as he wanted it for me, I guess I will keep this one. Doctor has at last said he would really rather have his watch than the one he wanted at first.

Dispatches from the front have just come in. They say Joseph wants a talk with General Howard. He says he is tired fighting. He was drawn into it by White Bird and other chiefs, and he wants to stop. We hear there is great dissatisfaction among the hostiles themselves. The squaws are wanting to know who it was among their men that took the responsibility upon themselves of getting into this war with the Whites. They have lost their homes, their food, their stock, etc. We feel much more secure and comfortable here for the last few days and can let all our anxieties and fears go to our friends in the front. We hear poor Captain Bancroft is wounded in the lungs. They have hopes of his recovery, though.

The artillery companies we were with in Sitka are on their way up here. I will be glad to see our old friends again, but I know how distressed their wives are, and I shall feel so sorry to see them move on to the front.

They talk of making Lapwai a big four company post with the headquarters of a regiment here, and there is no knowing, even if the war is soon ended, where we will all turn up next spring. Poor Mrs. Boyle says she hopes she won't be left here. She shall have a horror of Lapwai all her life. The Boyles had not been here a week until this trouble began.

Give much love to Uncle Owen.

Your loving daughter,
Emily FitzGerald

Fort Lapwai
July 18, 1877

Dear Sallie,

Mamma said she had sent a letter of mine to you, so I need not explain what a commotion we have been in. This morning our first warriors arrived, the first officers that have come in since the battle of the 11th and 12th, and they brought such good news. We have had, at least I can answer for myself, a very thankful day. Several officers came in early this morning and brought news that the Indians in bands have been giving themselves up for the last two days. Quite a number of Joseph's band came in, and they say Joseph himself wants to come in, but White Bird won't let him. The cavalry are out after those that are still hostile, but our officers think the war is practically over and that there will be no more fighting. They say that the fighting up to now has been horrible. They never saw such desperate fighting as these Indians did.

We are all pretty well but tired, and even though the war may be over, the fuss for this little post will not be. Eleven companies are on their way here from California, will be here this week, and will go into camp until things are settled. A whole regiment of infantry is also on the way. As soon as matters are a little more settled out in the front, General Howard intends leaving the cavalry to follow up the scattered bands out there, and bring the rest of command in here. From all the troops then gathered here, he plans to organize a body of men, six hundred strong, to go into the Spokane country to look after the Indians there. But we hear the Indians are all pretty well frightened, and we don't anticipate any more resistance from the Non-Treaty bands of other tribes in this Department. They are all to be forced on reservations, one after the other now, before the matter is let rest.

One of the officers, a nice fellow, walks in his sleep. He was unfortunate enough to get up in the night in camp and shoot the picket outside of his tent (one of his own men) and killed him instantly.

You never have told me how to wear the blue around my neck. I am waiting to know, and tell me how you fix your hair and what you wear in the way of little fixings. Since I have lost my fear of being murdered by the Indians, my desire to fix myself up and look young has returned.

Mrs. Perry and Ms. General Howard are coming to Lapwai tomorrow. We have had such a string of people at our table for this last month, poor Jennie thinks the world is upside down. Among other companies that are expected tomorrow is Captain Field's, who was with us in Sitka. In a few days all the wounded are to be brought in here, nearly thirty poor fellows. They say there are some awful wounds. Poor Captain Bancroft is wounded in the lungs. I expect Doctor will bring him here. And Mr. Williams will be taken to Major Boyle's. I should like so much to do a great deal more for everybody than I do. If I only had or could get better help than Jennie, but it just kills me to be in the kitchen this warm weather, and for that reason, I neglect asking a great many people whom I feel and know John thinks really ought to be asked in.

(Mrs. Hiestand said Emily had good cause to complain, for Jennie went on periodic drunken sprees. "I remember Jennie

had made a night of it just before a false alarm of an Indian attack," Mrs. Hiestand said. "She was sleeping off the 'effects' when the alarm came. Mother hurried us down to Major Boyle's quarters, behind the breastworks, forgetting Jennie in the excitement. Later she sent a soldier to waken her and bring her to us. The soldier came back laughing, saying that he could not rouse her. He would shake her and say, 'Indians coming. Get awake. Kill.' All he could get out of her was a mumble, 'Me no fraid Indians. Me injun, too.' ")

Friday, July 20 1877

All our troubles are upon us again and worse than ever. I feel even more upset, as John is ordered into the field and I will have to be here alone. He was to have gone with the troop that leaves tonight, but since morning, he has been ordered to wait and assist Dr. Sternberg to get the wounded comfortable and then follow with the next detachment. The wounded are being hurried in here. Some will arrive this afternoon, and it is so hot, I never in my life felt such weather. The thermometer in my shady sitting room (the coolest room in the house) stood yesterday at 98 degrees, and that was much less than it was at the hospital and on the porches.

The Indians had gone in full retreat towards the buffalo country. The cavalry went after them nearly a hundred miles and reported them all gone and impossible to follow, from the condition of the country. So General Howard started his command back here, leaving three companies up there to watch the place the Indians ford the river, the ford that leads to the mountains. We knew yesterday that General Howard's command was near Lapwai. In the evening, an officer, who had been sent on in advance, came in and said there were signal fires burning in the mountains. By and by, General Howard himself and some other officer came in, and in a great hurry. A messenger had just reached them from the three companies left to watch the ford saying the Indians were all back. So, of course, everything is in confusion again. General Howard did not wait to rest but started right back, and those poor, tired soldiers have to turn and do it all over. The companies of artillery and infantry that were expected are arriving here now and will march tonight. I don't know what we will do after John goes. I wish it was over! The confusion, outside of everything else which is even worse, will set me crazy!

I won't have time to write to Mamma again this week. I wish you would send her this scrawl, as I think she would like to know what is going on. They are going to leave all the Indian prisoners here and double this garrison. With the wounded here, and the Indian prisoners here, and Doctor gone, I think I should like to go, too, but I suppose I had better stay, as I have no friends near I could go to. To board somewhere would be lonely and worse than here, besides the expense which would be quite an item. I want to tell Mamma that such a nice little package came from her, and I will write to her about it next week. Some of the officers are going through here this morning from the front and say the war has just begun! I want to send this letter out now, as a mail is going out.

Lots of love to all, and write to me.

Yours affectionately,
Emily FitzGerald

Kamiah,
Indian Territory
July 29, 1877

My Precious Darling Wife,

Got here today at 10 A.M. without adventure of any sort. It seems a month and longer since I left you. Yet, excepting this feeling of long lapse of time, I have, after a fashion, enjoyed this nomad's existence of two days and nights. Made a long march yesterday and felt considerably fatigued when we got in, but Lt. Forse and I went down to the water with soap and towels and bathed our heads, hands, and feet. I found a nice, cool spot under some bushes where a great pine tree had fallen across the hollow, and served to keep the little pool of rain water cool. I sat for some time with my pantaloons and drawers rolled up and my boots off (of course), with my feet and legs up to the knees in that cool water, and with so much of my body in the water, of course, I was soon cool as a cucumber. Slept in open air, sound as a log. Got up at 3 A.M. and had my breakfast and enjoyed it. Mr. Otis was half sick all night with a terrible headache.

As I said, we got here about 10 A.M. The troops to go (and with whom my lot is cast) are all across the river, and stores are being crossed over. It looks like a war picture, indeed quite an army, and among them, I am glad to see about 25 Indian scouts who were brought through by Colonel Sanford. By the by, I go with Colonel Sanford who has Jackson's, Carr's, Bendire's, and Wagner's companies, 1st Cavalry, 200 strong. And Assistant Surgeon Newlands (nephew of Mr. Newlands—West Point) is my assistant. He is quite a boy in appearance and quite handsome.

I shall mess with Colonel Sanford, whose mess consists of Captain Carr, Mr. Cresson (1st Cavalry), and Doctor Newlands. Everybody here seems pleased to see me with them. Field also goes with this column and it is intended and arranged to go along together. The Indian scouts will be in the advance. It is said and believed here that Joseph's Indians are all over in Montana and peacefully disposed among the settlers in that region. Doctor Alexander says that I will be back at my post in 30 days. I hope so, Darling, for I feel that I have been away from you for an age already. I don't see how I can stand it for 30 days. You may rest assured, Darling, that absence for that time, or maybe a week or so longer, is all you have to fear on my account. The Infantry (15 companies including the artillery) numbers about 600 now, and the command altogether will be 800 or thereabouts.

Kamiah region is very beautiful and picturesque. Today, when we came out on the crest of hills overlooking the Indian settlement, I was astonished and delighted with the prospect spread out, as it were, at our feet and from 4 to 10 miles distant. Of course, it looked better at a distance than it does now, for down here on the scene, you come in contact with the more repulsive features of the still savage inhabitants. General Howard and others went down to hear preaching by some of the young proteges of Miss McBeth. How good it was or how bad, I don't know or care.

Major Jackson's Company is out about 2 miles on the Lolo Trail as a picket guard. No signs of Indians have yet been seen. I forgot to tell you our Indians all wear soldier's uniforms with a kind of blue sash of stripes and stars. It looks, in fact, like a piece of old garrison flag. They belong to the Bannock tribe of Indians farther to the south, and they can be depended on.

I forgot to say I found Captain Winters and Mr. Forse very pleasant travelling companions, but Winters remains behind with a command about Mount Idaho. Colonel Sumner also remains behind. He asked after you, as also did a dozen others, including General Howard. Colonel Sumner says he intends soon making a scout into Fort Lapwai and will call and see you. I have heard many remarks from Infantry officers about the general stampeded condition of several companies. And I must tell you this. I was to lunch (and such a lunch) with Doctor Alexander at General Howard's Headquarters, and the General asked after you and added, "And Mrs. Perry? She is well, is she? She went off into hysterics when she arrived."

I hardly know, Darling, what else to tell you. I suppose we will reach Missoula in a week at farthest. I was going to say you might write me there, but that would not do, as I suppose it would take two weeks for a letter to reach that place via San Francisco.

There will be one or more opportunities for you to write me by courier from Lapwai. Take care of yourself and the babies, and wait for me as patiently as you can. I am writing all this under a pine tree back from the river on this side in

Colonel Sumner's camp. I have a memorandum book on my knees for a table and am sitting flat down.

If I can, between now and the leaving of the courier tomorrow morning, I will add a P. S. to this long scrawl. I keep thinking of the long absence from you, my dear wife, but it must be. I suppose there are 30 or 40 more gentlemen in this command who have left their wives and babies, and who, in case of more fighting, will be in far greater danger than your man can possibly be in, but, honestly, I don't think we shall see an Indian hostile. I said to Colonel Miller, "Colonel, what are we all going to do over there?" He replied, "Oh, we will have a big mountain picnic with no Indians to trouble us," or words to that effect. The impression is general that we will have some hard marching only, with no fighting of any kind.

Be my patient, darling, sensible wife, as you always have been, and 'ere long I will be with you again. My ink is getting low, so goodbye, my honey, and believe me

Ever your faithful
John

Fort Lapwai
July 30, 1877

Mamma Dear,

I have had two letters and lots of nice bundles since I wrote last. John left on Friday and I am lonely without him, but I would not be any place else than here for anything, as here I can hear from him every time anything goes in or out to General Howard. I heard this morning from Kamiah, and I will enclose John's letter, as I can't tell you all he says.

The Indians, it is supposed, have gone off over that Lolo Trail to Montana. A dispatch from the Governor of Montana says a great number of ponies, women, and children, with a lot of wounded men, had come over the Lolo Trail, and he had not force to stop them. No one knows whether Joseph and his warriors have gone over there too, or whether they just got rid of their families and helpless men so they could make the better fight themselves. General Howard is determined to find them and has formed two columns. The one he commands himself will follow over the trail the Indians took into Montana. The other goes north through the Spokane country and joins General Howard's column sometime in September over at Missoula where General Sherman will meet them. Then, if the trouble is not over, a winter campaign will be organized, but we hope it will be over even before that. If it should be that John will be obliged to be out all winter, I will come home in the fall, as he would not want me to stay here alone so long, but I hope he will be with me here long before that.

Don't worry·about us here. We are comfortable and safe. I only wish I was nearer to you so I could either go to you or have you with me, for I am not very well and I am lonely without Doctor and often need comforting. There is nothing the matter with me, only I have so much company and have been so shaken up by the excitement and all, that I am completely run down. But now I am fortified with the greatest amount of tonics and have nothing to do but get a good rest, and I hope, by the time my dear John comes back, to be as strong as ever.

Colonel Perry, my next door neighbor, leaves tomorrow. Doctor speaks in his letter of Mrs. Perry. You will understand better when I tell you she is a very nervous and excitable woman. I feel sorry for her and pity her, for I know how hard it is to keep up myself, and know, too, if I do give way, it is all the harder afterwards. Colonel Perry goes with the Spokane expedition; Doctor goes the Lolo Trail.

Mrs. Hurlbut, the poor little laundress I have menioned in several of my letters, was here staying in my house at nights all that first month. She is expecting daily to have another baby, and she was afraid, in case of an alarm at night, she would not be able to get across the parade to the breastworks.

So she asked me if she could bring her children and sleep up with Jennie, which she did until lately, since our fear for the post is over. She is a very nice little woman, and her children are as nice as I know. She is left destitute. After her sickness, we will all help her. A purse will be raised to take her back to her friends. She is a helpless sort of a little woman, and I never saw such a look of distress in my life as has taken possession of her face. I have not seen her for the last week.

Now about the children's clothes. The bundles have all come, and I never saw such a nice lot of little clothes in my life, but I don't know when they are going to wear so many best clothes. I can't put them on to play over the woodpiles, and I can't keep them off the woodpiles for ten minutes at a time. Indeed, they do not want any more good clothes. They just run wild from morning until night, and I can't look after their clothes. So I want to put things on them that I don't feel badly about their spoiling. On Sundays I forbid the woodpiles and the dirt pile and the water barrels. But other days I just let them do as they like, and then scrub them up before I put them to bed.

The little gloves came this morning. They are cute little things and Bess was delighted. Bert seemed to think them rather a nuisance and objected very much to trying them on. Bert, you know, will be three years old in a few weeks, and Bess will be five this winter.

I have not had gloves on for three months. I have not been any place but to the next house in all that time, and Mrs. Boyle, who has been at the post a little more than two months, has never been outside the parade.

Doctor, I expect, is marching up the mountains today, farther and farther away from us. How I hate the army and wish he was out of it! I hope they won't find any Indians, and I hope he will come back to me safe and sound. I had made up my mind he would not be ordered from here, as the wounded are all here, and Dr. Sternberg can't do all the work. But Dr. Alexander said they must have FitzGerald in the field, and he would be sent back here as soon as he could be spared. Poor Dr. Sternberg is disgusted and worked to death. The hospital has 36 men in it, 28 or 29 wounded, and the others sick. I don't see what they do want with John on that Lolo Trail. They have four or five medical officers, and that ought to be enough. Sometimes when I think what might happen out there, I get half distracted, but I fight against it and keep my mind occupied with other things, and I plan for John's coming home. As long as there is a chance of John's coming back soon, I will stay here.

All the Indian prisoners are here, some 60 in all. They are horrid looking things, and I wish they would send them away. John said before he left he would not think of leaving us here unless he felt perfectly sure we were safe, so don't feel anxious about us, I am only anxious for the Doctor. Write soon. Lots of love to all.

Your affectionate daughter,
E. L. F.

Fort Lapwai
Sunday
August 5, 1877

Dear Mamma,

It is doleful living along this way without John and not knowing when he will come home. I don't know how much longer I can get along. Bess has not been well this week, but it always seems to me all my troubles come when John is away from me. We are four ladies at the post now. Dr. Sternberg sent for his wife, and she has arrived.

Yesterday the Indian prisoners were taken away from here down to Vancouver. The squaws seemed to feel awfully about being taken away. Some of them moaned and groaned over it at a great rate. I did feel sort of sorry for them, as parts of all their families are still up here. One poor woman moaned and cried and really looked distressed. Just before she left, she took some ornaments of beads and gave them to the interpreter to give to her little girl who is up somewhere near Kamiah. One old man cut the bead ornaments off his moccasins and left them for his wife.

We have not heard anything from General Howard's command up in the Lolo Trail for a week. I wish we could hear! We have had all sorts of rumors about the Indians, but we don't know anything. I had a note from John written Monday night at their first camp on the Trail. He said it was a hard mountain trail. They had been all day going 15 miles. It is a zigzag, winding, steep trail, in many places impossible for two to walk abreast, with either rocks or a dense pine forest close on all sides.

There are several companies of troops over on the other side in Montana, and we have heard that the Indians were allowed to pass, but we don't think it possible. We also hear the Indians have gotten back on General Howard's rear. Mrs. Monteith spent yesterday with me. I wish I had some of my home people with me all the time. I would miss John under any circumstances, but how much easier it would be to bear if you were here.

I was fixing up my boxes a little while ago and took a good, long look at my locket, and I don't like it. I do believe I will change it yet, if there is a possibility. I think John's watch is a beauty, but I think this locket is ugly, and I don't believe I will ever like it any better. That square thing in the middle is stiff and is put on dreadfully crooked. I have been trying to like it, as I did not want to change it and John seemed to like it, but I don't like it and can't. I have never worn it, and if you can change it without its being awkward for you, I will send it on at once.

Monday, August 6, 1877

Dear Mamma, it always does seem as if everything goes wrong when Doctor is away. Both children are just a little sick, just enough to make them fretful and worry me. I was awake with them a great many times last night. They seem better this morning and are playing, but my one wish is that the war was over and John home again.

Afternoon

Dr. Sternberg just came in to see the children. They are not well, either of them, and it is so hard to have them get this way when John is away. I can't help worrying about them, and you know how two fretful children can keep a mother trotting.

You should see some of the Indian garments that were taken from the camp the day of the battle when the Indians left in such a hurry. They are made of beautifully tanned skin, soft as chamois skin, and cut something like we used to cut our paper dollie dresses. The bottom is fringed, and the body part down to the waist is heavy beaded. You never saw such bead work, and the beads make them so heavy. These, of course, are their costumes for grand occasions. One of them I could not lift. Then they have leggings to match, and if it is a chief or big man, they have an outfit for his horse of the same style. Doctor Sternberg is an enthusiast on the subject of collecting curiosities, and he purchased from men who had gotten them, four or five of these garments. For one, he gave ten dollars in coin, and for another with a horse fixing, 25 dollars. So you see, they must be handsome.

I will write soon again. Do write to me often. I am awfully lonely, and do tell me if I can still change the locket. Lots of love to all.

Your affectionate daughter,
E. L. FitzGerald

August 7, 1877

I just had a letter from you handed in, and I am so glad to hear. In all my worry and confusion here, it is such a comfort to know that somebody is thinking about us and is interested in us. Just now, particularly while John is away, I feel doubly glad to get your letters and am anxious for more. Both the children are better this morning and are now playing.

I do hope we will hear from General Howard's command today. It seems so long to wait. Lots of love.

Yours,
Em

August 1, 1877
Camp Spurgin in the Field
Bitter Root Mountains

Darling Wife,

Last night we had rather an unpleasant time, but I was somewhat comforted with your letter of the Saturday after my departure, and was made happy in your saying that you are all well, or were so when I left. I said we had rather an unpleasant night of it, for we went to bed without our tents, and it began to rain about midnight. So I had to get up and make a shelter with a tent fly which I had laid on the ground as a sort of mattress. Doctor Newlands and I were bunking together. However, we finally made it comfortable and rain proof, and then slept on till morning.

Got up at 5 A.M. but did not march until 11 A.M., and then only went 8 miles and made the nicest camp we have yet had in among partially wooded hills, or rather, mountains. We had some fine mountain views yesterday and today. We were so high up that the whole extent of mountainous country was spread around us. Tomorrow we are to march about 18 miles and make camp on the Clearwater River, the same river that runs by the Agency, only we shall find it a mere mountain brook that can be easily forded by the men and horses. I shall think then of my darlings, and make the stream a little mental address about going down to Lapwai and leaving a message from me to those I so love.

Captain Spurgin, 21st Infantry, caught up with our army last night, and today some beef cattle arrived to serve as food for us all, poor things. We find for the last 3 nights hardly any grass for our horses and pack mules. It is very poor, indeed, and we shall not get any better for 3 or 4 days to come. We are still some 50 miles from the summit of the Bitter Root range of mountains which, you know, is the dividing line between Idaho and Montana Territory. Then we shall have 60 miles more to Missoula. No Indians have been heard of yet, and I suspect that our mountain climbing this week and next will not accomplish any substantial result. The life we lead on such a campaign is very rough, and it would puzzle many to account for the fact that it is, to some extent, enjoyable. Only when the elements frown upon us does it seem discouraging. Last evening and night, and also this morning, everyone looked disgusted with everything, but we made an early and very pleasant camp after a short day's march, and presto, everybody is changed, and a generally cheerful aspect prevails.

I hope, Darling, that this scribble will find you all well. Tell Bert that Papa is coming back to his place at table and home just as soon as he can. Tell him that when I was riding along in the big woods today, I came upon a poor little Indian pony which had been left behind, and it followed us into camp. If I was only going towards home, I would try and bring it in for him. Tell Bessie, my girl, that Papa yesterday saw a great many beautiful flowers along the way, and they made me think of my little girl. I wish I could send her some fresh ones. As it is, I will put in for you, Dear, and for her a sprig of heather in bloom which is all about our camp tonight. I gathered an armful of it to spread my blankets on for my bed tonight. I wish, Darling, you would write — every chance you get. I will endeavor to do the same.

Your loving,
John

Remember me to the Sternbergs and the Boyles.

Fort Lapwai
August 12, 1877

Dear Mamma,

Your letters have been coming somewhat irregularly lately.

I expect it is all owing to the trouble on the roads from the strikes. We have been so concerned about the war in this region that the troubles East have not been much talked of, but I have seen enough in the papers to make me sure you have all been excited and anxious.

I am still lonely, as, of course, I should always be without John. It had been nearly two weeks since I had heard from him until I had a note yesterday. It seemed so long since it was written that I wanted another one, as soon as I had read it, to tell me what he had been doing since. By John's note, I suppose General Howard had not, up to that date, heard of the Indians going North, but some official dispatches were brought back by an Indian that show the news reached him just about that time. He cut loose from his infantry and artillery and hurried on with his headquarters and cavalry and expected to be in that region on the seventh and then follow the Indians. This is the 12th, and I feel so anxious to hear what has happened.

We have heard two stories about the Indians. Both are believed by some of our people here. One is that Joseph is going North, as fast as he can, but is obliged to move slowly, sometimes making only a few miles a day, because his stock is worn out and he has a great many wounded to carry with him. The other story is that Joseph has come or is on his way back to this valley by the Elk City Trail, reinforced and ready for another fight. Two companies have been sent up the Elk City Trail, and we just wait here, not knowing anything. I am the only one at the post whose husband is with General Howard's command. Colonel Perry has gone on the Spokane expedition and will be back soon. How I wish it was over and John safe back home. I told you the 2nd Infantry was to come out here to this Department. They did not come out to the post but started for the Spokane country.

Bert and Bess have both added to their prayers lately, "Please, God, take care of our dear Papa and bring him home safe to us." Yesterday, Bert heard his Papa's letter read, and when he went to say his prayers, said, "Please, God, take care of my dear Papa, and bring the little Indian pony home safe to us." A great deal of love to all.

Your affectionate daughter,
Emily FitzGerald

P. S. We have had dreadful news this morning of a horrible fight. Eighty killed or wounded. When will it end? Oh, the aching hearts that must follow when the list of names is known. Poor Mrs. Hurlbut had her baby last night.

I got up this morning feeling awfully blue, and Bert almost set me off at the breakfast table. Bess, who notices everything, said, "Mamma, you look as if you were going to cry." I said, "No, dear. I am not crying, but Mamma feels badly this morning because Papa is so far away from us." Little Bert stopped his breakfast, leaned over his plate, and said, "Please, God, give our dear Papa a good breakfast, for Jesus Christ's sake," and then went on with his meal as if it was all settled. His faith is greater than mine. With much love and hoping to hear soon, I am,

Your loving daughter,
Emily FitzGerald

Fort Lapwai
August 12, 1877

Dear Aunt Annie,

I have not written to you lately. So much has interfered. Ever since John has gone, I find lots of little things to do. We are not afraid here at Lapwai, now that the trouble has gotten so far away from us. But I would much rather have had it keep up in the valley, for then we knew all that happened and could hear so often from our husbands. Now the Bitter Root Mountains are between us, and there is no way of hearing unless couriers are sent to and from General Howard. We have been living very quietly here for the last few weeks. Our only event is the arrival of the mails, which we all watch for anxiously.

You know General Howard followed the Indians over the Lolo Trail. There were a few regular troops and some volunteers over at the other side to stop the Indians until General Howard could catch up. Well, the Indians, when they got there, made a treaty with the volunteers promising not to molest them, if they would let them pass. There were only 20 soldiers, and they could do nothing, and the Indians all marched past and away. I think those volunteers ought to have an army turned against them! Think of it! They are the people that our poor soldiers have got to protect!

General Howard is following the Indians up, and I suppose, has reached them before this. I am very anxious to hear what has happened. We hear the Indians are short of ammunition, and over in that country they tried to buy cartridges, offering a dollar a piece for them.

There are some of these Nez Percés Indians that have, for a long time, been considered fine fellows. Some of them have been studying theology. Miss McBeth, who was a missionary among them, educated some of them quite thoroughly. I have a photograph here that I will send you. It may be interesting to you. It is a picture of four men that Mr. Thompson (the minister who baptised Bert) examined in theology a few months ago. They have since been licensed to preach. Mr. Thompson told us he had been astonished at the knowledge of these men, and he was delighted at the way they understood our plan of salvation. He said he asked them to give answers of their own to such questions as "What is faith?" and he was delighted with their answers. They were taken down to Portland, and they had this photo taken there. While these good fellows were preaching and praying in Portland, Joseph and White Bird and those other red devils were murdering the poor people up on Salmon River.

I must stop writing and get the children a lunch. Write to me often. We are all well but awfully lonely without the Doctor.

Your loving niece,
Emily FitzGerald

Camp on the East Lolo
20 miles from Missoula
August 7, 1877

Darling,

The last two days we have been in rather a handsome country, i. e., since we struck the eastern Lolo River, which is a tributary of the Bitter Root River. Last night we had the most picturesque camp I have ever seen — a very remarkable spot where there are 4 hot springs. The steam from them this morning rose up as if from a number of steam mills. I bathed my feet in one of them last night and found it as hot as I could bear comfortably. There was good trout fishing in the Lolo nearby, and Colonel Sanford and I got quite a fine string and had them for breakfast. Today we had a long hard march over the hill and got down on the Lolo again this evening for camp — and in a pretty place. Colonel Sanford and I again had some trout fishing.

We are 20 miles from Missoula, but we learn tonight that the Indians are about 60 miles off, and that General Gibbon is after them with about 200 infantry in wagons, and is within 30 miles of them. We are to push on tomorrow with the cavalry, with a view to overtake him. The Indians were allowed to pass through this valley by the scalawag population that bought their stolen horses. And it is said some of them traded ammunition, powder, etc., to the redskins for their stolen property, gold dust, etc. We hear that several watches have been traded for by citizens of Missoula, and it is possible that Mr. Theller's watch may be recovered. Mr. Fletcher went into Missoula this morning, and Mr. Ebstein is to go in tomorrow, but our command, the cavalry, is to turn off in another direction about 10 miles this side of Missoula tomorrow. The artillery and infantry are nearly two days behind us, but General Howard and staff are now with the cavalry commands. It seems to me that things look as if we should have an end of it all in a few days or weeks, as the Indians will either be whipped or driven across the line into British possessions. The rumor is that Joseph has left White Bird and Looking Glass and is somewhere in the mountains by himself with his band.

Our poor animals are tired and considerably run down. Old Bill is but the shadow of what he was when I left Lapwai.

Well, Darling wife, how are my precious ones? What a happy hub you will have when his "footsteps homeward he hath turned." I hope you are well. I am and have been, and a large part of the time have rather enjoyed this nomadic life. Do you know, or rather, can you realize, that for nearly every morning of this month we have found ice in our wash basins and buckets? It is rather rough on us to be roused out of our warm beds at 3, 4, or 5 A.M. It almost "takes the hair off," as they say.

Your old husband,
John

Fort Lapwai
August 19, 1877

Mamma Dear,

It has just dawned on me why I have not heard from you lately. The letters are directed to the Doctor and have gone on to the front, as all the mail for officers in the field is sent off from town. So I suppose sometime I will see them, but I will see the postmaster and get the rest myself. We have all been feeling very blue. Everything is so unsettled, and the Indians have been fortunate enough to kill so many good officers and men, we don't know when it will end. Today we got news that is a little encouraging. We heard that the loss to Gibbon's command was not quite so large and that the Indians did not get ammunition. We hope this is true. This is the fourth Sunday since John left, and I do get lonely and anxious. How I will enjoy our home going next summer, if we all live through this.

Tuesday
August 21, 1877

Such a doleful time as I have, getting along without John. How nice it will be to have him coming in and out again and to see him at the table. I have not heard from him for an age and do get blue. I expect he is busy over there with General Gibbon's wounded. There has been no mail back this way from General Howard for some time, but we expect news daily, indeed hourly.

Jennie got sick this week and was in bed all day yesterday. She got up and poked about this morning, but I got breakfast. The children are well and play all day.

Joseph, they say, is on his way back to this country. I wish it was so. I feel sure that would put an end to the trouble soon, for there is now a large force in the valley, and General Howard would push on after them, and they could not escape. Then, too, that would bring all the army back here, and I could hear of and from John almost daily.

I have never had such a lonely time in my life. The post is quite lively. There are three or four young officers here, and then we have the band of the 2nd Infantry. It plays an hour in the mornings and one in the evenings. I would think it very pleasant if only my husband was here. Colonel Perry got home this afternoon. The Spokane expedition was recalled. Six companies go into camp here, and three or four go up to reinforce Colonel Green's command. That will make Lapwai a big post for some months, maybe all winter. I wish I could send the children to you for a visit. I would so like you to see them, and I would like a rest myself. They are dear little things, and I do believe anyone would see a good deal that is winning about them, though, of course, they are great bothers sometimes. This afternoon they came to me quarreling about some cards. Bert had taken some of Bessie's white ones and wanted some green ones. Bert was crying, and I called them both up to inquire all about it. Bertie was the offender, though Bess had been very cross to him about it. Well, I talked to them and told them I had nothing to make me happy but my children, now that pappa was away from me, and if they were good, I was so pleased, etc. Bess went off, and in a few moments came back and handed Bertie half of her green cards. I smiled at her, and she threw her arms around my neck and squeezed me and whispered in my ear, "Mamma, God told me to do that." They are a great pleasure, and a great care! Do write soon, and direct to me here. I hope the dress you sent me has not gone out to General Howard for the Doctor.

Lots of love,
Your loving daughter,
Emily FitzGerald

I will enclose this note Mr. Miller, one of the officers in town, sent me, as I can't write it all.

Loewenberg Brothers,
Importers and Dealers in
Dry Goods, Clothing, Boots and Shoes, Groceries,
Farming and Mining Implements

Lewiston,
Indian Territory
August 1877, 8 P. M.

Mrs. FitzGerald,

Fearing that you may have unfounded rumors about the reported fight of General Gibbon in the Bitter Root country, I will give you all the news I have that is at all authentic. Lieutenant Jones, 4th Artillery, arrived here tonight and says that night before last, a rumor came to Walla Walla of a fight in the Bitter Root Valley, 100 men being reported killed. Yesterday morning he and Lieutenant Boutelle went to the telegraph office and obtained from the operator in Portland the following news, viz.

There has been a big fight, Indian camp charged and taken by General Gibbon's forces, and about 182 men were driven out with heavy loss of 80 men killed or wounded. Our last news from General Howard was on the 9th, 45 miles beyond Missoula. He telegraphed to Walla Walla, ordering General Wheaton not to move on any further but to go into camp. General Howard said he was moving with the cavalry in advance of the infantry.

I have written you all I know. I will send you anything that will be of interest to you. The Doctor is all right, and this note is for the purpose of keeping you from being needlessly anxious, as you might be if you listened to all the rumors. You asked me to send you the news, and this is all I can gather. I do not yet believe the reports of the fight. You know what terrible rumors came from Colonel Perry's fight at first. This, I think, will simmer down considerably. Undoubtedly there has been a fight, but General Howard's forces were not engaged.

Yours,
W. H. Miller

Fort Lapwai
August 23, 1877

Mamma Dear,

I only have time for a note to tell you the dress came safely and did not go out to the front to John, as I feared, but all your letters must have, as I have not had one letter in a month.

I am feeling blue, as we don't hear from the troops and everything is so unsettled. Six companies of the 2nd Infantry will be here this week to go into camp. Dr. Egbert (who knows you) is with them, and I will see him and tell him who I was. He might hear of me for years and be none the wiser. I hear he hurt his finger badly with a folding chair out in camp. The chair in some way folded on his finger and completely cut it off at the first joint. Captain Conrad, one of our old neighbors at West Point, also belongs to the 2nd Infantry and will be here. Now if only my husband would come home, how nice it would be.

General Howard is following the Indians up closely and his men are almost worn out. That was a dreadful fright of General Gibbon's, and we hear all those officers, both killed and wounded, are married men.

I hope you are all well, but I don't know anything about you, and the provoking part is that Doctor doesn't either, for all the mail is waiting for the command at Mt. Idaho. Do write as soon as you get this. I do hope you are not ill.

Your loving daughter,
Emily FitzGerald

Fort Lapwai
August 30, 1877

Dear Mamma,

I must write a note for fear you will think more is the matter with us than really is. I have felt almost too wretched to write letters for the last ten days. Indeed, I have never been so unhappy in my life. This uncertainty of everything in the future, and this not knowing or hearing anything is the hardest thing to bear I have ever gone through. I have heard nothing from Doctor himself for almost a month. No one has heard directly from the Command since the 10th, and except for those dispatches of General Howard's, we don't know anything. Our only consolation is that if anything had happened, we would know. I feel that we must hear soon. It can't last much longer. I am very anxious and worried about my dear husband. I would be, even if I could hear from him often, and am, of course, much more so, as I can't hear.

Then, too, what upsets me most of all is a talk of the likelihood of there being a winter campaign, and the probability of the troops, now in Montana, being left there for the winter. Of course, nobody knows, but the very idea is dreadful, and I hope and pray it may not be so. I don't feel that I could wait that long to see my dear John, even if he is spared through it all. Just think! They are way over in the Yellowstone country.

Everything is so unsettled. There are to be great changes at this post. It is to be made a four or six company post, and we will have to have a change of quarters. Then, too, here is the first of September on Saturday, and I am not thinking about being ready for fall for either myself, or the children, or John.

It is too provoking, but all your letters have gone to Mount

Idaho with the mail for the front, and there they have been for a month. I did speak to the postmaster, but I have not had one letter from you since Doctor left, and I don't know anything about you *either*. I wish all this war was over and John home again. I don't see how I can get through many more weeks.

As soon as I hear from you, I will send the children's measurements and get their fall things started. I don't want anything but what is on the list I send you. Mamma, I don't know what I should do if John has to remain over there for the winter. Much as I want to see you all, I don't want to go so far away from him. I don't believe I could undertake that long journey East alone with the babies, even if I wanted to. I hope that before another month closes, I will hear that the command is on its way back to this Department.

Do write at once and direct to Mrs. Doctor F. Lots of love to all. I hope so much that by the next time I write to you, I will have heard from John and also heard good news for the future.

Your loving daughter,
Emily FitzGerald

(*The following letter was written approximately August 14, 1877, or later. The first section is missing, but in it Doctor FitzGerald apparently told Emily that dispatches informed the officers of General Gibbon's encounter with the Indians.*)

The first thought was of sending two of us Doctors with an escort, but presently, it was thought best to make an early start with the cavalry and push on. So we lay down at 11 P.M., and got up at 3 and started. We marched about 20 miles by 12 o'clock, had lunch, and then Doctor Alexander and myself were sent forward with 30 soldiers and 6 citizen scouts, with our supplies on one pack mule. We pushed on and crossed over a long and weary mountain which was the divide between the waters of the Atlantic and Pacific Oceans and, as such, was part of the back bone of the Rockies. We got over it about 8 P.M. and then had easy travelling down a narrow prairie between forests and hills on either side. We rode on and on until 1 o'clock. When there being no indication of the near proximity of General Gibbon's camp, we tied our horses to the trees and waited through the chill and weary hours until dawn. I was so cold, it was impossible to sleep. It was thought, too, by some of the party, that we might have passed the camp and be in danger of running into the savages. I, however, was sure that such was not the case.

Daylight came at last and I was about the only one who had not managed to doze off. I was just on the point of rousing everyone for our start, when one of our citizen scouts came striding into the midst of us. I asked him where he had been, and he said he had been down the trail several miles, had run into a small party, 4 or 5 Indians, and had concluded to come back. I think now he made up the story.

We soon were in readiness to move and left our stopping place about half past three A.M., rode on and on, and finally reached General Gibbon's camp about 9 A.M. We found a horrible state of affairs. There were 39 wounded men without Surgeons or dressings, and many of them suffering intensely. General Gibbon had not taken any medical officer with him. He had followed the Indians for 5 or 6 days (day and night), finally got up with them on the 9th of August, and advanced on their village before daybreak and attacked at daylight. He charged through their village (his command was infantry) shooting down everything in sight, but the savages ran into the willow thickets along the stream and opened a murderous fire upon the troops which compelled them to seek shelter. They retreated to a wooded embankment above the stream and sheltered themselves behind logs and trees as best they could, but the Indians soon got possession of sheltered positions overlooking the soldiers and killed and wounded a great many. In fact, they actually corralled General Gibbon's command, and if General Howard's forces had not been following after him (of which fact the savages were informed), I think it probable they would have finally annihilated them (General Gibbon's soldiers). As it was, he "stood them off" for two days, when all but a few warriors left.

The savages sustained greater losses, however, than the soldiers, for we found over 30 dead bodies (mostly women and children). I saw them myself, and among them think I recognized those two large squaws who sat in the Council tent last April at Lapwai, one of whom you questioned about her bead work leggings and who refused to answer you. Also I saw the body of the large Indian who wore that robe trimmed with ermine skins. At all events, it was the same robe, or one just like it. I was told by one of General Gibbon's officers that the squaws were not shot at until two officers were wounded by them, and a soldier or two killed. Then the men shot every Indian they caught sight of — men, women, and children. I saw five or six children from 8 to 12 years old, as near as I could determine. I saw also six or seven braves, and the remainder of those I saw were squaws — eleven or twelve of them. I was informed that there were some eight or ten more bodies of men further down the stream.

Of General Gibbon's command, two officers were killed and five wounded, including himself. One of the wounded, 1st Lieutenant English of the 7th Infantry, will probably die. He was married only two or three months ago. There were 19 soldiers killed and 36 or 37 wounded, mostly slight wounds, however. I think it probable that one, at least, will die. There were no amputations. Five or six citizen volunteers were killed, and three or four were wounded. We made them all as comfortable as we could, and the next morning (yesterday) General Gibbon's command moved off in one direction for Fort Shaw, and we in another on the Indian trail, heading southeast.

Last evening, after we got into camp, a courier came in from Bannock City and reported that the Indians had killed ten men in the valley and run off 200 head of horses. They were moving rapidly toward headwaters of the Yellowstone River via a place on the maps designated Pleasant Valley. General Howard said last evening he would pursue them as far as that point. Then if he did not succeed in overtaking them, he would notify General McDowell and terminate the campaign, break up his command, and dispatch them toward their several ways and posts. How glad one Doctor will be on the consummation of that event you, darling wife, may imagine. I have had you in mind all day today, you and the babies! I hope this finds you all well. I have had only two letters from you since I left home. I feel sure, however, that it is due to the erratic character of our mail communications, and not to omission on yours.

From the battleground to this place, the country is very beautiful, being a succession of grass covered valleys with clear sparkling streams, and surrounded by a mighty wall of snowy mountains. Tell Bess Papa saw some beautiful blue bells this morning and wanted to get some to send to her, but I knew they would be all dry and spoiled before they could reach her. We passed a few deserted ranches and several large herds of cattle, and saw many buffalo heads and bones, indicating that those fine animals once roamed over the prairies but have been exterminated by man. The streams hereabouts are all tributary to the Missouri River, and the waters of the rivulet from which we make our coffee this evening will flow past Leavenworth, Kansas, in a week or ten days. Can you realize the fact that your husband is on the Atlantic side and you are on the Pacific side of the Rocky Mountains?

Darling, I must close. I fear this long scribble will make your dear eyes ache. I do hope you are all well and that I shall be on my way home before the close of another two weeks. Remember me to Doctor Sternberg and wife, to Major and Mrs. Boyle, and other inquirers.

Your old husband,
John.

Fort Lapwai
August 31, 1877

Darling, Darling Old Husband,

I was made such a happy old woman this morning by a letter from you. Oh, John, I was so glad to hear! This is the first for four weeks. I wish I was sure of your getting this, but I will send it off in the hope you will. I heard Colonel Weeks had been sent for to go to Fort Ellis, and I suppose, of course, he will have some communication with General Howard's command, so I will send it in his care. I am afraid to be too happy, for fear it will not all prove so, but the people seem to think the order for Colonel Weeks to go over there means an end to the war soon. Darling, I won't know how to love you enough if I get you back safe. I do hope it is so and, dear boy, I pray that you will be spared to me through it all. We are well, but I am, of course, anxious about you. You began this letter by saying you had just sent the first part of it (this was marked at Bannock City), so I suppose that was the mail that was lost by the courier, which I told you all about in a long letter that is probably at Mount Idaho for you now.

There are to be great changes here. Do hurry home before somebody wants our quarters. They say five or six companies are to be here, and there is lots of rank — seven or eight captains in the 2nd Infantry, to say nothing of the field officers floating around. Now, dear, dear husband, there are lots of things I would like to tell you if I was sure of this ever reaching you. The Boyles expect to be ordered from here at once. I heard from Sallie this morning saying your shirts were on the way, and I hear there is a bundle in town for me. I suppose that it is it. I wish I could send them to you. Oh, John, I am so much happier today than I have been for weeks. I hope and pray the idea of the campaign being about over is a true one.

The other day Colonel Parnell rode up. They all welcomed him, etc. Bess came in to me, leaned over my lap and said, "Mamma, I wish our Papa would come home, too." Darling,

I hope you will get this, and oh, how I hope it will find you on your way home. My dear, big, better half — good night.

Your loving wife
Emily FitzGerald

Camp on Henry's Lake
Montana Territory
August 23, 1877

My Darling Wife and Darling Precious Ones,

Since my last cheerful letter giving some promise of a speedy return, I have had reason to relinquish it altogether. Our prospect for remaining in the field for some long weeks further before we can hope to start homeward is practically assured.

Everyone, believe me, is sick and tired of a fruitless pursuit of these Indians. On the 20th inst. at 4 o'clock in the morning, a party of them rode through our camp, firing right and left and whooping like devils, and actually succeeded in running off nearly all our pack train of mules, one hundred and fifteen of them, and got away with them, too. One man was slightly wounded in camp, and, in the pursuit and skirmish following, one man was killed and eight more wounded in our Cavalry Command. General Howard seems determined to follow them up in the (vain) hope, I suppose, of overtaking them and recovering the pack mules. Poor man — and yet I do not think he deserves pity. Not many officers are in sympathy with him, and a great many think he is guilty of folly of the gravest kind to follow on at the expense of loss in men and animals in a hopeless pursuit.

Camp at head of
Henry's Lake
Montana Territory
August 25, 1877

My Darling Wife,

I left off at the foot of the preceding page on learning that the messenger had departed for Virginia City, Montana Territory, and on learning also that I would have another opportunity. We moved camp yesterday about 5 miles to the head of this beautiful lake. General Howard has gone into Virginia City to buy clothing and shoes for the men, I believe, with the intention of immediately resuming the pursuit of the Indians who have gone over into the Wind River Mountains on the headwaters of the Yellowstone River. If he does, we cannot hope to start homeward before the middle of October, and it would take at least six or seven weeks for us to march back.

Your old husband,
John

Fort Lapwai
September 7, 1877

Dear Mamma,

Day before yesterday I received your letter written just before you went to Columbia. I was very glad to get it, as I had not heard for so long, and then, too, it relieved me about the fall fixings for the children. I had not thought about that money and was not quite ready to send on some, as I had been waiting until I could send some mail to the Doctor to have some checks and papers signed. I am glad you are all well, and I am very much obliged to you for getting my things ready. I will send you some more money as soon as I can get mail to John. I don't know how much more of this waiting and waiting I can bear. It does seem to me sometimes that I will go crazy and cannot wait another day to see my husband. Then the days come and go, each one bringing nothing nearer the end than the one before. I am thankful, though, that they bring no bad news and pray this state of things is not going to last much longer. I have never been so unhappy in my life as I have been for these past six weeks.

Sunday morning
Sept. 9, 1877

I will send this off, as there is a mail going out. I have some things I wanted to write about, but I forgot them now and so will write again. I had a long letter from John last night. The last of it was written as late as the 27th. I will send you the first sheet, thinking it might be interesting to you. I am glad to know John is well, but the campaign is going to be much longer than anyone expected, so that I feel very unhappy to look forward to the weeks I must still wait for my husband to come home.

The children are both well and happy and send lots of love to Grandma. Lots of love. Write soon and often.

Your loving daughter,
Emily FitzGerald

Fort Lapwai
September 20, 1877

Mamma Dear,

I wrote you such a hurried scrawl the other day, I am afraid you won't be able to read it. This unsettled state of affairs will be the death of me. I never knew things in such confusion as they are among the army people out in this region now. The whole 2nd Infantry is near here, and this was to have been made a big post, but General Wheaton has been dispatched to stop building now and wait, as it has been found necessary to make a big post in the Spokane country. The Perrys hear they are to go to Walla Walla, the Boyles hear they are to go to Colville, Doctor Sternberg is still waiting here for Doctor FitzGerald to come back, we hear some new surgeon, Dr. McClennan, wants this post, and nobody knows anything! The Perrys moved out of their house, as General Wheaton wanted it, and took the Boyles', who moved into the next set. They are all in confusion, not knowing whether to fix up or not, and we just all sit and talk and wait. If I had my dear husband home, I would not care a bit for quarters and posts. All my anxiety is for news from General Howard. I expect we will change posts before winter sets in, if Doctor gets back. I don't care a bit, if he only gets back. What makes this confusion all the more trying is that our cold weather is upon us, and everybody wants to be settled. I have not heard from John since the 2nd of this month — four weeks ago. I know he was alive and well on the 15th by a dispatch, and that is a little comfort.

Bess and Bertie are fast asleep. I wish the winter things would hurry to us, as the children will soon need them. Bert is cold in his little calico shirt, and I was obliged to let him wear his little flannel sack over it.

How quickly the time passes in spite of it all. Here it is almost Christmas, and I had intended having such a nice one for my little family this time. Now I can't count on anything, not even on my dear John being home. I hope this state of things won't last long and that I soon can feel happy and cheerful again. I had no idea I could be such a miserable old thing as I have been for these past months. I will send this by tomorrow's mail and write a more connected, sensible letter this week. I hope the locket and the muff have arrived long ago. The babies would join me in love, if they were awake. They talk a great deal about you.

Affectionately,
Your daughter,
Emily FitzGerald

I am going to trouble you to get me some more things for Jennie. She wants three warm flannel shirts such as we wear, and she also wants another pair of buttoned boots, 4½. Jennie is sick this winter, and as soon as John comes home, I think I must send her back to her friends. I will feel better about it if she has a good outfit of clothing.

Emily

Camp on
Yellowstone River
Montana Territory
September 16, 1877

My Darling Precious Wife,

I came in very tired tonight from a long and tedious ride to find your two dear comforting letters of August 9th and 10th awaiting me. I have so much to tell you that I don't know where to begin. First, however, I must say how very happy I am to know my precious dear ones are all well. I approve, my darling, of all you do or may do, feeling that it is wisely done. Next I had a note from General Eaton about my July pay account enclosing it to me for transfer to the First National Bank with note etc. for signature, when I had firmly believed that you had it (the amount) long since in your possession. I fear you may be uncomfortably short of funds. If you are, you must borrow of the Leowenbergs. On the 26th, I sent my August and September accounts to General Eaton, Chief Paymaster, Portland, and told him to have them cashed and placed to your credit. I will write him now to have them cashed, if possible, without having to send them back to me. And, if he cannot, to hold them until I get back, or to your order.

And now, Darling, I must tell you the events of the past 4 days. On the 11th instant, General Sturgis, Commander of 6 companies, 7th Cavalry, joined the command about 65 miles from here. Colonel Merrill (Cousin Lewis Merrill) was with it. Also, Captains Bell and Nowland, and some of the young cadets who were cadets at West Point when we were there, Mr. Slocum for one. Cousin Lewis was astonished to see me. He has been in the field since last May, but hears often from his wife and family, all at Fort A. Lincoln.

Well, early on the 12th, General Howard instructed General Sturgis to make forced marches and overtake the Nez Percés. He had but one medical officer and asked for another, and Merrill said they wanted me. I told them they would have to give me a good horse, as mine was worn out, and Merrill said I should have one of his. So I was ordered out. Marched from 6:30 A.M. until 9 P.M. — a long and weary ride. It rained all afternoon and my boots and everybody else's got full of water. Made a wet and disagreeable camp with but little to eat.

We were off again early next day and crossed the Yellowstone River about 10 A.M. where it was concluded from the indications that the Nez Percés were too far off to be overtaken by our jaded horses. The General ordered his command into camp. He had scarcely given the order when up galloped one of his scouts who shouted, "General, the Nez Percés are very near, not more than four miles away, and are coming this way to fight."

The call "to horse" was sounded, and we started full tilt in the direction from which the scout had come. We rode rapidly about 5 miles when we came in sight of them — the whole herd — and began skirmishing with them, and it was a very handsome little fight and lasted until evening. Many ponies were captured and it is said that 6 or 8 Indians were killed. I have seen only two, and I made some effort to see all of them. They killed two soldiers and wounded eight, two mortally. We camped on the field and next day pursued them nearly 40 miles when our animals gave out, but many more horses were captured by the Crow Indians who took part with us in the fight.

Poor Nez Percés! There are not more than perhaps 140 or 150 of them, while we had about 400 soldiers and nearly as many Crow Indians. I am actually beginning to admire their bravery and endurance in the face of so many well equipped enemies.

Well, yesterday morning I started back to this Command (General Howard's). I made about 16 miles yesterday on our poor worn out horses, made the rest of the 40 miles today, and got in here tired and hungry about 4 o'clock. Now I hear General Howard is determined on following them up, even to the British line!

Your old husband,
John

(Orders transferring the FitzGeralds from Fort Lapwai to Boise City, Idaho, came between September 30 and October 16. The letter in which Emily announced the news to her mother is missing.)

Fort Lapwai
October 16, 1877

Dear Mamma,

Your letter of October 2nd, just before starting for Columbia, has just arrived. I think you got lots for 17 dollars, and I am very much obliged to you for using your own money and not disturbing that in the bank. I will send you 25 dollars within the next ten days, and ten more when we get over our journey. I wish my shirts would come before we start, but if they don't I will travel over the mountains in one of John's old thick ones. And talking about money, just tell Aunt Pace to tell Major Taylor that Doctor has already been obliged to pay eight hundred dollars. That's the reason we are so poor. His only hope now is that Congress may pass his bill and, in that case, he will have it paid back to him.

I hope the cloaks, and the thick skirts, and drawers for Bess, and the leggings, mittens, and caps will come before we start rushing about trying to get together enough warm things for the children on the trip. I should have sent to you earlier, but I never dreamed of this move. I am quite comfortable for the trip, all but shirts, and I would like to have had some dark stockings, but still I can do nicely. But the children are not ready. Of course, I will make them warm, even if I have to tie them up in blankets, but I would like them to look nice, as well as comfortable, for the journey.

October 17, 1877

I did not get to finish this last night. Some gentlemen came in. Goodness, how impatient I am getting to have John home. I feel almost sure he can't arrive this week, but I will look for him hourly next week. Just think! We will scarcely get fixed up in our new quarters at our new post before Christmas. I must have a nice little time for the children, as they are now old enough to know and watch for it, and they are already talking about it, but I am going to make very little do. I find there is nothing the children seem to keep their interest in longer than in toy animals. So when I get to Boise, I am going to send to you to get me some animals and a dollie for Bess, and I will get Bert either a dollie or a box of those Crandle's Acrobats. And that is to be the extent of my expenditure for this Christmas. I did want to get something for John, and if funds are not very low when we get over this journey, I will send for gloves and handkerchiefs for him, but, otherwise, I will not give him anything until we get East. He must have a thick pair of gloves, though, as he wore out those last on this campaign, I am afraid.

One lady arrived the other day, so I am not the only lady in the garrison, as I expected to be since the Boyles and Perrys left. She is Mrs. Cockren. She has two little children, and my two were delighted to have someone to play with. General Wheaton is living in the Perry house next door to us. He told me yesterday my children were the best he had ever seen in his life. I said I did not think them very bad, but they were far from good. He said if I didn't think them good, I should just compare them with other children. The Sternbergs, too, used to tell me that mine were remarkably good children. It is encouraging to have people say so, for I worry with them, and talk to them, and try never to let an opportunity pass that I think might benefit them by trying to teach them what is right and what is wrong. But I don't see that all my fussing does much good. They are wild little scamps yet that just love to have their own way. I often feel sure after a battle with one of them that I have been wrong myself, and it isn't a very comfortable feeling. My children are gentle, loving little things, and I do hope will grow up with a love of what is good and right.

I hope by the next time I write, my dear John will be with me. All my troubles are very little ones, as long as I am under his wing, and I hope this separation will do for our lifetime. With much love to you, Uncle Owen, and all, I am

Your loving daughter,
Emily F.

Lapwai, Indian Territory
October 21, 1877

Dear Mamma,

Returned from the recent Indian war on the 17th, finding my darlings all well. I was very glad to meet them and be with them again. I hope I shall never have occasion to repeat my past three months' experience.

I find that I am to change stations from this post to that of Fort Boise where there is a lively little town, Boise City, which, by the way, is the Territorial (Idaho) Capital. It will be nearly a week nearer home, and we shall have a daily mail, which we shall appreciate. I think it will be a good change when once effected, and that Emily will consider herself repaid for the fatigue and discomforts of a whole week of overland travel by the pleasanter surroundings of Fort Boise.

Fort Lapwai has been a horrible experience for her, and she will associate it in the future with memories of a very unhappy experience. I said in the beginning of this letter that I found my darlings all well. I perhaps ought not to have said so as to Em. She is not strong, and, for the last few days, has not felt well in the strict sense of that term. I think, however, she will now rapidly grow better. I find the babies grown and as lovely as children can be, and would give much to have the friends see them. We hope to come East next year. In fact, I feel morally sure of doing so, and mean to spend the winter of 1878 in Philadelphia, if all goes well.

Address us in the future at Fort Boise, Indian Territory. Please remember me to the family and friends generally.

Sincerely and
affectionately yours,
J. A. FitzGerald

PART IV

NINE DAYS FROM HOME

Fort Boise, Idaho — 1877

The FitzGeralds left Fort Lapwai October 28, 1877, and arrived in Walla Walla four days later. They apparently had to wait two days before taking the stage coach to Boise City. Mrs. Hiestand remembers quite vividly the rigors of the trip from Walla Walla. She said, "I remember my father held Bertie and me in his arms so that my mother could have both hands free to brace herself. At one time, the ride was so rough that I was thrown out of my father's arms. The driver stopped the stage, came back to see if we were all right, and apologized for the accident."

The FitzGeralds arrived in Boise City November 7, 1877, and Dr. FitzGerald reported to Fort Boise for duty as Post Surgeon November 8, 1877.

A great many of the letters which Emily undoubtedly wrote during her stay in Boise are missing.

Boise City
November 8, 1877

Dear Mamma,

I have about a thousand things I want to write to you, but I feel so tired, I don't know whether I will think of half of them. I have begun two or three letters to you at different places on the way, but I had not time to finish any of them. In the first place, the locket came just the night before we left

Lapwai. I think it much prettier than the other one, and Doctor likes it better, too, though he liked the first one. I will not exchange it again and think this will suit me better than anything else of the kind I have ever seen. The morning we left Lapwai I had a letter from you from Columbia, and this morning a bundle came with the little drawer leggings for the children and some real pretty pins from Aunt Annie. I will write to her just as soon as I get rested.

We got here yesterday afternoon from the hardest trip I have ever had in my life. Indeed, we were nearly dead, and are yet. I felt as if I had been ill for six months. We were four days going from Lapwai to Walla Walla. We went in an ambulance and stopped every night, but from Walla Walla here, we came in the stage and travelled day and night — three nights and days. Indeed, I never was so tired in my life. It was actual suffering. Fortunately, it was not cold, but the jolting and cramped position were terrible. Poor Doctor saved me all he could, but he looks as if he had been ill. He had not gotten over the hard campaign or the cold he brought home with him, and then this journey on top of it has made him feel it very much. I am worried about him, as the cold has clung to him now for more than six weeks.

We were so glad to get here, and this is a very pretty little town. We will stay here at the hotel for a few days until I am rested. Doctor is up at the fort this morning. It is just three quarters of a mile from here. I have spent all my time since our arrival on the bed, stretched out on the broad of my back. Doctor likes the fort very much and says we have pleasant little quarters. I will be glad to be in them. We sent Jennie back to her friends. I felt glad to have her go, as she was not much help since the children have gotten big.

I intended sending you some money, 25 or 30 dollars, to repay you for what you have spent and to get the other things I want, but as you kindly told me to send it at my convenience, I will not send it in this, but will wait until John gets some more checks from Portland. (It will be in about two weeks.) This horrible trip cost us two or three times as much as we expected, and as I don't know what the things we will need in the way of furnishing will cost, I think I better not lessen the amount in hand. I must get some table covers, and I think I had better send to you than try to get them here. I need two or three. Get the best you can for me for 10 dollars.

Doctor is so much pleased with his watch. He says it keeps such good time and he likes it better and better. As for the children's clothes, I need petticoats and flannel drawers for Bess particularly. Another thing I wanted to ask you about was how to have the ermine furs made up for Bess. I sent them all to the furriers before I left Lapwai and told him to hold them until I wrote him what to do with them. I wish I had not gotten the ermine. Some dark fur would have been so much prettier for her.

Another thing just dawned on me this morning. This is quite a town and I will necessarily have to dress a little more than at Lapwai. And then, too, I will want to go to church and expect I must have a new cloak. I had intended that my old one should do this winter, as next fall I will be East and, of course, will want something new. My old one is a short, blue cloth sack, trimmed with beaver, very comfortable and warm, but not very dressy looking now. What could I get that would not cost much? I would like some dark cloth fixing trimmed with that heavy braid.

Please write at once and tell me what you would do, and please send some table covers and the flannel drawers for Bess as soon as possible. There are a whole lot more things I want to write about, but I am too tired. I am sort of amazed that I have accomplished so much. With much love, I will stop and will write a more satisfactory letter soon.

Lovingly,
Your daughter,
Emily

Fort Boise
November 14, 1877

Dear Mamma,

Your letter directed to Boise arrived this morning. It took nine days, but they tell me we get mails several days earlier in the summer. I have never been even as near you as nine days for a long time.

I am getting rested and waiting for our quarters to be repaired. The painters and white washers are at work, and it will be very comfortable. For the first time, I have a nice room that I can fix up for a spare room. I won't do anything to it but have it painted and cleaned until you send me word you are coming. Then I will just be too glad to get it ready. And, Mamma, I don't see why not. You could easily come, and I feel so tired now, I think I shall want to stay here two or three years before starting another journey. If you come out here to see me, I will induce John to remain another year in this Department, and we will be all fixed.

Since I wrote, three packages have arrived. The shirts and shoes which Jennie wanted have been sent on to her. You asked me how those shoes wore. Jennie said she never had such good ones before. I am so glad to get the stockings and like them so much. Everything you tell me in your letter about the things you have gotten and are getting for me is just right.

Your loving daughter,
Emily F.

Fort Boise
December 27, 1877

Dear Mamma,

I think it about time for me to acknowledge the receipt of some of the nice bundles that have come to us from Chestnut Hill in the last week. Your letter came on Friday, and the bundles for Bess and Bert on Saturday, and the children have felt very rich in Christmas gifts. They were all just as nice as they could be. Bess was charmed with the dollie, and the shoes to come off nearly set her wild. We wanted the acrobats for Bertie, and I am glad you sent them. He plays with them a great deal. His Papa makes him all sorts of new combinations not on the list. The animals and magnetic toys were entirely new to the children, and they enjoy them ever so much. The books are too nice for common, and after putting them in their playhouses with all the rest for Christmas morning, I brought them to my bookshelves, in the sitting room, and only mean them for the evenings and Sundays.

I think, Mamma, the pin from you is beautiful. Doctor says he has not seen anything he liked so much for a long time. His handkerchief, too, he says, is the nicest one he has ever had, and we both are just as much pleased and obliged as we could possibly be. So many pretty things all coming at once nearly sets me beside myself.

I hope you had a lovely Christmas. We had a quiet one, but a very pleasant one. The children had a delightful one. They had a tree, trimmed up with what was left from last year, and Doctor made them each a playhouse. He got Bert a big wagon and Bess a trunk. Then I had a lot of little things for them, and we turned one of the upstairs rooms into a play room and had all their toys together. They had, and are having still, a very happy time.

I went down to the Methodist Church last Sunday to hear the Presbyterian minister, Mr. Stratton. Mr. Vollard, the Episcopal minister, came up to see me the other night with a Mr. Wells, who was the Episcopal minister at Walla Walla while I was at Lapwai. I often saw him, and I think ever so much of Mr. Wells. If he was to remain here, I would not look any further for a church. I don't believe Mr. Stratton will succeed in forming a Presbyterian one.

December 28, 1877

I did not get to finish this last night, but I will mail it now. What are you all going to do on New Year's day? Mr. and Mrs.

Ward and their little daughter Nellie are going to be with us all day. Mrs. Ward and I will have a luncheon for the gentlemen who call. Mrs. Ward is a dear, little woman, and I am glad they have come to the post. Mrs. Ward was Lizzie Dunn, daughter of Major Dunn of the 12th Infantry, and a first cousin of the Dunns at Leavenworth. Didn't you meet them there?

Did I tell you about Jennie? She went to Portland and intended looking for a place there and not going back to Sitka until spring. She had nearly a hundred dollars and some good clothes. I heard from the matron of the Helper's Home in Portland the other day telling me a girl who had lived with me was there and that she was very ill, and that she wanted her to write to me and ask me if I wouldn't help her to get back to Sitka, if she lived. Poor Jennie had lost all her money. The matron says she talks so much about the children and says she wishes she could see them once more. Poor Jennie! We sent her a little Christmas bundle of things from the children and also sent her shirts down. And I suppose I had better get the shoes she wanted. She liked those you got. I wish you would get them and send them to me, but don't get them until I write again.

We all join in lots of love,

Your daughter,
Emily

(*Jennie never reached Sitka again. Mrs. Hiestand said, "The matron wrote my mother she had everything done that could be done for her, but Jennie had taken ill with tuberculosis and had died in the hospital."*)

Fort Boise
January 7, 1878

Dear Sallie,

I just told Mamma a few days ago in a letter that I didn't think it would hurt you to write to me a little oftener. I suppose you think the same of me, but indeed, if you knew how much I like and want to hear from you, you would keep writing. I think you owe me a half dozen letters now, don't you?

Tell me about your Christmas. We had a very quiet one and didn't give each other anything. We are awfully poor, but I made up my mind I will not let another one go by without some little presents, no matter how small they are. This move to Boise just took all the money we had been able to save at Lapwai, and as we felt poorer than Job's turkeys, we concluded not to count each other in for this year.

How the money goes! I feel disgusted when I think of all the wants and the small amount of bills to supply them with. I have just paid Mamma up. She has spent 40 or 50 dollars for me, and I also sent her some more to get a couple of dresses fixed, and now I feel as if I had been awfully extravagant.

I want to have a little whist party for Doctor on his birthday and thought a long time this morning before I decided I could buy some more cards. Those you sent me at Lapwai were carried off this summer. I am going to get you to buy me two more packs. I think you gave 60 or 62 cents for them. Get the two packs with different colors on the backs. You know, they sometimes use two packs, and they are bad to sort when they all are the same. Now this is the last money (except to pay for a hat) I am going to spend until Doctor's bill passes. But alas, I fear it won't even pass, and I will continue feeling poor until the end of the chapter.

I am going out to return some calls this afternoon. I am going to wear the black cashmere dress I had made while I was in Sitka, and the hat I got when I came out here, and a pair of kid gloves Mamma gave me before I left West Point. Now don't you think I am an economical woman?

Tell me just everything about your winter outfit, and what you mean to do and have for spring. Let me know how your hats look, and about what sort of things people wear generally. Sallie, tell me, too, if they wear the skirts long or short in the streets.

I expect my furs will be here this week, and just think, they won't be a particle of use to me. I have no cloak but the old heavy one I have trimmed with beaver, and I can't wear a mink muff and boa with that or carry a silver fox muff. What would you do?

With lots of love, I will close. Answer all my questions. John joins me in love and says he would be glad to hear from Brainard. Lovingly,

Your sister
Em FitzGerald

Fort Boise
February 17, 1878

Mamma Dear,

I have not written for a while. In the meantime, ever so many things have come from Chestnut Hill, and I will begin with the first. The evening I sent off my last letter, "Red Riding Hood" and "Cinderella" came. The children have never had any books like them, and I kept them for Bessie's birthday which was only a few days off. Then the little brown hoods came — and then my hat! When I tried it on, it came just down over my head all round to my nose. Wasn't it too big for you? Well, it is just the shape I like, and after thinking it over a while, I find it is so high, I can cut it off about an inch all around and then it will fit. I like the velvet and the plume ever so much, and I can make it a very pretty looking hat, much better than it is now. As it stands, there is about one half too much trimming on it.

I like my blue dress better every time I wear it. It is so comfortable. I don't like a street dress long, though, and intend to shorten the underskirt.

This week has been the week in the year that all the great days in our family come. Doctor's birthday came first, and we gave him his little gifts and had a little extra good dinner. Then came the anniversary of our wedding. I did want to do something to celebrate the day, and I concluded to have all the post people in to a whist party and lunch. At first I thought I could not afford it, but going over it all, I had a nice fat turkey left of a pair Doctor got in the holidays, and I had a fruit cake, and I had material in the house to make a salad. I found I could have my lunch just as I wanted it, and only spend two dollars — one for cream and one for sherry wine (not to drink — but for jelly). So we had them all (the twelve post people), and we had a real merry time. My table was lovely. My silver is pretty, and I have pretty glass. I haven't seen as nice a looking table anywhere else since I came here.

Then Bessie's birthday came. She wanted, above all things, another dollie — she never gets enough. So Doctor got her one, and I had the "Red Riding Hood" and "Cinderella" and a little book you sent her a long time ago — it seemed too old for her and I put it away until now — and gave it to her from Grandma. Then I had a cake baked for her and iced it. It was a cake with raisins — her delight — in it, and I put 5 little candles in it with pins. She invited all the children in and we lighted the candles, and when they burned down, Bess cut the cake, and they had a regular spree. As I said to Doctor, they had just as good a time as if I had gone to a great deal of trouble and had them a party.

I am sorry the children are getting so old before you see them. I thought last night, as I was giving them their baths, how big they are getting to be. I love them very much sometimes when they seem to me to be wonderfully good children, and at other times, I feel like taking their heads off. Bert still keeps some of his pretty baby ways, though he, too, is growing fast.

I am getting very much interested in this little church struggling into life here. It will finally organize next Sunday with a membership of about 16 for a beginning. I like Mr. Stratton so much, and I do wish he was going to stay.

I wanted to tell you more about the church affairs, but must stop on account of my eyes which trouble me quite often again. I hope you are all well. I am counting the months off until we will start eastward. I only know that it will be this year. Write often. With lots of love from the children who constantly talk of you, I am

Your loving child
Emily FitzGerald

Fort Boise
March 1, 1878

Mamma Dear,

We heard of a man who took pictures and who has "set up" in town, so we went down to interview him with the results which I enclose. His photographs were awful. You could not tell who they were intended for, so we tried some of these, and out of four or five we selected two of each of the children which we thought did look like them, and took them to send to their two grandmothers. I am really surprised that they are as good as they are. Wriggling children, and a one horse artist, and fixings, and such dirty fingers (his finger marks you see on the pictures) don't make very finished pictures. I only send them, as I know you will like to see how the children are growing.

My own was unexpected. I did not go down fixed to have a picture taken but sat for fun while the chicks were getting rested, and thought the picture was so good, I took it to send you. When they saw it, Doctor and the rest made such comments on it, I really began to think I might be better looking than the picture. Until then, I really thought it very flattering. That spot on the chin is NOT on my chin. It was on his glass!

Sallie will recognize on Bert the little sack she made. He stood better than Bess. She is such a nervous, wriggling sort of a child. It almost kills her to be still.

I have intended writing and telling you about our little church which has just been organized. I have been so much pleased and interested in it all, but I can't write about that now. Will send this note as an excuse for a longer one. I am glad you are all well. Hasn't Bep had any photographs taken lately? I would like to have one of him.

With much love, I am
Your loving daughter,
Emily FitzGerald

P. S. I would have had John have a picture of this kind taken to add to this group, but the ones you have of him are so much better than any he could get here, I did not insist. He is well and sends love. He is a darling husband, and we are all very happy except that we are far away from all of you.

Fort Boise
March 11, 1878

Mamma Dear,

Your letter of the 28th arrived Thursday night. I was glad to get it, though it was a short one.

Doctor and I, between us, have just manufactured such a comfortable lounge. You know furniture out here costs a fortune, and we couldn't think of having a lounge at the prices they ask here. So I thought of the plan of the old one you used to have, and Doctor said he would manage the frame if I did the rest. I had two square hair pillows I had at Lapwai and some red cretonne. I had Mrs. Burroughs make me a mattress and had it stuffed with hay. Doctor tacked it for me just like a bed mattress, and you don't know what a fine lounge we have. Indeed, we have set the fashion. There are two on the way being made like it now, and the carpenter came in a few minutes ago and asked if he could see my lounge frame. He is going to work on a third just like it for Mrs. Riley.

I had a very nice birthday which I must tell you about. When I was getting out of bed, Doctor called the children into the sitting room and they came back carrying between them one of those boxes that has these long, thin bottles of that nice cologne, and gave it to me as a birthday gift. There was a poem on the cover, too. Then Bess gave me a package from her Papa with another poem on it which I had better not exhibit. That package had in it a pair of slippers. I had remarked in the last few days I wanted a new pair and did not think there were such nice ones out here as these John found. The children got into the fever of giving, and Bess began telling me what she would give me and Papa from her playthings just as soon as she got dressed. Poor Bert had broken up all his Christmas toys and had only one whole thing left — a little tin cart. He got up into my bed, kissed me fervently, and said, "Mamma, just as soon as I get my coaties on, I will give you a beautiful little tin cart for my birthday gift." When Bess got dressed, she did divide up all her possessions and brought me some pictures which she insisted on my sending you. After breakfast, Mrs. Ward sent me up a prettily bound book. Considering that I wasn't thinking of it being my birthday at all, I think I fared very well.

You should hear Bess and Bertie talk. Bess, at any rate, leaves Sallie and me way behind in the amount of talking she can do in a short space of time. She is quick in everything, and Doctor is delighted to see how she reasons. We were out in the hills walking yesterday, and Bess and Bert were fishing by a little creek. Bess brought her Papa a piece of stone or glass and said, "See, Papa, I found a piece of flint or glass. I found it in some ashes by the creek. I guess somebody has been camping there and had a fire. Don't you think so?" What pleased John was the idea of a child of her age reasoning from the ashes there had been a camp there. It is too funny to hear these children. You know that Doctor is always poking into and taking an interest in everything when we are out-of-doors wandering around, and, as he often has the children with him, they, too, gather up stones and roots and bones, etc., and discuss what they are. Bess, and even Bert, can talk as learnedly about rocks with mica in them, and gold ore, and flint arrowheads, etc., as an old man. Little Indian arrowheads, flints, and obsidian are found around here, and Doctor has often picked up little scales of flint and told the children about the Indians who scaled off

ie FitzGerald (Mrs. Elizabeth Hiestand) with her dollie from Grandmother, Christmas 1877.

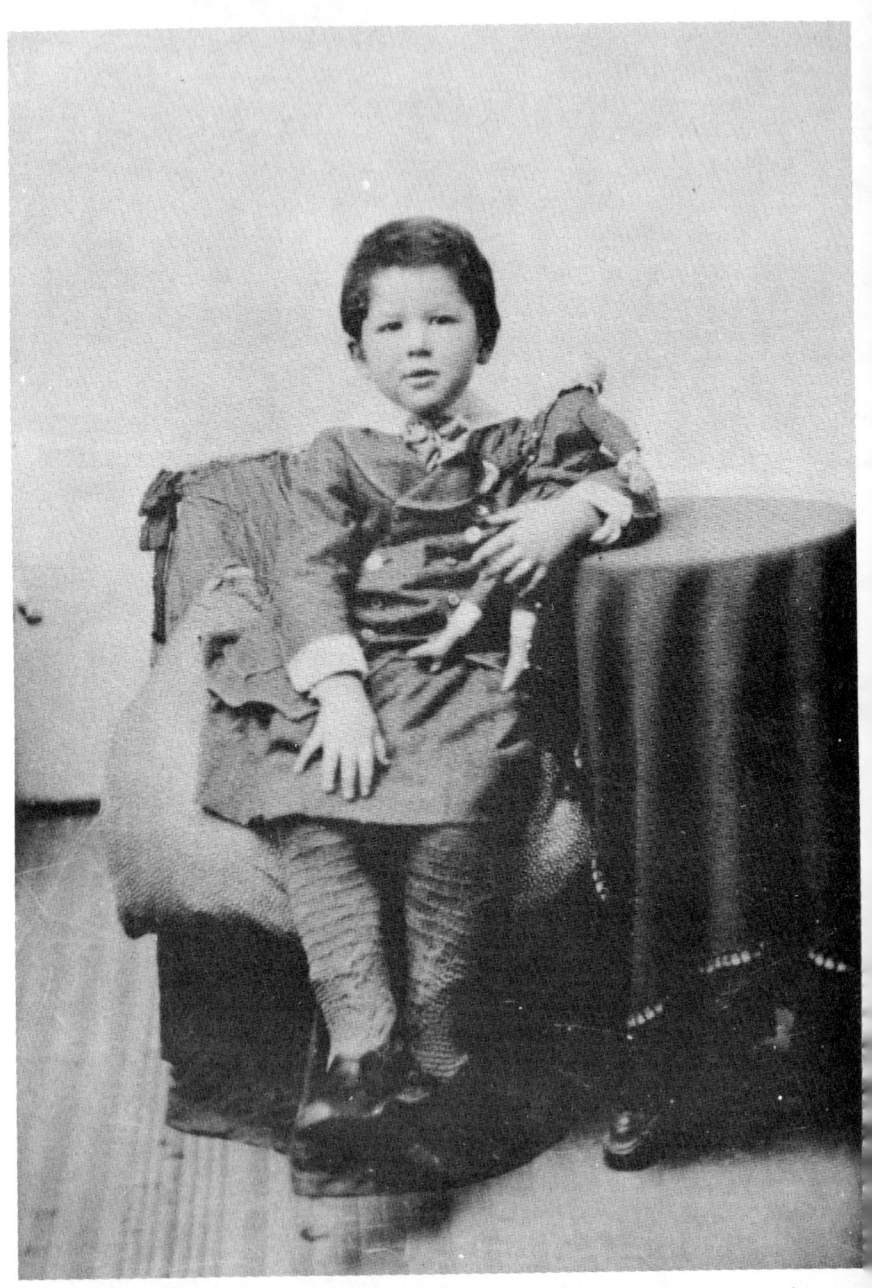

Bertie (Herbert) FitzGerald, four years old, his picture and Bessie's were taken at Fort Boise in March 1878.

those pieces when they were making arrowheads, and told them other things about it. Now, Miss Bessie picks them up often, and knows them, too, and discusses flint scales with the other children, and tells them about the Indians. Bert hunts stones and tells the other children, who all go to him, which is mica and which is not, just like an old geologist.

I think Bess will learn quickly, and she seems very anxious to. She has taught herself all the letters, big and little, with her blocks, though b, q, p, and d of the small letters still puzzle her. A few weeks ago she started school but went only once. It is just a little school for just a few hours every day in a young lady's house. As Bess wanted to go, and some of the older post children went down every day in the ambulance, I thought Bess might try. She went and was delighted, but that very day we heard of a fresh outbreak of diphtheria in town, and Doctor concluded he would rather the children would not have any connection with the town at all for the rest of the winter. So poor Bess didn't get much schooling, but every now and then she shows me something she learned at school that day. She learned to make nearly all the capital letters on her slate, and to draw a plum, and, as she says, "Mamma, I knew how to spell it that day, too, but I don't now."

We like Mr. Knowles here very much. He has been preaching on this coast for some years but lately has had a charge in New York. He was sent here by the Board of Home Missions to take charge of this little church which is just coming into existence, but all looks very promising. We are going to have a nice little church building of our own. That has been decided on. I believe the Board gives a proportion towards it, and the rest must be subscribed. I like Mr. Knowles and I like the nice, plain people who go to our church. There are some very nice, pleasant people here and this little party of Presbyterians all seem to feel such a friendly interest in each other. It is delightful.

John is well. He has quite a number of sick people on his hands and is consequently anxious and worried. He always gets just as much interested in and anxious about anyone very sick as he would if it was one of us. I get quite indignant at him sometimes for his anxieties. He has brought a couple of patients through since we came here (that some of the other physicians had about given up) that have gotten him quite a reputation. Everybody he attends seems devoted to him afterwards, and I don't wonder, as he is always kind and watchful if anyone is ill. I must close. We all join in love. Write soon.

Your loving daughter,
Emily FitzGerald

Fort Boise
March 19, 1878

Mamma Dear,

I have not heard from home nearly as often as I thought I ought to lately, but your last letter, received night before last, tells me you missed one week, so that accounts for my short allowance. I am glad you are all well and wish I could go into the city with you on some of your shopping expeditions and see all the lovely things you tell me about.

Such lovely but unseasonable weather as we have been having, I never saw before. This is March and the weather has been like late May or June. For 2 weeks the children have played out-of-doors without anything on them, and for the last three Sundays, Mrs. Ward and I have gone to church without any cloaks or wraps. The sun has been so hot, I was obliged to put the children in sundowns. They play all day long now on the hillside, picking wild flowers and digging holes.

My blue hat has been very much admired. I find, with my eyes troubling me, a hat that shades my eyes is so much more comfortable than one that does not, though I like the latter. I have concluded all I will get for a summer hat will be a little straw sundown, and that will do to wear every time I go to town, to church, to call, and everything. You know, I have positively no use for a dress hat here. The town ladies, I find, do just about as I thought they would here. They wear nothing but calico dresses all summer long, and I don't want anything else.

Before I leave the subject of clothes, please do tell me how much a pair of good, dark stockings (purple or gray — or blue or red and gray — or some such grave color) for myself would cost. I want to send for three pairs when I send the next lot of money.

This a little country town, a real pleasant town, but none the less country. I like Boise and am particularly interested in our little church. We are now beginning to think of building a little room that will do for a wing or addition to the main building, when there can be money enough raised to build the church proper. Mr. Knowles is so earnest and, I think, a worker. He is not well off in this world's goods, though, as our ministers usually are not. Some one went to call on Mr. Knowles and found his room so bare and uncomfortable that we ladies felt we ought to try to help him fix it. He has been at some expense coming out here, and the support the Board gives him, we know, is not more than will support him. So some of the ladies (they are very good, plain, working people — not much means) contributed, and we got him a nice lounge and hope to get him an easy chair. Mr. Knowles, I know, is good and will do good. He is well-born, well educated, and refined.

The people here are good, and I like them. Doctor says he is beginning to think we must be older than he had concluded we were, as I always get intimate with the old ladies. Now I see more of Mrs. Braymin who has grandchildren older than I am. No, they are not either, for I believe her oldest grandchild is 20, but I like Mrs. Braymin very much. She is from the East and is congenial.

About our coming home, we don't know anything. In the unsettled state of this part of the country, all the movements of the troops are uncertain. The Indians have been favored by this open winter and have been holding Councils and having big talks and dances all over the country. They are very ugly and seem determined to resist any movement towards putting them on reservations or to resist interference from the Whites. The settlers, who are scattered through this upper country, are all anxious. Some are removing to the towns, and others are preparing places of safety and defense for their women and children. The governor is urging General McDowell to hurry troops into this region before the spring opens. The Columbia River Indians have been holding talks all winter, and they say old Moses of the Spokanes, who we feared would fall on us at Lapwai last summer, is certainly preparing for war. Everybody is anxious and we army people have about given up the idea of having our husbands at home with us this summer. There will certainly be scouting parties out all summer from here.

I forgot to tell you Boise is to be made a five company post with a major in command. The tribes around here are all feeling very sore and are behaving in a very threatening manner. That surprise and surrender of the Bannock camp was all a farce. The Indians were prepared for it, had driven off all their war ponies, and had hidden all their good arms. They weren't quite ready to fight. Oh, they are a cunning foe, and I wish we were out of this horrid Department.

I would like to hear from you soon. Bert's shirts will be acceptable as soon as they can be made.

Lots of love to you all,
Your daughter,
Emily

Fort Boise
March 25, 1878

Mamma Dear,

I have had company today. The paymaster, who is one we know and like very much, Major Canby, and his brother lunched with us, and just as we were going to an early dinner (John wanted to go down town) we saw Governor and Mrs. Braymin coming up the hill. They came in and went to dinner with us and then sat for a couple of hours. I do like her so much. She reminds me, not of any one in particular, but of the sort of people you all are at home. She is an old lady and a good one, too. She likes me, too, and says I remind her of her daughters, and she likes to be with me as much as I do with her.

Mamma, I want some summer stockings for John. I will have to send some more money, as I want them as good as the winter ones you got him. Mrs. Burroughs has just made me such comfortable nightgowns for the babies. I had them made four apiece, and good and big, so they would not outgrow them. Bessie's look big enough for me.

Now when I will have sent off this letter and paid up all my small amounts here, I will have spent all my money again. Do you know I don't believe I will ever be rich enough to come home and buy all the pretty things I want unless John finds that gold mine. Do you know, I think your advice — to just send for what I want and pay for it when I can — is very bad. Now what sort of advice would that be for you to give a foolish sort of woman who would? Why she would always be spending money before she got it, and you know that is bad and unsatisfactory. Really, I have no real genuine wants which are not supplied. Of course, I could spend more money if we had it, but I really don't need anything, and I do feel as if we should spend less than we do. There is no hope of our having more of an income than we have now for years and years, and we will, as the children grow older, have more expenses. We spend just about all monthly, and I feel we should save a little. We have no debts, but that is not all. We ought not to spend all our income, and I do so want to get a start at saving that I am willing to do even with less than now. Now don't you go to giving me such advice any more. What you ought to tell me is to wait until I can spare the money for what I really need and then send, and that is what I am going to try to do.

Will you please find out from some hair store what a good black braid will cost? I promised to write about one for my ferocious domestic. I don't believe I ever told you about her.

She has been with me now four months and I think myself very fortunate. We call her "The Duchess." She wants a good braid, and would not like to give more than 15 or 16 dollars. She doesn't want one of short hair, but wants one of long hair from the top down. Will you please price some and tell me? I will be much obliged.

Write soon.

Your loving daughter,
Emily

PART V

THE FRONT LINES, 1878

John's Letters from the Bannock Campaign

(*With the exception of two short notes written across the backs of Doctor FitzGerald's letters in June and July, the remainder of Emily's correspondence to her mother is missing.*

Doctor FitzGerald was assigned to temporary field duty in the Bannock Campaign and left Fort Boise May 30, 1878.)

Camp at Sheep Ranch,
Oregon
June 15, 1878

Dear Old Woman,

I got here about an hour ago, about a quarter to 4 A. M., without misadventure. There is nothing later than I wrote of last night. Only Sarah Winnemucca, the Indian woman, was sent out 3 days ago. (She is the daughter of the old Chief of that name). She said she would have her people bring all the Bannocks in as prisoners. She was very sanguine about being able to have the Bannocks arrested, etc.

The command is waiting for that of Colonel Whipple which will join tonight, probably, and then maybe it will start on the Indians' trail. I am very tired and did not get any sleep. Will write again in the next 48 hours and tell you further of what is to be done.

Mr. Riley is here and says it is not decided whether he is to go on, remain with this command, or go back to Boise. He just came up and asked me to say as much for Mrs. Riley's information.

All are well here and wish to be remembered.

Your hub,
John

Camp Sheep Ranch
in the field, Oregon
June 16, 1878

Dear Old Woman and Darling Wife,

The Indian Woman, Sarah Winnemucca, came in last night greatly excited. She says the Bannocks and other hostiles have disarmed the Piutes generally (i. e., her people) and threaten them if they will not join them. They are congregated at Steins Mountains and are in considerable force, and include the renegades of several tribes.

For the present, I am to accompany Colonel Bernard's command. Whipple and Bomus will join tonight or tomorrow, but we will move on slowly today. General Howard goes back toward old Camp Lyon to join Major Stewart's command and hurry them up. All the other troops are being directed this way, too, and it may be that the war can be ended at or near Steins Mountains. Stewart's command, with General Howard, will get to Steins Mountains in a week or less, when I shall be again with Headquarters Company. Dr. Spencer will remain at Boise for the present. We are now nearly ready to start, so I must hurry and close this letter. I hope you are all well, darling. I will write again my first chance and keep you posted. Kind regards to all.

Tell Mrs. Riley her husband is to remain here for a week or so and then return to Fort Boise. Do not borrow trouble on my account, for I am comfortable, and, save for being absent from you, I rather enjoy this thing. We will, I trust, have a short campaign, and then you and I will take our chicks and go East and have a good time generally.

Your loving husband,
John

(*Emily wrote the following note on the backs of the two preceding letters.*)

Dear Mamma,

I will enclose two notes received from John yesterday. We are all anxious, as there are so many Indians and so few soldiers. Doctor is about a hundred miles from here, and the command he is with is close on the Indians' trail. I hope there will be no meeting until more troops get out there.

I have not heard from you for some time, but there are two reasons why letters might be lost. One is that the mails are so irregular, and another is that a lot of mail directed to Doctor has been sent to him from the office without my seeing it. As you often direct to him, some of your letters may have gone out. We are all pretty well. I am wondering whether my stockings are lost or not. I hope not, as I must have some, and if these don't come this week, I will have to get some here, as I can't wait to send again.

It was very inconvenient for the Indians to break out just now. They have completely upset all my arrangements. I hope you are well. We have been in a constant stir here. Troops are continually going and coming, and old friends are coming up to see us. I saw nearly everybody in the Department last summer at Lapwai, and now, this summer, I meet them all again. There are so few soldiers out here and none, or very few, that can come from other departments. If they still cut down the army, I hope the Indians will get clear to Washington and clear out Congress. I really do wish they would cut out one medical official known to us, and we could let the Army alone forever. I am just lost with the Doctor away this way. I feel as if the bottom was knocked out of everything. Write soon and direct your letter to me. The children are both well. I can't write anything connected until this war is over, so will close. With much love, I am, as ever,

Your loving daughter
Emily FitzGerald

Cumming's Ranch
John Day's Valley,
Oregon
July 2, 1878

My Darling Wife,

We rested over yesterday at this place in order to get supplies from Canion City, 20 miles distant. But this A. M., we pull out again about 6 o'clock for Fox Valley, about 20 miles northeast from here and where the savages are supposed to be. The report is that there were from 200 to 300 Umatilla Indians there with their families the day before yesterday, and it is known that the hostiles we are pursuing have gotten in among them, and the probabilities are that they will unite, although the Umatillas have been offering to fight the hostiles as our allies within the past week. A man came in yesterday saying that the Umatillas had sent off their families, which is significant. I do not think the Indians will make any stand but keep right on, either for the impregnable Salmon River Mountains, or towards the Columbia River to gain other allies from the Spokanes and other tribes. It will yet take all the troops in this Department to subdue them. I am sure it will be an all-the-year business, in any event. General Howard and his toiling infantry column are back in the mountains over which we have come, although he is looked for now daily. He ought to mount his infantry and hurry up, for it would thereby be possible to overtake these Indians and fight them to advantage. I have nothing else of importance to write of.

By the way, if that check comes for June's pay, I think they will cash it at the bank by your endorsement, or Major Collins would take it and let you have the money if you are in need.

I have no use for more than I carried away, so rest easy about that.

Still more am I, this morning, of the opinion that the war will be a long one, and that it would be wisest for you to make preparations at your leisure, and, when ready, to go East by easy stages. I am sorry I cannot go with you and take as much of the bother and worry off you as possible, but it is not possible, and so you will have to do it all by yourself, Darling.

Be of good cheer as you can, and all will go well, and I will join you in the fall. It will be the best thing that could happen to the children to leave their present surroundings. I guess you and I will have to leave them at Chestnut Hill when we go to our next post and let them stay 2 or 3 years there to counteract or whitewash the evil they have learned in the last six months.

But I must close. I may have an opportunity to send this letter this morning, but if I don't, I will do so tonight or tomorrow — with further items, if there should be any.

Your loving hub,
John

Fox Valley
July 3, 1878

Darling Wife,

We got here last evening. It is a very pretty little prairie bordered by wooded hills. There are a few sheep ranches hereabout, but all are abandoned. The Indians were camped here yesterday, but, with the Umatillas, have all passed on to some point we are yet to find. They are supposed to have passed over into Long Valley, about 14 miles off, and are probably making for the Salmon River Mountains, though it is almost equally probable they are going to cross the Columbia in the expectation of having their numbers recruited from the Spokane and other tribes.

This valley is quite elevated and cool. The morning is dark and cloudy and threatening rain. Several cool sprinkles have already fallen. Yesterday, on leaving the other camp, some fellows who had started back for General Howard's command returned saying the General and Staff had all left that command 4 days ago to join this one, but they had not been heard from since. A few hours afterward, though, a messenger came in from General Howard saying they were in camp, one day's march back of us, etc. I heard one of the captains, five or six days ago, animadverting on the General's rashness in riding ahead of his Command with only a few men as escort. The captain said he should not so much mind being killed in fair fight, but to run the daily risk General Howard did to be shot from ambush was more than he could stand. When we got that report yesterday, no one seemed to think it improbable but what might naturally be expected.

I consider myself safer with this fighting command than I would be with the General. We move shortly for the trail which we are to follow on — on — and on — with but little prospect of overtaking them. Should you have any sure prospect of sending me anything, please send me that other new pair of soldier pants I have, and also one pair of my best. I expect we shall pass over into the Grand Ronde Valley on to that stage road from Boise to Umatilla. If you hear that we are near Baker City or La Grande, you may send them to either place. In haste, goodbye, my darling. Many kisses and all my love for you and my babies.

Your loving hub,
John

Camp, Head of
Birch Creek
Blue Mountains, Oregon
July 8, 1878

My Darling Wife,

We have had another field day of it — a battle of the hills this time. This A. M. at 6 o'clock, we moved out westward and had gone about 2 or 3 miles, when a scout came galloping in saying the Indians were just ahead of us in force. We went forward at a lope and soon came in sight of quite a number. Then we moved down and up deep canyons and high hills. You will recollect the kind of hills just before you get into the timber on the Blue Mountains on the Walla Walla side. The Indians were full 4 miles away, and our horses were almost out of breath before the fight began. Then, suddenly, a high hilltop swarmed with Indians and the skirmish fight became very scenic, but the savages gave way, even when they had fine natural fortifications, and the fight became a running one and passed over about 3 or 4 miles of mountain ground — half of it wooded. They left packs, and dead horses, and live horses all along the way. Two or three packs fell in my way as I followed up the line of battle, and I got several things for you and the children. I got you a fine beaded squaw robe, so you need not go to the expense of a new dress to go East in. This will just fit you. Tell Bess I got a whole lot of bead necklaces for her, and tell Bert I got a whip for him.

Our loss is 5 men wounded, one probably fatally, and a lot of horses killed and wounded, but we captured some 200 horses from them, and killed and wounded a number of horses for them. They are not half as formidable enemies as were the Nez Percés, but now, I suppose, we will have to chase them all over creation until the end of time. I suppose the General is much pleased with the day's work. If the country had been favorable, we would have ridden over them. Seven companies of cavalry are not often under the command of a captain, and Bernard has reason to feel pleased. Everybody is tired tonight. The horses are very tired. I shall send the wounded to Walla Walla tomorrow, and I suppose we will move on the trail which now leads back toward Boise. Maybe I will write further before I post this.

Your loving hub,
John

Camp on Head of
Birch Creek
6 o'clock A. M.
July 9, 1878

Dearest Wife,

I will only add that we have news to the effect that yesterday, Captain Kress, Ordinance Department, on an armed steamer not far from Umatilla, attacked and defeated a large body of Indians crossing over. They are supposed to be Columbia River Indians, mainly. He captured a large quantity of their camp plunder and destroyed canoes, etc. He used howitzers and rifle guns. He had 40 men on board the boat. So you see, the Indians are being put to it and have been "hooped" up pretty lively. This outfit we encountered yesterday are supposed to be the Piutes and the Bannocks. The gorgeous new dress I got for you yesterday belonged to a Piute high society lady — upper ten, according to Sarah Winnemucca, who is still at Headquarters. She wanted me to give it to her, but I declined.

We shall not leave camp yet for some hours, as we do not know where to find the Indian trail. We have sent scouts out for that purpose. Our command is in high feather now, and would be only too pleased to be able to get at the savages on fair ground, or, in fact, on any ground.

I hope this finds my darlings well. Am afraid my dreadful scribbles will hurt your poor eyes, so I guess I will give you a rest by writing less often than I have been doing.

All day yesterday we were passing back over the route on which we came, having fought the Indians right on the road on which we were marching the day before, only we had faced right about. We are to march back toward Camas Prairie today, and maybe we will have to pursue these Indians back toward the Grand Ronde and over toward the Salmon River Mountains.

One of our 5 wounded men died this morning. The other 4 are only slightly wounded.

Your loving hub,
John

Camp on McKay Creek
10 miles below
Cayuse Station
Oregon

Dearest Old Wife,

We left our battleground camp this morning and made a short march of 13 miles across the hills. General Howard and one company of cavalry went on to Cayuse Station to get telegraphic communication with the outside world. I could tell you a good many items of various sorts if I had time, but I must hurry up so this note can go out tonight. I made a bundle of that squaw robe and other things for Bess and Bert. Tell Bess this afternoon we camped near an Indian ranch where they had recently been living in a common lodge, and a nice little kitten came out and sat on my lap while I was sewing up that bundle. It made me think of my dear baby girl who I know would have been pleased to have found a kitty under such circumstances. I am almost tempted to try to send it to Bess, but I guess we shall have to leave it in camp.

This place is on the Umatilla reservation, and the stream in every respect reminds me so forcibly of the Lapwai, that I keep thinking I must be near that post. The hostile Indians, it seems, have passed Cayuse Station on the mountains and are making for the Grande Ronde or Wallowa Valleys. We shall move on past Cayuse Station. Miles' command is now within a few miles of us, and I suppose we shall be within cooperating distance if we should possibly overtake the savages again, although we have cavalry enough to lick them, whenever found. I am in hopes that we may give them another blow soon, which would go far toward making them give up. Otherwise, we shall have a tedious summer and fall campaign. I would so like to make a run into Boise to see you, Darling, if only for 24 hours and return, if only to see you for a few hours. I dreamed of you last night, and my dreams were full of terrors. I trust, though, you are having a peaceful time, even though it may be a little monotonous, all deserted by your husband as you are. I do hope the war will soon close out, and that we may get our release from service in this Department. We are all well and I have no wants. Should you hear that we are coming along the stage road, send those pants (one pair of my best) and the pair of soldier trousers (new), and also one more pair of the heaviest drawers, and my new boots. They can be done up in a compact bundle and sent by express to me with Colonel Bernard's command, via Baker City, or La Grande.

Your loving husband,
John

Camp Battalion,
1st Cavalry in the Field,
Walla Walla, W. T.
July 13, 1878

My Darling Wife,

Yesterday, through a blinding dust more difficult to bear than any other feature of the campaign, save absence from my darlings, we arrived at Fort Walla Walla and went into camp under the post, back of the officers' quarters. Have been very busy since and have been endeavoring to get possession of our probable future movements for your information.

I have met most of the people here. We had dinner with Mr. and Mrs. Bomus yesterday. I saw your letter to her of the 2nd, which gratified me much, as the last I had from you was of June 24 and 25. General Forsyth takes command of this outfit, and we move for Lewiston and Mount Idaho at 1 P. M. General Howard has preceded us, going yesterday. In the meantime, we learn that Cayuse Station, where we were two days ago, has been burned, and that two men out of the five who were there are missing. We hear this A. M. that the Spokane Indians, or at least the Columbia River Indians, have commenced business on the other side of the river by killing several people. You have heard, I suppose, of the shelling of the Indians lately who were crossing the Columbia. There were 3 of the river steamers plying up and down the river, and all of them found Indians crossing, and fired into them. So I suppose they have commenced to retaliate, although I suppose they would have done so anyhow. Our present movement is intended to overawe those Indians and to head off those we have been following who are making for the Wallowa and Salmon River region. I have little expectation that this war will end before late fall at furthest, and, Darling Old Woman, I am sorry for you, as well as for myself, for I have no prospect whatever of release from this duty. You must bear it, however, with what patience you can until I return. Make your preparations at once and go home.

I signed my pay accounts for July today and gave them to Major Keefer, who, with his family, is stationed here, having arrived last week. He will forward the amount to you by express, as soon as he gets the money for July. The other check for June he says he forwarded to me before he left Portland. You can get the money on it by depositing it with the bank, or Major Collins, no doubt, would give you the money for it. Then write home for some money, enough to take you home. I do not think it would be wise for you to lose any time but to get East as soon as possible. Sell out everything.

I am afraid that this command will not do the work now that it would have done under Bernard, I mean the work that would help to end this war. And this long, round about move, too, I can see no reason for, although the General, no doubt, has good reasons for the move. I think it would have been much better to have followed the trail.

I hope, darling, you are well. I regret to have to write as unencouragingly as I do, but I cannot see it in any other light. Of course, I shall be ordered East just as soon as it is over, and then we will have a good and pleasant time together among our friends. I look forward to it with the keenest delight. You must be my good, courageous old woman, and don't keep yourself thin with fretting. Other wives are in the same fix, and perhaps worse. I shall avoid all risks and will write to you as often as possible.

Mr. Ward is Quartermaster and Mr. Hunter is Adjutant General. Tower goes on recruiting service, and Forsyth commands the regiment. He brought me pleasant messages from Sandy Forsyth, and I was told that he expressed himself as pleased to have me for his medical officer.

Kind regards to all the neighbors. Kiss the babies for me and tell them they must be good.

Your loving husband,
John

Camp, 1st Cavalry
Meachane's Ranch
July 16, 1878

Darling Old Wife,

I ought to have written you early this morning, for then we had a mail going out, but I was just starting off about a mile from camp on an errand for the Medical Museum. Yesterday morning, the Umatillas had a fight with the hostiles and killed 11 of them, one of them being the Piute Chief Egan. Well, I went out and got the latter's head and was back in less than half an hour. I went with about 25 scouts and Umatillas. We were encamped some 4 miles north of this station. The hostiles have incontinently fled, and just now we are joined by nearly 100 Umatilla warriors, all eager for the pursuit, and now thoroughly committed by the fight yesterday.

This is the best news I have had so far to give you, for it will go far to end this war, I think. There had been a good deal of doubt about the Umatillas, and nearly everyone said they certainly would go with the hostiles. We shall take the trail in half an hour which leads westward, and I think we shall catch and use them quite up altogether. I do hope so. I sent off a letter to you yesterday with other news, but I hope this will go on in advance of it.

Later

I wish you could see our wild allies in their paint and fine horses and outfits. I expect they would be as formidable as the Nez Percés if at war with us, for they are generally well armed. I notice a few them with bows and arrows, in addition to their guns, and their ponies are very superior horses as compared to those of other Indian tribes.

Yesterday, on this road near the summit, this side of Cayuse, we found a wagon train which had been taken by the savages, and the bodies of four of the teamsters. The wagons had been partially rifled of their contents, mainly provisions — flour, bacon, hams, etc. There is nothing of further interest to write. This will go through to La Grande by volunteer scouts or courier. General Wheaton is coming up now, four or five miles away.

We are all well and hope we see in the events of the past 24 hours a faint prospect of the beginning of the end of this war. I hope my darlings are all well. I gave you a long lecture in yesterday's letter, and was almost sorry after it was off that I had done so, but you will forgive me, I know, and behave yourself better, too, in consequence. We will go East this fall and forget, in the pleasant association of friends, all about these Indian troubles.

Kiss my babies for me and take care of them and yourself, too. I shall take the greatest care of myself and avoid all unnecessary danger for your sake.

Kindest regards to neighbors and friends. In haste,

Your loving husband,
John

Camp 1st Cavalry in the
Field, Blue Mountains
Head of the
Grande Ronde River
July 18, 1878

My Own Dear Wife,

I have so much to tell that I almost despair of putting it on paper. When I last wrote from Meachane's, I said we were to take the trail that evening, but we did not. General Wheaton came up just as we were starting, and so did a drizzling rain, and by his orders we went into camp. The Umatilla Indians, some 75, were sent out with two or three white scouts to locate the hostiles. They sent back word as to the general direction taken, and we were ordered out at 6 A. M., taking the steep road toward La Grande and Boise for 10 miles, when we diverged on the old Immigrant Road to the south and west to strike the head of Grand Ronde Valley. We crossed that stream some six or eight miles from the stage road, and then followed the valley up stream, passing some fine scenery all the way, finding an occasional settlement where the valley opened out into a basin, which it did every few miles. We followed really what is marked on the maps as the "Daily Road," and finally, toward evening, reached the Daily ranch in a fine, indeed beautiful, round valley. The houses and barns were substantially built, and fat cattle and cows were visible all around. There was a fine garden from which I got some splendid lettuce and onions, and enjoyed them amazingly. There was a buttery there, too, but they had hid away (cached) all the butter on hand. That was about 28 miles we had made from Meachane's.

The scouts who had gone out with the Umatillas came in and reported that they had struck the trail of the Snakes (hostiles) and had encountered one of them and killed him and were in sight of the whole outfit. They wanted General Forsyth to come right on that night (a distance of 20 miles) as they were to wait for us there. We were already tired, and the animals (horses) were more so, and yet it was decided to go after a rest of 2 or 3 hours and supper. The horses were turned into a green field of timothy hay, which was almost as good as grain, and at 9 P. M., we started, and shortly after the full moon rose and lighted up our trail. We entered upon a succession of open glades and pine groves. We could see our scouts, about a dozen of them, ahead of us a quarter of a mile. I was riding with Colonel Bernard, when suddenly we saw a light to our left, half a mile away, as if someone was lighting a pipe. The scouts came shortly to a halt, and as we rode up they said, "Did you see the signal fire?" They were quite excited, but we had one Umatilla Indian as a guide, and he and one other man went cautiously forward toward the place where the light had appeared in an open grove of pines. They were gone only a few minutes, our column meanwhile coming to a halt, when we heard a whoop which was followed by a regular series of Indian war whoops and sounds of Indians running awāy on horseback. But presently they sounded nearer, and then there was loud talking in the Indian tongue. Then we heard a shout from the scout who had gone ahead, and then we all moved forward toward the grove, and we were amazed to see all the Umatillas there, some mounted, some on foot, and all in a commotion. We also heard children crying, and we soon learned that after the Umatillas sent on word to the general, they had encountered the Snakes, charged them, killed 10 or 15 and captured 22 or 23 women and children and about 35 horses. They did not lose a man (the Umatillas). Two or three Indians were waving or flourishing some scalps and talking excitedly. The Snakes, they said, *hi-u, Clat-a-wa-ie,* ran like pick-pockets, and the Umatillas thought best to come back to meet us.

We gathered in and around the captives, poor, wretched things, and the group was illuminated by a lurid, blazing fire of pine boughs and knots. The men, by companies drawn up in line, were conspicuous by moonlight. The captors were mounted or in picturesque groups of color. The scene was one I shall not soon forget, and, like Mr. Darwin, when he first saw the wild shore dwellers of Patagonia, I thought, "Such, or very similar, were our ancestors." The captive women appeared more sad than frightened, and made feeble attempts to hush their wailing babies. (There were 6 or 8 squaws with young babies.) Well, after a little parleying, it was thought best to go back to our camp at Daily's ranch, 2 or 3 miles back, and camp for the night — and we did accordingly.

We were roused at 6 A. M., and after two hours, we resumed

the march, all our Umatillas allies, meanwhile, putting in an appearance for some rations. We got off about 8 o'clock, leaving the Indians at breakfast, and started on the trail, marched 10 miles, and found their battleground and the dead hostiles, and then followed on the trail to this place 10 miles further where we are in camp on a little open valley surrounded by forests.

Now I have a sensation for you. Just as we were coming into this open place this evening, one of the men of Company G heard a baby crying in the bushes. He dismounted and found a poor, little, black-eyed, Indian baby girl, about 8 or 10 months old, that had been abandoned by its savage mother. I heard the men calling, and, riding up, the man (Sergeant Chaffie) called to me, and asked, "Doctor, won't you take it?" I hesitated a moment, then concluded to take it. She was old enough to be alarmed at the commotion, and cried in a terrified way. Fortunately, we had brought along some of the Umatillas who had one of the captive Piute women with them, so I turned the baby over to her, and shortly after fixed some rice water and sugar for it, and gave the baby its supper. It was almost famished, although it looked (as to cleanliness) as if the mother had not left it very long. It fed greedily, and then I found some condensed milk. Mr. Hunter has taken the baby under his supervision and furnished the condensed milk. I have fixed up a nursing bottle for it, and I suppose it will get on tolerably for the present. I want you to tell Bess and Bert all about this and ask them if they would like to have a little Indian baby sister. Shall I bring it home to you, dear?

(I confess I have not the remotest idea of such a thing, so rest easy!)

I could tell you much more, but it is now growing dark and we are to move early on the trail, but the hostiles are completely stampeded and have separated into small bands and gone off in different directions. I do not think that we shall encounter a single hostile Indian again during the summer, so you can rest easy on that score, too.

We are all well. Remember me to friends and neighbors, and write to me soon. I think the best direction is to Hd, Qm, 1st Cavalry in the Field.

Many kisses for my darlings,

Your loving husband,
John

P. S. I had rather campaign a year in the mountains than 2 months of summer in Walla Walla Valley.

(*Emily wrote the following note on the last page of the letter.*)

Dear Mamma,

I had a batch of letters from John last night and will send these two on to you, as it saves me the writing of what I want to tell you of him and his whereabouts. I have not heard from you yet to know whether you care enough for the Indian news to read all of them. Of course, as I have said before, I would not let anybody but you see what my husband writes for my eyes only, but I know you are interested in both of us. I feel, too, perhaps through his letters you will get to know my precious old husband better than you do. His letters are just like him. He is always kind. Sometime he is indifferent, or seems so — sort of abstracted — and when he is anxious or worried or busy, he is always so. But he is always thoughtful for me, and I am always sure of his interest and sympathy, and I always know just where to find him. Hope you are all well and will soon send me some more stockings and tell me how much they cost.

Lovingly,
Em

Dr. FitzGerald returned to Fort Boise, August 6, 1878, and resumed his duties as Post Surgeon. He was due for a promotion to a Majority, and Emily anticipated a return to the old home. On October 5, 1878, the FitzGeralds left Fort Boise and went to Columbia, Pa. Captain FitzGerald reported to the

Army Medical Board in New York on October 14, and then was granted a four months' leave. He and Emily spent a few happy weeks with her family in Columbia and at Chestnut Hill in Philadelphia. The happiness was short lived, however, for he was confined to bed with an inflammation of the lungs on January 21, 1879. The wound he had received during the Civil War at Rasaces and the severe cold he had contracted in the Nez Percés campaign added further complications. He died August 11, 1879. Emily lived, much of the time in memories, until 1912. They lie buried side by side in the cemetery at Columbia, Pa.